1997
TEXAS
GARDEN ALMANAC

TEXAS
TEXAS
TEXAS
TEXAS
TEXAS
TEXAS
TEXAS
TEXAS
TEXAS

Mike Peters — Editor
Cynthia Ryan — Research Editor
Jeff Wolf — Art Director

Harvey Hooker — Sales Manager
Tiffany McMillen — Account Executive

Rick McMillen — Publisher
Marna McMillen — Chief Financial Officer
Bambi McMillen — Circulation Manager

© 1996 McMillen Publishing, LLC
5819 Highway 6 South, Suite 370
Missouri City, TX 77459
(713) 261-6077 — Fax (713) 261-5999

ISBN # 0-96543-780-9
Distributed by Gulf Publishing, Inc.

DEDICATION

To George Stewart,
Texas vegetable gardener
extraordinaire,
who undoubtedly will be
out tending his beets
on his 90th birthday this year.

LETTER FROM THE EDITOR

"

Exactly why "gardening by the moon" works is a mystery. But even skeptics have noted that gardeners who are guided by moon phases and signs tend to have the prettiest and most productive gardens.

Through lunar gardening, some find oneness with the cosmos and with ancient wisdom. Some find science: water pressure within plants, affected by lunar gravity as tides are, probably affects the plants' growth cycles.

I suspect that one right answer is the simplest one. Lunar gardening provides a structure — almost a schedule — that stimulates us to spend more time in the garden.

A wise person once wrote, "The best fertilizer is the gardener's shadow." The sort of gardener who reads an almanac is a person who keeps the soil rich and friable, who plants good varieties at appropriate times, and who pulls weeds before they are large enough to provide shade. One who trusts the earth to provide.

This almanac has a 25-year history on the Texas Gulf Coast, and we're very proud to expand it statewide. At 256 pages, this edition is the largest ever and includes several writers we admire. The resulting diversity of opinion is, we believe, stimulating. (The gospel according to A&M and the gospel according to Howard Garrett, for example, don't always come from the same bible!)

I hope this book stimulates you to spend more time with a good pair of gloves and your favorite trowel. (And those funny foam kneepads are neither silly nor self-indulgent; they're a blessing to gardeners of any age.) I also wish you companionship in the garden: sassy robins, pollinating bees, parasitic wasps and perhaps a child who can share the wonder of growing things.

The earth will provide. It always has.

"

Mike Peters

CONTRIBUTORS FOR THIS EDITION

Brian Anderson is a Houston-based freelance writer and part-time college instructor. His book reviews and articles have appeared in the Houston Chronicle and other local and national publications. His article on the Aztec calendar begins on page 14.

Liz Druitt is a garden writer, designer, consultant and experienced rose rustler. She is the author of *The Organic Rose Garden* and co-author (with G. Michael Shoup) of *Landscaping with Antique Roses*. She is a host of PBS's environmentally oriented gardening series *The New Garden*. A board member of the Heritage Rose Foundation, she lives in Linden, Texas. Her story on Thomas Affleck and the original Texas garden almanac begins on page 256.

J. Howard Garrett writes about organic gardening for the Dallas Morning News, and is the author of several books, including *Plants of the Metroplex*, *The Dirt Doctor's Guide to Organic Gardening* and *J. Howard Garrett's Organic Manual*. His radio show can be heard on WBAP, news/talk 820 on Saturdays, 11 a.m.-noon and Sundays, 8 a.m.-noon. His organic gardening guide begins on page 65.

Madalene Hill is past president of the Herb Society of America and, with her late husband, Jim, founded the Hilltop Herb Farm in Cleveland, Texas. She and daughter **Gwen Barclay** are co-authors of *Southern Herb Growing* and also wrote the well-known "Thyme Being" column for *Houston Home & Garden* magazine. At the Festival Hill Institute in Round Top,

they continue to grow herbs, cook delicious food, teach workshops and write on their favorite subject. Their article on thyme begins on page 162.

Jerral D. Johnson, Charles L. Cole, James V. Robinson and **George Ray McEachern** have written many bulletins for the Texas Agricultural Extension Service, and have published articles on pecan- and fruit-tree growing in both trade and popular magazines. Their guide to spraying fruit trees begins on page 30.

Bob Randall is director of Urban Harvest, a community garden and orchard program of The Park People, Inc., in Houston. His article on community gardens begins on page 170.

Cynthia Thomas is a feature writer for the *Houston Chronicle*, and a host of "Chicks on Film" on public-access TV in Houston. Her article on the Vegetable Improvement Center at Texsa A&M begins on page 173.

Albert Wong is chairman of the Department of Art at The University of Texas at El Paso. He received his BFA in advertising art from the Columbus College of Art & Design, and his MFA in painting from Kent State University. His work is part of the permanent collections of Chase Manhattan Bank, Coca-Cola Co., Benson and Hedges, Tennessee Valley Authority and the Akron Art Museum. He lives in El Paso. His original illustration is reproduced on the cover.

TABLE OF CONTENTS

Calendar/Geography/Weather

Features

How-To: Do It Yourself

TABLE OF CONTENTS

Region Sections

All regions include: Soil Conditions, Agriculture and Forestry, Local Climate Data, Temperature Records, Chill Hours, Annual Rainfall, Recommended Vegetable Varieties, Vegetable Harvest Guide, Recommended Fruit & Nut Varieties, and Where To Find Local Resources.

TABLE OF CONTENTS

And The Winners Are . . .

Gardening By The Month

All months include: Phases of the Moon; Historical Events;
Times for Sunrise, Sunset, Moonrise and Moonset;
Best Dates For Planting and Maintenance;
Journal Pages For Your Garden Record.

MOODY GARDENS:
A Natural Wonder

Acres of lush gardens. A beautiful tropical paradise.

Rainforest Pyramid
Explore the rainforests of Africa, Asia and The Americas. Discover the Bat Cave in our 10-story glass pyramid filled with tropical plants, birds, fish and butterflies.

IMAX 3D Theater
Sit back, relax, and put on your 3D glasses to experience adventure in IMAX 3D. Images seem to leap from the 6-story screen, drawing you right into the action.

Palm Beach
A secluded paradise featuring soft white sand, freshwater lagoons, tropical vegetation, and a yellow submarine for the little ones. Open Memorial Day through Labor Day.

1-800-582-4673

Moody Gardens is a public, non-profit botanical garden utilizing animals and nature in the process of healing, rehabilitation, education, research and recreation.

MOODY GARDENS
GALVESTON ISLAND

RAINFOREST PYRAMID   IMAX 3D   PALM BEACH   CONVENTION & CONFERENCE CENTER

1997 CALENDAR

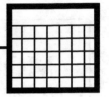

January
S	M	T	W	T	F	S
			1	2	3	4
5	6	7	8	9	10	11
12	13	14	15	16	17	18
19	20	21	22	23	24	25
26	27	28	29	30	31	

February
S	M	T	W	T	F	S
						1
2	3	4	5	6	7	8
9	10	11	12	13	14	15
16	17	18	19	20	21	22
23	24	25	26	27	28	

March
S	M	T	W	T	F	S
						1
2	3	4	5	6	7	8
9	10	11	12	13	14	15
16	17	18	19	20	21	22
23	24	25	26	27	28	29
30	31					

April
S	M	T	W	T	F	S
		1	2	3	4	5
6	7	8	9	10	11	12
13	14	15	16	17	18	19
20	21	22	23	24	25	26
27	28	29	30			

May
S	M	T	W	T	F	S
				1	2	3
4	5	6	7	8	9	10
11	12	13	14	15	16	17
18	19	20	21	22	23	24
25	26	27	28	29	30	31

June
S	M	T	W	T	F	S
1	2	3	4	5	6	7
8	9	10	11	12	13	14
15	16	17	18	19	20	21
22	23	24	25	26	27	28
29	30					

July
S	M	T	W	T	F	S
		1	2	3	4	5
6	7	8	9	10	11	12
13	14	15	16	17	18	19
20	21	22	23	24	25	26
27	28	29	30	31		

August
S	M	T	W	T	F	S
					1	2
3	4	5	6	7	8	9
10	11	12	13	14	15	16
17	18	19	20	21	22	23
24	25	26	27	28	29	30
31						

September
S	M	T	W	T	F	S
	1	2	3	4	5	6
7	8	9	10	11	12	13
14	15	16	17	18	19	20
21	22	23	24	25	26	27
28	29	30				

October
S	M	T	W	T	F	S
			1	2	3	4
5	6	7	8	9	10	11
12	13	14	15	16	17	18
19	20	21	22	23	24	25
26	27	28	29	30	31	

November
S	M	T	W	T	F	S
						1
2	3	4	5	6	7	8
9	10	11	12	13	14	15
16	17	18	19	20	21	22
23	24	25	26	27	28	29
30						

December
S	M	T	W	T	F	S
	1	2	3	4	5	6
7	8	9	10	11	12	13
14	15	16	17	18	19	20
21	22	23	24	25	26	27
28	29	30	31			

Civil Calendar

New Year's Day .... Wednesday, Jan. 1
Martin Luther King Day .... Monday, Jan. 20
Presidents' Day .... Monday, Feb. 17
Mother's Day .... Sunday, May 11
Armed Forces Day .... Saturday, May 17
Memorial Day .... Monday, May 26
Father's Day .... Sunday, June 15
Flag Day .... Saturday, June 14
Independence Day .... Friday, July 4
Labor Day .... Monday, Sept. 1
Columbus Day .... Monday, Oct. 13
Halloween .... Friday, Oct. 31
General Election Day .... Tuesday, Nov. 4
Veteran's Day .... Tuesday, Nov. 11
Thanksgiving Day .... Thursday, Nov. 27

Texas Calendar

Sam Rayburn Day .... Monday, Jan. 6
Confederate Heroes Day .... Monday, Jan. 20
Texas Independence Day .... Sunday, Mar. 2
Sam Houston Day .... Sunday, Mar. 2
Texas Flag Day .... Sunday, Mar. 2
San Jacinto Day .... Monday, April 21
Emancipation Day in Texas .... Thursday, June 19

Religious Calendar *

Epiphany .... Monday, Jan. 6
First Day of Ramadan (Tabular) .... Friday, Jan. 10
Ash Wednesday .... Wednesday, Feb. 12
Palm Sunday .... Sunday, Mar. 23
Good Friday .... Friday, Mar. 28
Easter Sunday .... Sunday, Mar. 30
First Day of Passover (Tabular) (Pasach) .... Tuesday, Apr. 22
Ascension Day .... Thursday, May 8
Islamic New Year (Tabular) .... Friday, May 9
Whit Sunday, Pentecost .... Sunday, May 18
Trinity Sunday .... Sunday, May 25
Feast of Weeks (Tabular) (Shavuot) .... Wednesday, June 11
Jewish New Year (Tabular) (Rosh Hashanah) ...... Thursday, Oct. 2
Day of Atonement (Tabular) (Yom Kippur) .... Saturday, Oct. 11
First Day of Tabernacles (Tabular) (Succoth) .... Thursday, Oct. 16
First Sunday of Advent .... Sunday, Nov. 30
First Day of Hanukkah (Tabular) .... Saturday, Dec. 6
Hanukkah .... Wednesday, Dec. 24
Christmas Day .... Thursday, Dec. 25
First Day of Ramadan .... Wednesday, Dec. 31

The Jewish and Islamic dates are tabular dates which begin at sunset on the previous evening and end on the day tabulated. In practice, the dates of the Jewish and Islamic fasts and festivals are detemined by an actual sighting of the appropriate new moon.

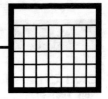

Visibility Of Planets In Morning & Evening Twilight

Morning Stars

Venus	Jan. 1 - Feb. 21
Mars	Jan. 1 - Mar. 17
Jupiter	Feb. 2 - Aug. 9
Saturn	Apr. 17 - Oct. 10

Evening Stars

Jupiter	Jan. 1- Jan. 6; Aug. 9 - Dec. 31
Saturn	Jan. 1 - Mar. 13; Oct. 10 - Dec. 31
Mars	Mar. 17 - Dec. 31
Venus	May 12- Dec. 31

Eclipses

Total Eclipse of the Sun   Mar. 8-9
Viewable throughout the Americas except northwest, and from Iceland, Greenland, Arctic, West Africa, part of Antarctica, Europe except extreme east.

Partial Eclipse of the Moon   Mar. 24
Viewable throughout the Americas except northwest, and from Iceland, Greenland, Arctic, West Africa, part of Antarctica, Europe except extreme east.

Partial Eclipse of the Sun   Sept. 1-2
Australia, New Zealand, Southeastern Indian Ocean, part of Antarctica, southwestern Pacific Ocean

Total Eclipse of the Moon   Sept. 16
Australasia, Asia except extreme northeast, Indian Ocean, Africa, Europe, southeastern Atlantic Ocean, Antarctica, western Pacific Ocean.

Daylight Savings Time

Spring Ahead — First Sunday in APRIL, set clocks ahead 1 hour
Fall Back — Last Sunday in OCTOBER, set clocks back 1 hour

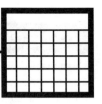

The Almanac Eras

The background behind the calendar cycles and eras described in this almanac as they relate to the Christian calendar:

The **Christian** (Gregorian) calendar is calculated from the starting point of the birth of Christ.

The **Byzantine** calendar has its starting point at the creation of the world, as narrated in the Book of Genesis, calculated to be the year 5509 B.C.

The **Jewish** calendar — Jewish Era (A.M., *anno mundi*, Latin for "year of the world") also has the creation of the world as its starting point, but calculates that date to be 3761 B.C.

The **Chinese** era bases its beginning — 2637 B.C. — on a legendary date, the founding of the Chinese Empire by the equally legendary emperor, Fo-Hi.

The **Japanese** calendar uses as its starting point the legendary creation of the Japanese island by the Sun Goddess in 660 B.C.

The **Aztec** calendar (see page 14) represents cycles of 52 years, starting over at Year 1 every 53rd year. They were not recorded linearly, at least as far as current scholarship can determine.

The calendars of **Nabonassar**, **Seleucid** (or Grecian) and **Diocletian** are named for individuals, and are important for astronomers and historians as their names appear on dated lists of Roman kings and rulers whose births, exploits, deaths are recorded and can be cross-checked and correlated.

The **Roman** calendar, which was used for thousands of years until the Christian calendar started to be used in the 6th century A.D., counted its years from the traditional founding of Rome in 753 B.C. — Roman Era (A.U.C., *ab urbe condita*, Latin for "from the founding of the city.")

Chronological Cycles & Eras

Dominical Letter	E
Epact	21
Golden No. (Lunar Cycle)	III
Julian Period	6710
Roman Indiction	5
Solar Cycle	8

All dates are given in terms of the Gregorian Calendar in which 1997 January 14 corresponds to 1997 January 1 of the Julian Calendar.

Era	Year	Begins
Byzantine	7506	Sep. 14
Jewish (A.M.)*	5758	Oct. 1
Chinese (Ding-chou)	4634	Feb. 7
Roman (A.U.C.)*	750	Jan. 14
Nabonassar	2746	Apr. 24
Japanese	2657	Jan. 1
Grecian (Seleucidae)	2309	Sep. 14
		(or Oct. 14)
Indian (Saka)	1919	Mar. 22
Diocletian	1714	Sep. 11
Islamic (Hegira)*	1418	May 8

*(* Year begins at sunset)*

ARBOR DAY

National Arbor Day is April 25. In the past, the state of Texas and some cities have at times marked their own Arbor Days in January, when it makes more sense to establish trees in the ground here. It's not clear whether politics or John Denver was too much to resist; unfortunately, many of the January dates have been abandoned even by enlightened municipalities.

Our solution: Find a grand specimen of a native Texas tree and plant it in the landscape in late January. Then in April, raise your glass in a toast to trees everywhere.

Some Great Trees For Texas

Shade Trees
Texas Green Ash
Bur Oak
Red Oak
Chinquapin Oak
Caddo Maple
Bald Cypress
Big Tooth Maple
Austrian Pine
Pecan
Ponderosa Pine
Chinese Pistache
Red Cedar

Ornamental Trees
Possumhaw
Mexican Plum
Sumac, Flame
Wax Myrtle
Desert Willow
Eve's Necklace
Yaupon Holly
Mexican Buckeye
Washington Hawthorn
Japanese Maple
Redbud, Texas
Rusty Blackhaw Viburnum

Tulip Time in Holland
— Spring 1997 —

An 8-Day Garden Tour Sponsored By
Texas Garden Almanac and
Texas Gulf Coast Gardening
(Includes Travel Days)

Join Us And . . .

- Enjoy a panoramic city tour of 700-year-old Amsterdam, including the Royal Palace on Dam Square, Central Station, Mint Tower, Skinny Bridge and the Flower District.
- Visit the largest flower show on earth: 70 acres of blooming tulips and other Dutch bulbs in famous Kuekenhof Gardens at Lisse. Stop at Frans Roozen Nursery to shop and ship bulbs for your home garden.
- Enjoy a drive along the scenic River Vecht, visit an historic private garden and the Palace Het Loo, where the group will tour the formal royal summer residence and its Versailles-like sculptured gardens.
- Tour Hoge Veluwe National Park and several private gardens in the area.
- Visit Leiden and the Hortus Botanicus, where the first tulip was brought from Turkey. Tour the Hague and a Delft Blue pottery factory. Time out to shop!
- Spend the last full day in Amsterdam. Start at the Aalsmeer flower auction, which sells and ships millions of flowers worldwide every day. Visit the Hortus Bulborum at Limmen to see its unique collection, more than 100 tulip varieties. Afternoon tour options: the Anne Frank House, the Rijkmuseum, the floating flower market, the Van Gogh Museum or a relaxing canal cruise.

Cost: Approximately $1,400 U.S., double occupancy, plus airfare.
Single supplement approx. $300.

*** *Optional 3-Day Rhine Cruise afterward* ***
(approx. $225)

A Dream-Come-True Christmas Gift!

AZTEC CALENDAR

By Brian Anderson

When the ancient Aztecs first planted seed corn in the rich soils of the Valley of Mexico — the lakes region where Mexico City now lies — they got more than simple maize stalks in return. They found a new and better way of living, and in time, unearthed the timeless secrets of social stability and economic power.

In fact, experts often cite the Aztecs' advanced farming skill as a key factor in the civilization's rise to domination in central Mexico after the 1300s. By perfecting the cultivation of maize, the Aztecs learned to support a stable population, and in the process, transformed themselves from a poor, nomadic tribe into a powerful kingdom of millions.

Like many ancient civilizations, the Aztecs strived to understand the forces of untold power that held sway over the yearly crops and other life events. Though some of the ways Aztecs attempted to control nature, including human sacrifice, seem unspeakably barbaric to the modern mind, the Aztec calendar stands as a monument to aesthetic style and mathematical grace.

The Aztecs measured the passage of time with two calendars, and each influenced the regulation of planting and harvesting. The 365-day solar calendar, the *xiuhpohualli*, was divided into 18 sections of 20 days each, later called *veintenas* by the Spanish, plus five "hollow" days at the end of the year.

These "hollow" days were believed to be unlucky, and Aztecs avoided danger at these times by retreating into inactivity. Scholars believe a sixth hollow day was added every four years to correct for the true length of the solar year.

Each *veintena*, or "month," had a special festival tied to the agricultural calendar. Before the planting of maize in spring, for instance, the Aztecs celebrated "The Ceasing of Water" and the "Flaying of Men" festivals, appeasing the gods with sacrifices, offerings, and ceremonial dances in hopes of a fertile and productive season. During the growing season, priests fasted for rain and the Aztec lords danced with maize stalks. The harvesting season prompted ceremonies in honor of the merciful fertility of the earth goddess.

While the *xiuhpohualli* calendar is similar to the modern Christian calendar, scholars have been puzzled by its companion, the 260-day calendar called *tonalpohualli*. The 260-day cycle was most likely inspired by the fact that the sun, on its annual passage from south to north, crosses an observed zenith point at a latitude near the Mayan city of Copán every 260 days.

Known as the "counting of the days," this circular calendar was divided into two cycles of 20 named days and 13 numbers. According to Aztec scholar Richard Townsend, each of the 20 days was given a separate name, such as alligator, rabbit, or flint knife, represented by a picture on the calendar wheel. After every rotation of the calendar, each animal or object day was engaged with a new number, represented by dots on the calendar. Thus, each day within the 260-day cycle was identified by both a number and an animal or object Day-Name.

The 260-day cycle was also divided into 20 periods of 13 days each, called trecenas by the Spaniards. Each "week" began with the number "1" and the Day-Name which happened to came up in rotation. This gave each day within the 260-day cycle a totally unique identity, represented by an animal or object, a number, and the week.

The resulting confusion was in one sense by design. The Aztec noble classes controlled access to the sacred *tonalpohualli* — kept in elaborate screenfold books called *tonalamatls* — and the mystical calendar likely served as a powerful tool in manipulating the hopes and fears of the masses.

The nobles trained experts to understand and interpret the meanings behind the *tonalpohualli* calendar combinations. In addition to making predictions in all areas of Aztec life, these diviners were called upon to help set the agricultural calendar and determine the best days for planting and harvesting. The results have interesting parallels to the way the zodiac has been used in other cultures. According to historian Diego Durán, Aztec diviners took great pains to coordinate their

THE 'CALENDAR ROUND' COMBINES BOTH AZTEC CALENDARS IN A 52-YEAR CYCLE.

own predictions with the festival calendar, natural agricultural seasons, and weather conditions. "All this was done with superstitious order and care," Durán wrote. "If chili was not sown on a certain day ... the people felt there would be great damage."

The two Aztec calendars merged in a 52-year cycle called the *xiuhmopilli*, sometimes known as the "Calendar Round." Any date could be designated by its position on the 52-year cycle, but, as frustrated historians have discovered, the 52-year cycles were not differentiated from each other in historical records.

The period at the end of each 52-year cycle was a time of great anxiety and foreboding, as the people waited for the end of the world foretold in Aztec creation myth. In expectation of the catastrophic events, when the stars and planets would devour the earth, all fires were extinguished and business activity ceased. People marked the end of the cycle by cleaning house, throwing out useless items, and smashing pottery.

Those who tended the *chinampas*, the famous Aztec farming plots built on reclaimed swamp lands, regulated planting and sowing activities more pragmatically, in order to maximize crop production. These "floating gardens," formed by dredging swamps and constructing artificial islands of fertile mud and aquatic plants, supplied the mighty Aztec cities with flowers, chilies, tomatoes, squashes, and maize. Planting times were carefully timed so that the plots produced crops year-round, and the professional diviners were not likely to interfere with this efficient production.

The Aztecs revered the sacred calendar system as a transcendent representation of the divine, and memorialized it in like fashion. The largest representation of the Aztec calendar, and the largest known Aztec carving, was discovered at Tenochtitlán in 1790. Known simply as the Calendar Stone or Sun Stone (for the grim-faced sun at the center of the carving), the circular monument spans 12 feet and weighs 24 tons. While not a working calendar, the design summarizes the story of the Aztec creation myths and includes the 20-animal and -object calendar Day-Signs in a band around the inner circle of the monument.

The Spanish conquest ushered in the end of the world as the Aztecs knew it, but the end did not come at the close of a 52-year cycle, nor did earthquakes swallow the sun as predicted in creation myths. The sun kept burning and the earth kept spinning. And like the sun, Aztec farming culture continues to thrive in small pockets throughout the Valley, producing flowers, tomatoes, and chilies in much the same fashion as the ancients did. The calendar wheel, too, continues to turn endlessly round, mimicking the spinning cosmos and the interlocking of earthly time and heavenly eternity.

MOON PLANTING SIGNS

Moon signs have guided the way humans plant for about as long as humans have planted. After centuries of controlled experiments and tradition, here's the basic idea: plant above-ground crops while the moon increases from new to full, and plant root crops as the moon decreases from full to new.

Why this should work is rather mysterious to seasoned gardeners and PhD'd horticulturists alike. Is it gravitational force between moon and earth, and the resulting change in water pressure within plant cells? Or biomagnetic force lines on our planet, in turn affected by the sun and moon? For some of us, the moon signs rule because "Grandma always did it that way." Author Christine Allison admits being in the "plant it whenever" group of gardeners, but adds, "I cannot dispute that of all the gardeners I know, the wisest, gentlest and most methodical ones — who also have the most spectacular gardens — do follow the moon's phases in their gardening."

If you're doubtful, experiment! Plant a row "by the moon" and another row "the wrong week," and compare for yourself.

"Dark of the moon" doesn't mean to plant your potatoes at midnight. The term simply refers to the moon's waning days from full to new. "Light of the moon" is the opposite — those days the moon grows from new to full, ideal for leafy crops and other good things that make food above the ground. But look to weather and common sense: a 4" tomato transplanted during a freeze won't do well, no matter how the heavens align.

In the course of agricultural history, here's how growers have made the best use of waxing and waning moons:

New Moon: First Phase, increasing; from time of new moon to first quarter. Plant annuals producing above ground, especially leafy types with the seed formed outside the fruit. (Corn and rice, lettuce and cabbage; ornamental flowers.)

First Quarter: Second Phase, increasing; from first quarter to full moon. Plant annuals for above-ground harvests, especially those that form seed within the fruit. (Beans, melons, tomatoes, some flowers.) These plants will generally thrive if planted in the first or second phase.

Full Moon: Third Phase, decreasing; from full moon to last quarter. Plant below-ground crops (beets, peanuts, potatoes) and flowering bulbs, rhizomes, corms, etc. A good time of the month to establish trees, shrubs, perennials and biennials (plants you establish this year for production next year, such as onion sets, parsley, strawberries).

Last Quarter: Fourth Phase, decreasing; from last quarter to new moon. This is not a planting time. Use these days to pull weeds, stalk and slay pests, prune and cultivate.

MOON PLANTING SIGNS

To further refine lunar planning and planting, consider the Zodiac signs. When "the moon is in Aquarius," that means the moon in the sky is within that particular constellation at that time. This can make you dizzy if you study it too closely, because astronomers and astrologers are about 30 degrees apart thanks to the precession of the equinoxes. Because this (and most) almanacs calculate planting times based on the moon phase and the zodiac sign, siding with the astrologer, we're off 30 degrees from what you'd see through a telescope.

Fruitful signs are Taurus, Cancer, Scorpio and Pisces; Capricorn rates as somewhat fruitful. Virgo and especially Libra are productive signs for planting flowers. Barren signs are Aries, Gemini, Leo, Virgo, Libra (except for flowers), Sagittarius and Aquarius. You won't catch most lunar gardeners planting on those dates, though some will put fruit crops in the ground on a Sagittarius date. Follow this guide when the moon is in:

Aries: Barren sign; a time to destroy weeds and pests.
Taurus: Productive sign; plant hardy crops such as potatoes and cabbages.
Gemini: Barren; prune, cultivate and spray as needed.
Cancer: Very productive; the most fruitful sign.
Virgo: Again, barren; dig, prune, spray.
Libra: Semi-productive; a good time to plant and tend flowers.
Scorpio: Very productive, most fruitful sign after Cancer.
Sagittarius: Barren; don't plant now. Unleash the weed whacker, and greet slugs with a brick in each hand.
Capricorn: Fairly productive; good for root crops.
Aquarius: Barren; hoe and aerate, replenish compost, prune and spray as needed.
Leo: Barren; weed, water and dream of Pisces.
Pisces: Very productive. Sow, fertilize, reap the harvest. Smell the flowers.

ZODIAC Rules!

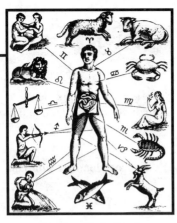

Ram....................... **ARIES** ...... Head and Face
March 21 to April 19
Twins .... **GEMINI**..................... Arms
May 20 to June 21
Lion......................... **LEO** .... Heart
July 22 to August 22
Balance ....**LIBRA** .... Veins
September 23 to October 23
Archer .... **SAGITTARIUS** .... Thighs
November 21 to December 22
Waterman .... **AQUARIUS** .... Legs
January 20 to February 19
Bull .... **TAURUS** .... Neck
April 19 to May 20
Crab .... **CANCER** .... Breast
June 21 to July 22
Virgin .... **VIRGO** .... Bowels
August 22 to September 23
Scorpion .... **SCORPIO** .... Secrets
October 23 to November 21
Goat .... **CAPRICORN** .... Knees
December 22 to January 20
Fish .... **PISCES** .... Feet
February 19 to March 21

***Ruling Periods of
the Twelve Signs of
the Zodiac and
Their Relation
to the Body***

Traditionally, gatherers of medicinal herbs follow the moon's phase and its position in the Zodiac — always remembering that the weather must be dry when you are harvesting herbs. Herbs picked to heal or strengthen those parts of the body governed by the Zodiac sign of the gathering day are said to be particularly effective.

Sign	Gather Herbs For...
Capricorn:	Bone and joint problems, skin diseases
Aquarius:	Vein diseases
Pisces:	Foot complaints
Aries:	Headaches, eye problems
Taurus:	Sore throat, ear ailments
Gemini:	Tension in the shoulders, lung complaints (for inhalation)
Cancer:	Bronchitis; stomach, liver and gall-bladder complaints
Leo:	Heart and circulation complaints
Virgo:	Digestive disorders, pancreas, nervous complaints
Libra:	Hip ailments, kidney and gall-bladder diseases
Scorpio:	Diseases of sexual and eliminating organs; good gathering sign for all herbs.
Sagittarius:	Vein diseases

MOON LORE

Sufferers of every sort of complaint have turned to plants for relief for centuries; it's no coincidence that most of modern pharmacy still has its origin in the plant kingdom. Following is a sample of remedies from traditional herbal medicine:

Effect	Plants
Improve bladder function	Chamomile, dandelion, stinging nettle, white dead nettle, rhubarb, yarrow
Lower blood pressure	Garlic, onion, field horsetail, mistletoe
Purifying blood	Dandelion, fennel, stinging nettle, pansy, yarrow
Lowering blood sugar	Bilberry leaves, dandelion, elder leaves, stinging nettle, onion, valerian, watercress
Improving blood	Carrot, black currant, cress, celery, field horsetail, garlic, lovage, marigold, stinging nettle, onion, parsley, radish, St. John's wort, thyme
Gynaelogical disorders	Lady's mantle, stinging nettles, sage, shepherd's purse, yarrow
Reduce inflammation	Agrimony, chamomile, comfrey, coltsfoot, great plantain, ribwort plantain
Activate gall bladder	Agrimony, lesser bindweed, buck-bean, chamomile, dandelion, garlic, gentian, peppermint, radish, St. John's wort
Pain, cramp relief	Apple (infusion of peel; drink very hot), balm, birch leaves, chamomile, heather, field horsetail, common knotgrass, peppermint, rosemary, sage, St. John's wort, savory, silverweed, valerian, yarrow
Elimination	Alder bark, buckthorn, fumintory, dandelion roots, senna leaves, yarrow
Strengthen connective tissue*	Agrimony, barley, french bean, comfrey, cucumber, heather, field horsetail, marjoram, stinging nettle, onion, spinach
Improve lung function	Beetroot, field horsetail, marjoram, mullein, onion, plantain, sage, watercress, yarrow

* Active ingredient is silicic acid; use young plants if harvesting your own, as little acid is released from older specimens. For best effect, gather these herbs when the moon is waning.

MOON LORE

	Activity	Moon's Phase	Moon Sign
Hair	Cutting To Decrease Growth	Full Moon or Last Quarter	Gemini, Leo, Virgo
	Cutting To Increase Growth	New Moon or First Quarter	Cancer, Pisces, Scorpio
	Cutting For Thickness	Full Moon	Any sign except Virgo
	Permanent Waves	New Moon	Aquarius
Weight	Start Diet To Lose Weight	New Moon or First Quarter	Aries, Leo, Virgo, Aquarius, Sagittarius
	Start Diet To Gain Weight	New Moon or First Quarter	Cancer, Pisces, Scorpio
Teeth	Filling	Full Moon or Last Quarter	Taurus, Leo, Scorpio, Aquarius
	Removing	New Moon or First Quarter	Gemini, Virgo, Sagittarius, Pisces, Capricorn
Laying Shingles		Full Moon or Last Quarter	Taurus, Leo, Aquarius, Pisces
Setting Fence Posts		Full Moon or Last Quarter	Taurus, Leo, Aquarius, Pisces
Surgery		New Moon or First Quarter	Aquarius, Gemini, Capricorn
Weaning		Full Moon or Last Quarter	Aquarius, Pisces, Sagittarius, Capricorn

Herbs gathered for their medicinal value are generally harvested young, when their active ingredients are released more easily. Herbs picked for the stewpot have the most agreeable pungency as youngsters, too. Spring is thus the favored time to harvest, though many herbs and other edibles will produce young plants and leaves later in the year.

Roots are best gathered at night, early in the morning or early in the evening. If your eye is on the moon, choose a day when it's full, waning or new; old herbals consider new-moon harvesting ideal because the "powers" of the plant have gone down to the roots.

Gather **leaves** after the morning dew has dried but before midday sun starts to wilt them. (Most books describe that point of happy medium as "late morning," but in Texas in

NORTH TEXAS (Zones 6-7)

Herb	Spring Planting	Fall Planting
Horseradish	Feb-Mar-Apr	**Sep-Oct**-Nov
Cilantro		**Oct**-Nov
Cumin	**Apr**-May	
Dill	**Mar**	**Sep-Oct**
Fennel	**Mar**	Sep-Oct
Parsley	**Jan 15-Feb**	Aug-Sep-**Oct**-Nov
Lemongrass	**Apr**-May	
Ginger root	**Apr-May**	
Turmeric root	**Apr-May**	
Basil	**Apr**-May-Jun	
Lemon balm	**Mar**	**Oct 15**-Nov
Mint	Mar-Apr	**Oct-Nov**
Oregano	Mar-Apr	Oct 15-Nov
Perilla	Mar 15-**Apr**	
Rosemary	Feb-**Mar**	Oct 15-Nov
Sage	**Mar**-Apr	**Oct 15**-Nov
Summer savory	**Feb**-Mar	**Oct**
Thyme	**Mar**-Apr	
Onion bulb		Oct-**Nov 15**
Onion seed	Jan-Feb	**Oct-Nov**
Onion, multiplying (seeds)		Oct-**Nov 15**
Onion, multiplying (plants)	**Jan-Feb-Mar**	Aug-Sep-Oct-Nov
Garlic		**Oct-Nov**
Garlic chives	**Feb-Mar-Apr-May**-Jun-Jul	Aug-**Sep**-Oct-Nov
Leeks (seeds)		Oct-Nov
Chile peppers (plants)	**Apr 15**-May 15	
Sorrel		**Oct**
Tomatillo (seeds)	Mar-**Apr**-May-Jun-**Jul**	
Tomatillo (plants)	Mar 15-**Apr**-May-Jun-**Jul**	

*(Ideal months are in **bold**.)*

How To...

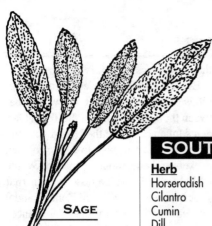

SAGE

warm seasons, 9 a.m. is plenty late.) Timing is especially important with broad-leafed, pungent herbs such as basil: as the sun warms the leaf surface, the essential oils will be stimulated to the detriment of flavor. You can harvest herbs in rainy weather if you plan to use them right away; otherwise, wait for a drier day to harvest herbs for preservation.

Pick **flowers** in the sunny hours, when they are fully unfolded; don't wait until they are on the verge of fading.

Collect **seeds and fruit** any time of day; they aren't so sensitive as other parts of the plant. (Avoid the heat of midday, for your own sake as well as the plant's!)

SOUTH TEXAS (Zones 8-9)

Herb	Spring Planting	Fall Planting
Horseradish	Jan-Feb-Mar	**Sep-Oct**-Nov-Dec
Cilantro		**Oct**-Nov
Cumin	**Apr**-May	
Dill	**Feb**	Sep-Oct
Fennel	**Feb**	Sep-**Oct**
Parsley	**Jan 15-Feb**	Aug-Sep-**Oct**-Nov
Lemongrass	Mar 15-**Apr**	
Ginger root	**Apr-May**	
Turmeric root	**Apr-May**	
Basil	**Mar-Apr**-May-Jun	
Lemon balm	**Feb**	**Oct 15-Nov**
Mint	**Feb**-Mar-Apr	**Oct**-Nov
Oregano	Mar	Oct 15-Nov
Perilla	Mar 15-**Apr**	
Rosemary	Feb-**Mar**	Oct 15-Nov
Sage	**Mar**-Apr	**Oct 15**-Nov
Summer savory	**Feb**-Mar	**Oct**
Thyme	**Mar**-Apr	
Onion bulb		Oct 15-**Nov 15**
Onion seed	Jan-Feb	**Oct 15-Nov**-Dec
Onion, multiplying (seeds)		Oct-**Nov 15**
Onion, multiplying (plants)	**Jan-Feb-Mar**	Aug-Sep-Oct-**Nov-Dec**
Garlic		**Oct**-Nov
Garlic chives	Jan 15-**Feb-Mar-Apr-May**-Jun-Jul	Aug-**Sep-Oct**-Nov
Leeks (seeds)		Oct-**Nov**
Chile peppers (plants)	**Mar 15**-Apr 15	
Sorrel		**Oct**
Tomatillo (seeds)	Mar-**Apr**-May-Jun-**Jul**-Aug	
Tomatillo (plants)	Mar 15-**Apr**-May-Jun-**Jul**-Aug	

*(Ideal months are in **bold**.)*

TEXAS GARDENING

Texans who write about Texas are fond of the phrase, "nowhere else but." Consider the topic of gardening in Texas and the phrase is hard to avoid. Only California rivals the Lone Star State's north-south stretch through so many of the USDA's growing zones. But Texas is even wider than it is tall, encompassing coastal woodlands, high interior plains, great river basins and western deserts in almost every zone.

So variety is the spice of our gardening lives, from bugs to soils to weather to the fungus among us. In this book, we've covered problems and growing conditions particular to Texas — and made some distinctions between our many climates and ecosystems. Dr. Sam Cotner, author, home gardener, and chairman of the horticulture department at Texas A&M University, insists that choosing good varieties for your area is a critical piece of the gardening puzzle. In the regional sections that begin on page 178, you'll find recommendations from extension agents around the state. Their experience and

their successes are yours to share.

Every book that includes "gardening regions of Texas" seems to draw lines between them differently. In the Texas Garden Almanac, we use the USDA growing zones to make it easy to relate to seed packets and other sources that follow the USDA map (next pages). Within that structure, we have divided Zones 8 and 9 into east and west, to make allowances for humidity, topography and soils that make a Zone 8 garden in Tyler rather different from a Zone 8 garden in El Paso.

The result, like most things in life, isn't perfect. "Greater Houston" straddles the line between Zone 9 and Zone 8, and Houstonians in northern suburbs should be successful with both Zone 8 and Zone 9 recommendations. Corpus Christi could have fallen on either side of our east-west division of Zone 9; the same applies to Bryan and College Station in Zone 8. They are the Switzerlands of Texas gardening, absorbing the horticulture of neighbors from all sides!

ZONE 6
ZONE 7
ZONE 8E
ZONE 8W
ZONE 9E
ZONE 9W

TEXAS WEATHER TRIVIA

COLDEST DAY IN TEXAS

-23°F

It happened twice:
Tulia
  (Swisher County, Feb. 8, 1899)
Seminole
  (Gaines County, Feb. 12, 1933)

HOTTEST DAY IN TEXAS

120°F

Also twice:
Seymour
  (Baylor County, August 12, 1936)
Monahans
  (Ward County, June 28, 1994)

MOST ANNUAL RAINFALL

109.38 inches
Clarksville 1873

LEAST ANNUAL RAINFALL

1.76 inches
Wink 1956

GREATEST SINGLE SNOW STORM

33.0 inches
Hale Center, Feb. 2-5, 1956
  The snow deposit on the ground at
  Hale Center on Feb. 5, 1956
  measured 33.0 inches, also a record.

HIGHEST SUSTAINED WIND

145 mph (over one mile)
Measured on two sites,
Matagorda and Port Lavaca,
during Hurricane Carla,
on Sept. 11, 1961.

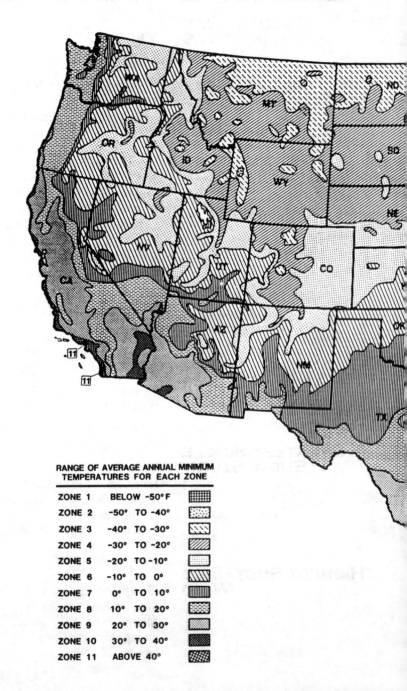

RANGE OF AVERAGE ANNUAL MINIMUM TEMPERATURES FOR EACH ZONE

ZONE 1	BELOW -50° F	
ZONE 2	-50° TO -40°	
ZONE 3	-40° TO -30°	
ZONE 4	-30° TO -20°	
ZONE 5	-20° TO -10°	
ZONE 6	-10° TO 0°	
ZONE 7	0° TO 10°	
ZONE 8	10° TO 20°	
ZONE 9	20° TO 30°	
ZONE 10	30° TO 40°	
ZONE 11	ABOVE 40°	

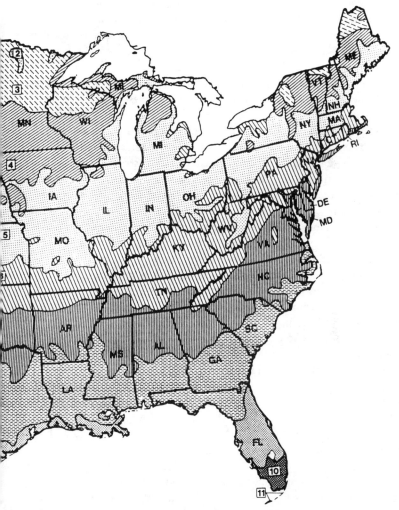

PLANT HARDINESS ZONE MAP

Years ago the U.S. Department of Agriculture in cooperation with the American Horticultural Society prepared a plant hardiness zone map. Revised periodically, it is the accepted norm in the horticultural field. These are the zones you see referred to in gardening books. This is the *1991* edition.

Temperature and day length are critical factors for most vegetable culture. Follow the planting charts for spring (page 98) and fall (page 138) for best results.

The notes below reflect more details needs and concerns for specific vegetables; all temperatures are Farenheit.

BEETS should mature when daytime temperatures average between 60° and 65°.

BIENNIALS (Carrots, parsley, etc.) are plants which normally have a two-year life cycle, growing vegetatively the first year and then flowering and setting seed in the second year. If carrots grow for a period of time, and then experience temperatures of 45° and below, they can "bolt" (be induced to flower) in the first year. In the case of carrots, this seriously impairs good root growth after that.

BROCCOLI produces more and better-quality heads when temperatures are between 45° and 70°. The best spring planting date, therefore, is two weeks before the normal last freeze date; in fall, planting 10-12 weeks before the firt killing frost allows time for plants to be harvested before freezing weather damages plants. (On the Gulf Coast, broccoli can often be harvested all winter.)

CABBAGES that mature when temperatures average 60°-65° produce the best heads. While cabbages are cold and even freeze tolerant, a sudden light freeze can burn them if they are not conditioned by cool weather first. In Texas, warm weather is the biggest problem: if cabbages haven't matured by the time temperatures are consistently above 75°, some heads will be loose and others won't form at all. (Choosing good varieties for your area helps.)

CARROTS like a temperature range of 40°-85° for best production.

COLLARDS and **KALE** develop sugar in their leaves after a frost, making their flavor sweeter and milder.

CUCUMBERS need night temperatures above 55° for best production. Sensitive to both soil and air temperature, cucumbers won't respond to early planting unless you provide protective cover for the plant and black plastic mulch to warm the soil.

KOHLRABI produces best when average temperatures stay below 70°, though it tolerates a wider cool-to-warm range than turnips do. Biennial (see above).

LETTUCE seed will germinate in soils ranging from freezing to about 85°, but you need soil temperatures under 75° to get a good harvest of lettuce. Leaf lettuce is easier to grow in most of Texas than heading types, primarily because leaf varieties mature in about 55 days while the headers fool around for up to 90 days. That means spring-planted head lettuce will be maturing when it's hot in most of Texas. Even leaf lettuce will be poor quality if it matures in temperatures that average above 80°.

MUSTARD GREENS should be mature by the time daytime temperatures average 70° or more. Warmer temperatures and longer days prompt the greens to bolt, and make them taste "hot."

OKRA likes it hot: don't plant it until the surface soil has warmed to 68° and nighttime low temperature stays above 50° for five consecutive days. Ideal soil temperature for germination: 75°-90°.

ONIONS, like any true bulb, grow in response to day length. In Texas, that makes choosing the right variety critical. Short-day varieties need 10-11 hours of daylight to start bulbing; intermediate varieties need 12-13 hours and long-day varieties need 14-16. On the Gulf Coast and in South Texas, the longest day of summer is less than 14 hours, observes Sam Cotner, author and chairman of the horticulture department at Texas A&M. "That means the long-day varieties will never bulb, but make giant green onions instead." In North Texas, where summer days are longer, the long-day types will make bulbs, but the intermediate-day varieties will make bigger and better ones.

Planted at the right time, short-day varieties perform well all over Texas. They are also less pungent than long-day varieties. The 1015Y and other sweet onions from Texas are all short-day varieties.

Onions are biennial (see page 28).

PEPPERS need soil temperatures above 55° for good root growth and overall plant humor. To plant a fall crop in central and south Texas, set out tranplants about 100 days before the first frost date. (In north Texas, spring planted peppers are more likely to produce through the summer and into the fall.)

POTATOES (cured cut seed pieces) can be planted once temperatures reach 65°, ideally in high humidity.

PUMPKINS require planting long before we start thinking about jack-o-lanterns, since they can take 100 days or more to mature. For fall planting, count back 100 days from the first freeze date, and add another 20 days for weather insurance. In the spring, wait until frost danger is past and soil temperatures reach at least 70°.

RADISHES won't sprout in soil cooler than 45°, and the seed will germinate much faster at 55°-65°.

SPINACH should be planted in the fall once soil temperatures are below 75°; that's usually 8-10 weeks before first frost in most of Texas. Plants are cold tolerant into the low 20s, but harder freezes will damage or destroy spinach.

SWEET CORN should not be planted until the soil is at least 50° at the seedling depth and all danger of frost is past.

TOMATOES need to bloom while nighttime temperatures are below 75° and daytime temperatures are below 92°. That's why you should always start with transplants, not seed, in the garden: the window of time between the last frost and warm days (and especially nights) is too short in Texas.

Tomatillos have similar temperature requirements and are even more fussy. Many growers got plenty of flowers but no tomatillos in 1996.

TURNIP seeds will germinate (and quickly) when soils are warmer than 60°.

WATERMELON should be planted (seed) once the soil temperature reaches 70°. Planting early generally is futile unless you artificially warm the soil to this temperature with black plastic mulch or other material.

Average Amount By City (% of total amount possible)

	Jan	Feb	Mar	Apr	May	Jun	Jul	Aug	Sep	Oct	Nov	Dec
Abilene	62	64	70	71	70	78	79	77	70	72	68	64
Amarillo	69	68	71	74	73	78	79	78	73	75	72	67
Austin	49	52	55	54	57	69	76	75	67	64	55	50
Brownsville	42	48	53	58	65	74	80	76	68	65	51	43
Corpus Christi	45	50	55	56	60	73	80	77	68	68	55	45
Dallas/Fort Worth	55	56	60	64	61	70	76	74	69	62	58	55
El Paso	90	91	92	93	96	96	89	85	78	92	79	79
Galveston	48	50	56	61	67	75	72	71	67	71	59	49
Houston	43	48	50	54	58	64	66	65	62	61	49	51
Lubbock	66	66	72	73	72	76	77	77	70	74	69	65
Midland/Odessa	69	66	73	76	77	78	79	73	76	70	72	65
San Antonio	48	52	57	55	55	67	74	73	66	64	55	49
Port Arthur	42	52	52	52	64	69	65	63	62	67	57	47

Source: Based on data from U.S. Department of Commerce, *Local Climatological Data,* 1990.

HUMIDITY IN TEXAS

Average Relative Humidity (%)

	January				April				July				October			
	6a	12p	6p	12a	6a	12p	6p	12a	6a	12p	6p	12a	6a	12p	6p	12a
Abilene	72	54	49	66	71	46	39	62	71	45	38	57	75	52	49	67
Amarillo	70	50	47	64	68	38	31	56	73	42	37	61	73	44	42	65
Austin	78	60	57	72	82	57	52	75	88	51	46	74	84	55	54	75
Beaumont/Port Arthur	87	68	75	86	90	62	69	87	94	65	71	92	91	58	73	88
Brownsville	88	67	74	87	88	59	67	86	91	55	63	86	89	59	69	86
Corpus Christi	88	68	71	85	90	62	68	87	92	57	63	88	90	59	68	85
Dallas/Fort Worth	79	59	57	72	82	56	52	73	80	48	44	67	82	54	55	73
Del Rio	76	55	46	66	77	52	40	62	79	52	39	59	82	57	50	71
El Paso	37	28	48	64	27	19	33	48	45	39	63	77	37	29	53	70
Galveston	85	77	80	83	86	75	80	85	81	70	73	80	80	65	71	75
Houston	85	63	67	82	89	57	60	85	92	58	62	86	91	56	68	88
Lubbock	73	50	46	65	68	39	32	54	75	47	39	61	78	48	45	67
Midland/Odessa	71	46	41	63	66	34	27	53	72	41	34	57	80	47	44	71
San Angelo	76	52	47	68	74	43	36	62	77	44	37	60	83	52	50	74
San Antonio	80	59	57	75	82	56	51	76	87	51	45	75	84	54	52	77
Victoria	86	64	68	84	88	59	63	84	92	56	60	87	90	56	65	86
Waco	82	63	61	77	84	58	54	75	81	48	44	68	85	55	57	76
Wichita Falls	80	56	55	73	80	49	46	72	78	43	39	66	84	51	54	74

6a — 6:00 a.m.
12p — noon
6p — 6:00 p.m.
12a — midnight

Note: All times are local standard.

Source: Based on data from U.S. Department of Commerce, *Local Climatological Data,* 1990.

PRECIPITATION In Texas

Average Number Of Days With 0.10" Or More Rain

	Jan	Feb	Mar	Apr	May	Jun	Jul	Aug	Sep	Oct	Nov	Dec
Abilene (40 days annually)	2	3	3	3	4	4	3	4	4	4	3	2
Alpine (35 days)	1	1	1	1	2	4	6	6	6	3	1	1
Amarillo (38 days)	2	2	2	3	4	6	5	6	4	3	2	1
Austin (49 days)	4	4	4	4	6	5	3	3	5	5	4	4
Brownsville (40 days)	4	2	1	2	3	4	3	4	7	4	3	3
Chisos Basin (36 days)	2	2	1	1	3	4	5	6	6	3	1	1
College Station (56 days)	5	5	5	4	6	5	4	4	5	5	5	5
Corpus Christi (43 days)	4	3	2	2	5	4	3	4	6	4	3	3
Corsicana (55 days)	4	5	5	5	6	5	3	3	5	4	5	5
Dallas/Fort Worth (50 days)	4	4	5	5	6	4	3	3	5	4	4	4
El Paso (22 days)	1	1	1	1	1	2	4	4	3	2	1	2
Fort Stockton (29 days)	1	2	1	1	3	3	3	4	4	3	2	1
Fredericksburg (45 days)	3	4	3	4	5	4	3	4	5	4	3	3
Galveston (56 days)	6	4	3	3	4	5	5	5	6	4	5	5
Houston (Hobby) (64 days)	6	5	5	4	5	6	6	6	7	5	5	5
Huntsville (65 days)	6	5	5	4	6	6	5	5	6	4	6	6
Kerrville (49 days)	3	4	4	4	6	4	3	4	5	5	4	3
Laredo (31 days)	2	2	1	2	3	3	2	3	4	3	2	2
Longview (65 days)	6	6	6	5	6	6	4	4	5	5	5	6

PRECIPITATION In Texas

	Jan	Feb	Mar	Apr	May	Jun	Jul	Aug	Sep	Oct	Nov	Dec
Lubbock (36 days)	1	2	2	2	4	5	4	4	4	3	2	2
Lufkin (63 days)	6	5	5	4	6	6	5	4	5	5	5	5
Marfa (34 days)	1	1	1	1	3	5	5	6	5	3	1	1
McAllen (35 days)	3	3	1	2	4	4	3	4	5	3	2	2
McKinney (54 days)	4	5	5	6	6	5	3	3	5	4	4	4
Midland/Odessa (27 days)	1	2	1	2	3	3	3	3	4	3	1	1
Pecos (24 days)	1	1	1	1	2	2	3	3	4	3	1	1
Port Arthur (67 days)	7	5	5	4	6	5	7	7	7	4	5	6
Presidio (22 days)	1	1	*	1	1	3	3	4	3	2	1	1
San Angelo (35 days)	2	2	2	3	5	4	2	3	4	3	2	2
San Antonio (46 days)	4	4	3	4	5	5	3	4	5	5	4	3
Temple (50 days)	4	5	4	4	6	4	3	3	5	4	5	4
Tyler (62 days)	5	6	6	5	6	5	4	3	5	5	5	6
Uvalde (38 days)	2	3	2	4	5	4	2	3	4	4	2	2
Van Horn (27 days)	1	1	1	1	1	2	4	5	4	2	1	1
Victoria (52 days)	4	4	3	3	5	5	5	5	6	4	4	4
Waco (48 days)	4	4	4	4	5	5	2	3	4	4	4	4
Wichita Falls (45 days)	2	3	4	5	6	4	3	4	5	4	3	3

Note: In some instances the sum of the monthly values does not equal the annual total because of rounding.
* Less than one-half day.

Source: Based on data for the period 1961-1990.

HOW TO...
SPRAY FRUIT & NUT TREES

By Jerral D. Johnson, Charles L. Cole, James V. Robinson & George Ray McEachern

Editor's note: This homeowner's guide is reprinted courtesy of the Texas Agricultural Extension Service.

Homeowners should be familiar with pests and diseases, their life cycles and damage. Problems must be identified and the proper control methods selected. The situation is often complex because such problems vary from one area of Texas to another and with the time of year. It is important to keep records of pest and disease occurrence to assist in making control decisions, such as timing of pesticide applications. (The journal pages inside this almanac, starting on page 105, offer a handy place to record this activity.)

CULTURAL PRACTICES: Healthy plants are less susceptible to insect and disease attack. Optimum tree growth is maintained by following a well-balanced fertility program, selecting adapted disease-resistant varieties and practicing proper pruning and other cultural practices.

Proper clean-up and plant residue disposal are important in reducing plum curculio, hickory shuck-worm, brown rot of peach and pecan scab.

PESTICIDE SAFETY: Before using any pesticide, carefully read all instructions on the container. Note any special instructions such as the need to wear protective clothing. Take necessary precautions when applying pesticides to avoid unnecessary chemical exposure.

Mix pesticides in a well-ventilated area or outdoors. Avoid chemical contact with the skin and do not breathe chemical vapors.

Apply pesticides at the proper rate. Using less chemical than prescribed may result in poor control, while using more than recommended may damage plants or leave excess residue on the fruit. It is also a waste of money.

Store chemicals in a secure area away from pets and children. Prepare only the amount required for one application. Properly dispose of any unused, diluted sprays and empty pesticide containers. Never store pesticides in unmarked jars, cans or bottles.

SPRAY EQUIPMENT: A number of different sprayers can be used to apply insecticides and fungicides.

Compressed air sprayers range in size from 1 to 10 gallons; because of cost and handling ease, most homeowners prefer sprayers with reservoirs that hold 2-1/2 or 3 gallons. Hose-on sprayers are less expensive but require a high volume of water, moderate pressure and a convenient water outlet. Applying wettable powders with a hose-on sprayer is difficult.

Once a sprayer has been used, it is considered a used pesticide container and requires proper handling and storage. Proper cleaning prolongs its life. Do not apply insecticides and fungicides with a sprayer previously used to apply herbicides; this may cause plant damage.

The pesticides suggested in the accompanying tables are registered and labeled by the Environmental Protection Agency and the Texas Department of Agriculture. The status of pesticide label clearances is subject to change, and may have changed since this publication was printed. County extension agents and appropriate specialists are advised of changes as they occur.

The user always is responsible for the effects of pesticide residues on livestock and crops, as well as problems that arise from drift or movement of the pesticide from his property to that of others. *Always read and carefully follow the instructions on the container label.*

For further information, contact your county extension agent (see "Where to Find It" in the appropriate regional section of this almanac or your telephone book).

PECAN SPRAY SCHEDULE

Timing	Pest	Pesticide	* Rate/ 1 gal. Water
	Insects		
DORMANT SEASON (winter)	scale insects phylloxera	97% oil emulsion	.25-.33 pt.

Spray tree trunks and branchs thoroughly.

	Nutritional		
BUDBREAK (just as the buds begin to split and show green color) - terminal bud growth should be 2 inches in length	rosette	Zinc sulfate WP or Zinc nitrate liquid	2 tsps.

Zinc sprays are essential for early season pecan growth. Early, frequent applications will give the best response. Elemental zinc is toxic to most plants other than pecans and grapes; therefore, avoid drift. If drift is a possibility, use NZN. Do not use any zinc product at higher than labeled rates since foliage burn can result. When applying more than one zinc spray in two weeks, reduce rate by one-half. Never spray young trees that are not actively growing.

	Insects		
	phylloxera	Malathion® 50% EC (several formulations)	2 tsps.

If dormant oil was not used, then treat trees where a history of phylloxera damage indicates a need for control.

	Diseases		
	scab and other foliage and nut diseases	Benomyl 50% DF (several formulations) or	1/2-1 TBS.
		Thiophanatemethyl (Topsin-M® 70% WP)	1/2-1 TBS.

Thiophanate-methyl is also available as a flowable and wettable dry granule.

Timing	Pest	Pesticide	* Rate/ 1 gal. Water
	Nutritional		
PREPOLLINATION (when leaves are one-third grown and before pollen is shed) - mid-April	rosette	same as Budbreak	
	Diseases		
	scab and other foliage diseases	same as Budbreak	
	Insects		
	fall webworm walnut caterpillar	Bacillus thuringiensis (several formulations)	Refer to label
		or	
		Diazinon® 25% EC (several formulations)	Refer to label
		or	
		Malathion® 50% EC (several formulations)	2 tsps.
		or	
		Sevin® liquid (several formulations)	Refer to label

Repeat insect sprays as pest problem recurs.

	Nutritional		
POLLINATION (when casebearer eggs appear on tips of nutlets) - May	rosette	same as Budbreak	
	Insects		
	pecan nut casebearer	same as Prepollination	

Apply during egg hatch (consult your county extension agent for precise local timing.)

	Diseases		
	scab and other foliage and nut diseases	same as Budbreak	

	Insects		
SECOND GENERATION CASEBEARER (42 days after first casebearer spray)	pecan nut casebearer	same as Prepollination	
	aphids	Diazinon® 25% EC (several formulations)	Refer to label
		or	
		Malathion® 50% EC (several formulations)	2 tsps.
		or	
		Cygon® 2 EC	Refer to label

Treat yellow aphids where an average of 25 per compound leaf are found or when excessive honeydew is produced. Repeated use of insecticides can result in strains of aphids that are resistant to insecticides. This can result in increased losses.

Timing	Pest	Pesticide	* Rate/ 1 gal. Water
SECOND GENERATION CASEBEARER (cont'd)	**Diseases** scab and other foliage and nut diseases	same as Budbreak	

Additional sprays at 10- to 14-day intervals may be required during extended periods of rainfall or high humidity.

COVER SPRAYS	**Diseases** scab	same as Budbreak	

WATER STAGE (when inside of the nut fills with water) - mid- to late July	**Diseases** scab and other foliage and nut diseases	same as Budbreak	

Treat where there is a history of disease problems and during high humidity.

HALF-SHELL HARDENING (- mid- to late August)	**Insects** aphids	same as for aphids listed in Second Generation Casebearer	

Treat yellow aphids when an average of 25 insects per compound leaf are found or when excessive honeydew is produced and aphid populations persist.

	hickory shuckworm	Diazinon® 25% EC or Sevin liquid (several formulations)	Refer to label Refer to label
	pecan weevil	Sevin liquid (several formulations)	Refer to label

Treat areas with a history of pecan weevil infestation. One to three treatments of 10- to 14-day intervals are needed for heavy weevil infestations.

	Diseases scab and other foliage and nut diseases	same as Budbreak	

KEY — Spray Schedules
* Due to variation in concentration of pesticides in different products, refer to label for specific rate per one gallon spray solution.
 WP = wettable powder
 EC = emulsifiable concentrate
 DF = dry flowable

HOW TO...

Timing	Pest	Pesticide	* Rate/ 1 gal. Water
	Insects		
DORMANT SEASON	scale insects	97% dormant oil	.25 pt.

Apply when temperature is between 40° and 70° F. Use only once.

	Diseases		
LATE DORMANT	peach leaf curl	Chlorothalonil (Bravo 720® 54.0% F)	1.33 tsps.
		or	
		(Ortho Multi-purpose Fungicide Daconil 2787® 29.6% F)	2.25 tsps.

Apply if fall copper or chlorothalonil applications were not made.

	Diseases		
PINK BUD (just before bloom when buds show color)	brown rot	Captan® 50% WP	2.66 TBS.
		or	
		Sulfur 97% WP	8 TBS.
		or	
		Benomyl 50% DF (several formulations)	1.5-2.25 TBS.
		or	
		Thiophanate-methyl (Topsin-M® 70% WP)	1.5-2.25 TBS.
		or	
		Chlorothalonil (same as Late Dormant)	

Treat where there is a history of disease problems.

	Insects		
PETAL-FALL (when flower petals begin to fall)	plum curculio	Malathion® 50% EC (several formulations)	2.5 tsps.

Apply when 75% of petals have fallen, and there is a history of insect damage.

		Sevin liquid (several formulations)	Refer to label
		or	
	peach twig borer	Diazinon® 25% EC (several formulations)	Refer to label

The peach twig borer usually is a problem only in West Central Texas.

Timing	Pest	Pesticide	* Rate/ 1 gal. Water
	Insects		
PETAL-FALL (cont'd)	lesser peach tree borer	Endosulfan (Thiodan® 9.7% EC)	2 TBS.

Make two applications approximately three weeks apart. Thoroughly wet tree limbs with spray.

	Diseases		
	scab	same fungicides as for Pink Bud	

	Insects		
SHUCK SPLIT (when the calux separates from base of newly formed fruit)	catfacing insects plum curculio	same insecticides as for Petal Fall	

Treat where there is a history of catfacing insects and/or plum curculio.

	Diseases		
	scab	same fungicides as for Pink Bud	

	Insects		
FIRST COVER (14 days after shuck split)	catfacing insects plum curculio	same as Petal Fall	
	Diseases		
	scab	Captan 50% WP (several formulations)	2.66 TBS.
		or	
		Sulfur 97% WP	8 TBS.
		or	
		Benomyl 50% DF (several formulations)	1.5-2.25 TBS.
		or	
		Thiophanate-methyl (Topsin-M® 70% WP)	1.5-2.25 TBS.

Treat where there is a history of disease problems. Benomyl and thiophanate-methyl are the most effective fungicides for the control of brown rot and should be used in areas where the disease has been a major problem.

	Insects		
COVER SPRAYS (at 14-day intervals)	catfacing insects	same insecticides as for Petal Fall	
	Diseases		
	brown rot	Captan 50% WP (several formulations)	2.66 TBS.
		or	
		Sulfur 97% WP	8 TBS.

Timing	Pest	Pesticide	* Rate/ 1 gal. Water
	Insects		
PRE-HARVEST	June beetles	Carbaryl (Sevin 21.3% LF)	4 tsps.
	Diseases		
	brown rot	Benomyl 50% DF (several formulations) or	1.5-2.25 TBS.
		Thiophanate-methyl (Topsin-M® 80% WP)	1.5-2.25 TBS.

Do not apply Benomyl within 3 days of harvest. Thiophanate-methyl can be applied on day of harvest. Wash all fruit before eating.

Timing	Pest	Pesticide	Rate
	Insects		
POST-HARVEST (mid- to late August)	peach tree borer	Chlorpyrifos (Lorsban® 12.9%) or	2 TBS.
		Lindane (Lindane® 20% EC) or	1 TBS.
		Endosulfan (Thiodan® 9.7% EC)	2 TBS.

Thoroughly wet from base of tree up to first scaffold limbs.

	Diseases		
	peach rust	Chlorothalonil (Bravo 720® 54.0%) or	1.33 tsps.
		(Ortho Multi-purpose Fungicide with Daconil 2787® 29.6%)	2.25 tsps.

Begin applications at first sign of rust and continue at 2- to 3-week intervals. Rust is a problem in counties south of a line from Houston to Hallettsville and Rio Grande City.

Timing	Pest	Pesticide	Rate
	Diseases		
OCTOBER 15 to DECEMBER 1	peach leaf curl	Copper hydroxide (Kocide® 77% DF) (Champion® 77% WP) or	0.5 TBS.
		Chlorothalonil (Bravo 720® 54.0%) (Ortho Multi-purpose Fungicide Daconil 2787® 29.6%)	1.33 tsps. 2.25 tsps.

Apply when leaves are falling from tree. Spray to run-off. Apply copper only during dormant season.

How To...

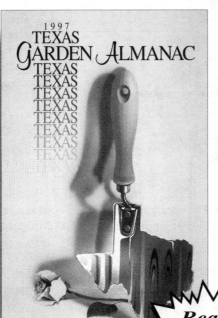

EDIBLE FLOWERS GUIDE

Many of us grow flowers and vegetables separately, at least in our minds: flowers are "ornamentals" and vegetables are "edibles." So how do we classify edible flowers, those trendy morsels that have enthralled the world of cuisine?

Squash blossoms are as prized by some harvesters as the squash fruits. Pick the flowers in quantity and there will be fewer fruits to harvest, which could have an interesting impact on prices and availability of both. Squash blossoms add color and texture to plates of food and

BUSH HONEYSUCKLE sometimes serving as a casing to stuff with paté or other filling (the flowers may be served both fresh or deep fried).

Consider edible flowers as both colorful garnishes and as savory additions to your favorite recipes, unless you suffer from hay fever or allergies. Cathy Wilkinson Barash, who has written extensively about edible flowers, advises against eating flowers that appear on your plate at a restaurant — unless you know they are safe to eat. Some kitchens may brighten your entrée with a chemically grown flower, never expecting you to snack on this decoration.

You may hesitate to sacrifice your garden beauties by making them lunch. But remember that individual blossoms of hibiscus and daylilies, for example, don't last more than a day or two in the garden anyway. And if greens such as arugula bolt and bloom, the flowers give you another way to savor these plants.

PETUNIA

TIPS FOR PREPARING EDIBLE FLOWERS...

- Harvest early in the morning, but after dew has dried (as you would basil).
- Do not use any pesticides or fungicides on any plants you intend to harvest for edible flowers.
- Wash the picked flowers thoroughly; check for critters hiding among the petals (there are more palatable sources of protein).
- Remove pistils and stamens from most flowers; generally eat petals only.
- Remove stems just before using.
- Don't eat flowers from a florist, nursery, or any other source where there may be a history of chemical treatment.
- You can store flowers on wet paper in an air-tight container, but their durability varies.

EDIBLE FLOWERS GUIDE

Here's a partial list of flowers that have much to offer
in the kitchen as well as the garden:

Flower	Flavor
Anise hyssop	Licorice
This "licorice mint" is now popular in garden centers	
Arugula	Spicy, peppery
Bachelor's button	Mild
Basils	Strong, spicy
Beans, snap or pole	Beany, floral
Beebalm *(Monarda didyma)*	Hot, minty
Strong raw; best used in sauces	
Begonia (tuberous)	Crisp, lemony
Borage	Mild, cucumbery
Calendula *(Calendula officinalis)*	Mild leafy
Petals in salad or soup	
Chamomile, German	Slightly bitter
For teas	
Chervil	Anise-parsley
Chives	Tangy, oniony
Chrysanthemum	Mild to strong, bitter
Collard greens	Sweet, mild
Coriander	Bold sage to tangy citrus
Daylily *(Hemerocallis)**	Green bean/asparagus
Use unopened buds in soups or deep fried; use open flowers as a garnish	
Dianthus	Mild to sweet spice
Dill	Mild aniseed flavor
Spicy aroma	
Fennel	Mild anise
Garlic chives	Garlicky
Geraniums, scented	Floral
Use flowers and dried leaves to flavor jams and preserves	
Hibiscus	Mild, varies
Hollyhock *(Alcea rosea)*	Mild to sweet, okralike
Use flowers in salads and leaves in gumbo-type soups	
Honeysuckle	Sweet nectar
Mildly bitter petals	
Impatiens *(Impatiens wallerana)*	Citrusy
Last-minute garnish; wilts quickly	
Johnny jump-up	Mild, cinnamon or root beer
Mints	Varies
Mullein	Mild

NASTURTIUM

DILL

**GLAUCOUS
HONEYSUCKLE**

EDIBLE FLOWERS GUIDE

Flower	Flavor
Mustard	Pleasantly hot
Nasturtium *(Tropaeolum majus)*	Peppery

In salads and soups; accompany meat

Oregano	Warm, savory
Pansy *(Viola x wittrockiana)*	Mild, leafy

Dazzling garnish; bitter stems

Petunia** *(Petunia x hybrida)*	Mild, leafy

Mild flavor blends well with salads

Pineapple guava	Sweet

Spongy, marshmallowlike

Primula	Slightly bitter

Add to salads and sweet gelatin molds

Rose *(Rosa spp.)*	Slightly floral

PANSY

*Petals and buds used in jam, tea, syrups and garnishes.
Old-fashioned, fragrant types are most flavorful,
though some will have a metallic aftertaste.*
Best choices: R. rugosu, *Damask and Gallica types.*

Snapdragon** *(Antirrhium majus L.)*	Somewhat bitter

Salads, decoration for cakes

Society garlic *(Tulbaghia)*	Garlicky
Squashes	Mild
Sunflower *(Helianthus annus)*	Mild, leafy

Pull off petals and use to decorate desserts, etc.

Thyme	Varies
Violet	Sweet, very floral
Yucca	Sweet, herbal

Add to soups or steam with other foods

ROSE

---

* True lilies only
   (calla, Aztec and
   many other so-called
   "lilies" are poisonous)
** Not all references
   agree

SUNFLOWER

HOW TO... HARDEN OFF TRANSPLANTS

When you buy tomato plants from a nursery or garden center, they are often not ready to make the plunge into your garden.

Why? "Because they are 'babies,'" says El Paso County extension horticulturist Willam S. Peavy. "Their tissues are soft and they are not in an outdoor growing mode." They may still think they are in a greenhouse, he adds, where they began life in an ideal, protected environment with a small root system and no wind.

These plants must be toughed up or "hardened" to help them survive and grow well in the outdoors. To do this, expose them to outdoor conditions gradually. Otherwise, the transplant shock will be so traumatic that, if they survive, the transplants will be stunted and produce smaller and later yields.

Peavy recommends the following step-by-step method. If the plants wilt during the first four days, give them a little water and revive them.

DAY	WHAT TO DO	REMARKS
1-4	Decrease watering	Indoors. Let the root ball dry down.
5-6	Move plants outdoors into shade, where they are protected from wind.	Protect from frost at night Bring indoors if needed.
7	Expose plants to 2 hours direct sunlight	Water as needed.
8	Expose to 4 hours sunlight, some wind	Water as needed.
9	Expose to 6 hours sunlight, some wind	Water as needed.
10	Expose plants to sun and wind all day	Water as needed.
11	Transplant outdoors	Water as needed.

WILDFLOWERS OF TEXAS

In much of Texas, we like to complain about having no seasons. This is most commonly heard in October, when television brings images of Vermont maples and Colorado aspens into our living rooms. Two months later, when our front yards are still quite handsome and Vermont is covered with the dirty gray mess of old snow, we're a bit less jealous.

And we bide our time. Because thanks to wildflowers, we get our own magical season in March and April. Eagerness touches all ages — schoolchildren to seniors — as we await the first bluebonnet of spring. Once those blankets of blue start filling out on the highways, we plan a drive to the Hill Country or another out-of-the-city spot. The destination is secondary; at this time it is truly better to travel than to arrive.

> " **ON TEXAS HIGHWAYS IN SPRINGTIME, IT IS BETTER TO TRAVEL THAN TO ARRIVE.** "

Wildflower seed has become a popular item at garden centers, but home gardeners who get the itch should remember:

• Wildflowers look better in a large mass, viewed from a distance. Most yards just can't deliver the effect of, say, driving into Brenham on Easter Sunday. Lady Bird Johnson — God love her! — and the Texas highway department have a big edge over home gardeners: they have big canvases for their Indian paintbrushes. You can grow many wildflowers yourself, but give them some space.

• Wildflowers excite us in the spring, but they should be planted in the fall. Unfortunately, too many nurseries take advantage of our bluebonnet awe by setting out big spring displays of seed. Bedding plants of colorful wildflowers — bluebonnet, gallardia and purple coneflower are just three that are widely available — can be set out in the spring. But seeds are pretty much a waste of time; plant them in the fall. More detailed planting guides, and lists of wildflowers for specific parts of Texas, can be obtained from the Texas Agricultural Extension Service in any county. *Roadside Flowers of Texas* (UT Press), available in paperback, makes identifying wildflowers easy and also includes the natural range of each plant.

• Texas is huge, and a plant that is wild or "native" in San Antonio isn't necessarily a natural in Beaumont. Know the preferred growing conditions (especially drainage) before you sow.

Brenda Beust Smith, the *Houston Chronicle*'s "Lazy Gardener," enjoys wildflowers both for their beauty and their vital role in our ecology. "Yet every spring, thousands of children pick wildflowers for school projects," she wrote recently. "This not only affects our environment but also teaches children a certain disrespect for our wild plants. They can't be very important if you can pick all you want and then throw them away.

"I wish elementary school teachers would encourage children to draw or photograph wildflowers instead of picking them," she adds.

BLUEBONNET OUR STATE FLOWER

The bluebonnet is a Lone Star symbol we take for granted, but as recently as 1971, the identity of Texas' state flower was the object of debate.

The Colonial Dames of Texas pressed the legislature to so designate the bluebonnet in 1901. Not everyone agreed. One business leader championed the white cotton boll, "the white flower of commerce." Uvalde's John Nance Garner, later famous as the vice president who compared that job unfavorably with a bucket of warm spit, sang the praises of the prickly pear cactus.

The bluebonnet ultimately got the nod, but the debate continued. The 1901 resolution specifically cited *Lupinus subcarnosus*, "not considered by bluebonnet lovers to be the most attractive of the six species discovered so far in the state," writes Elizabeth Silverstone in *Legends and Lore of Texas Wildflowers* (Texas A&M Press). Many wanted *Lupinus texensis*, the blue-carpeting "Texas bluebonnet," made the official designee. In 1971, the legislature declared both species and "any other variety of Bluebonnet not heretofore recorded" to be the state flower.

One of the bluebonnet's common names, "buffalo clover," grew out of the mistaken belief that buffalo savored this plant. In fact, only goats and sheep like them; cattle and horses avoid bluebonnets, and deer will eat them if nothing better is on the menu. "Past generations sometimes called bluebonnets 'wolf flowers' because they seemed to rob the soil and make it poor," writes Silverstone, "just as wolves robbed shepherds of their sheep. The scientific name *Lupinus* (from the Latin *lupus*, meaning wolf) arose from the same erroneous belief." The opposite actually is true. Lupines enrich the soil by putting nitrogen into it — a fact which was known by scholars as ancient as Pliny, who wrote, "there is nothing more beneficial than to turn up a crop of lupines before they have set pod."

This is so because beneficial bacteria inhabit (and swell) the roots of lupines and other members of the pea family. These bacteria combine nitrogen in the air with plant carbohydrates, forming nitrogen compounds which the plant can use as food. After being "turned up" or plowed under, when the lupines decay the nitrogen compounds are taken up by the soil in a form that other kinds of plants can use.

The pollination of bluebonnet flowers is interesting, as recorded by Howard S. Irwin in Roadside *Flowers of Texas*: "...the two low est petals are united to form an envelope (the keel), which contains the pollen-bearing stamens and the egg-bearing pistil. While the flower is still in the bud stage, the pollen is shed at the base of this tube and the stalks of the stamens thicken to form, en masse, a sort of piston. The stalks then lengthen as the flower opens, pushing the pollen forward to the outer opening of the keel. The receptive end of the pistil, the stigma, lies in the opening and although it ultimately becomes immersed in pollen, its receptivity depends on its being rubbed, most likely by a hungry bee dusted with pollen from other flowers."

PLANTING BLUEBONNET SEED

September and October are good months to sow bluebonnets in Texas. If your seed isn't pre-treated, you can soften up the hard seed coat and hasten germination:. Either soak them in warm water for several days (change the water daily) or "scarify" the seed by scratching them. Using a file or sandpaper is OK if you have just a few; otherwise:

- Spread a handful of seeds at a time on a driveway or brick patio, and gently rub a brick over the top of them for several passes.
- A tip from Lynn Schoepfle at Cornelius Nurseries in Houston: Put the seeds in a coffee can with some fine gravel, and take the container to a paint store. A minute or two of shake, rattle and roll does the rest.

Several legends about the bluebonnet's origin have been recorded by the Texas Folklore Society:

- Indians who had gone to the happy hunting grounds engaged in a terrific battle. They knocked chunks from the blue sky which fell to earth, shattered and became bluebonnets.

- An Aztec maiden, about to be offered as a human sacrifice, dropped her blue headdress as she was led up a mountainside to the sacrificial altar. The next day the ground nearby was covered with blue flowers in the shape of her headdress.

- After a great drought and a bitter winter, a young Indian girl heard the Great Spirit demand that her tribe make a burnt offering of its most valued possession and scatter the ashes to the four winds. She made a fire and placed in it her beloved doll, with its soft deerskin robe and a headdress made of blue-jay feathers. The next morning, the land was covered with lovely blue flowers, and the people knew the Great Spirit had forgiven them.

ENDANGERED PLANTS OF TEXAS

By Mike Peters
Illustrations by Lee McAffree

When you hear the phrase "endangered species," what picture comes to your mind? A big-eyed Florida panther? The last of the great whales?

Such photogenic creatures get most of the attention and the conservation dollars, but many professionals in the field believe that dwindling plant species pose the biggest threat to biodiversity.

"Losing a single plant can threaten as many as 10 animals with extinction," says Greg Wieland, staff botanist at Mercer Arboretum in north Houston, "because that plant supports other plants and animals on the chain of life." Our future food, clothing, shelter, fuel and medi-

BIG RED SAGE

cine are threatened when even a "nuisance plant" is lost, he says.

Consider that a bread mold gave us our first antibiotic, penicillin. The Pacific yew, a "weed" once cavalierly scraped away by logging skids, recently showed anti-cancer potential. A close relative, the "stinking cedar," is now so rare that too little remains to test for promising compounds.

In partnership with the national Center For Plant Conservation, Mercer Arboretum accepted both a challenge and a stake in vanishing plants. Mercer's Endangered Species Garden, which is curated by Wieland, provides a haven for this region's imperiled flora. (The only other formally curated garden of endangered and threatened flora in Texas was recently dedicated at Stephen F. Austin

TEXAS PLANTS CURRENTLY LISTED AS "ENDANGERED" BY THE FEDERAL GOVERNMENT.

Ambrosia, South Texas (*Ambrosia cheiranthifolia*)
Ayenia, Texas (*Ayenia limitaris*)
Bladderpod, white (*Lesquerella pallida*)
Cactus, black lace (*Echinocereus reichenbachii* var. *albertii*)
Cactus, Lloyd's hedgehog (*Echinocereus lloydii*)
Cactus, Nellie cory (*Coryphantha minima*)
Cactus, Sneed pincusion (*Coryphantha sneedii* var. *sneedii*)
Cactus, star (*Astrophytum asterias*)
Cactus, Tobusch fishhook (*Ancistrocactus tobuschii*)
Cat's eye, Terlingua Creek (*Cryptantha crassipes*)
Dogweed, ashy (*Dyssodia tephroleuca*)
Johnston's frankenia (*Frankenia johnstonii*)

ENDANGERED PLANTS OF TEXAS

State University in Nacogdoches.)

Surrounded by the sweeps of color flaunted by Mercer's other display gardens, the rare plants strike a scruffy note in some seasons. But this collection lies at the heart of a botanic garden's mission — if we expect more from a botanic garden than a green version of Disney World.

Why not let the strong survive and the weak perish? The surprising fact (to nonscience types, anyway) is that many endangered plants are survivors in tough terrains, which means they harbor some very hardy genes. Vital crops such as potatoes, corn and rice, when romanced by otherwise poor cousins, have been bolstered when the resulting hybrids delivered a critical strength. One of the most-watched plants in the world is the punkiest looking little corn plant you can imagine — thrilling to botanists because, unlike any other corn species, it is perennial.

Twenty-three Texas plants are currently listed as "endangered," and about an equal number, less rare, have been designated "threatened." Fostered by interested botanists and botanic institutions, dozens of elusive Texas plants may have a new future in the wild, including:

HINCKLEY OAK

Big red sage (Salvia penstemonoides): What? You say. I saw that plant at Wolfe's! It's possible, since this big beauty has been quietly cultivated by some growers in the nursery trade. But in the wild, only 300 specimens are known on a total of five sites, thanks to herbicides, dropping water tables, grazing, collecting and erosion. A perennial, it likes seasonally wet clay or silt soils in creekbeds and seepage soils of limestone canyons. *Status: Threatened.*

Ladies'-tresses, Navasota *(Spiranthes parksii)*
Manioc, Walker's *(Manihot walkerae)*
Pitaya, Davis' green *(Echinocereus viridiflorus* var. *davisii)*
Phlox, Texas trailing *(Phlox nivalis* ssp. *texensis)*
Prairie dawn *(Hymenoxys texana)*
Pondweed, Little Aguja *(Potamogeton clystocarpus)*
Poppy mallow, Texas *(Callirhoe scabriuscula*
Rush-pea, slender *(Hoffmannseggia tenella*
Snowbells, Texas *(Styrax texana*
Verbena, Large-fruited sand *(Abronia macrocarpa*
Wild rice, Texas *(Zizania texana*

Davis' green pitaya *(Echinocereus viridiflorus var. davisii)*: Barely an inch tall with pale yellow flowers that appear in late March or early April, this is one of seven cacti currently protected by federal and state law. (The total of number of endangered and threatened plants in Texas is 18). Both the Davis' green pitaya and Nellie cory cactus grow in rocky soil on low ridges in west Texas, often under mats of selaginella. Thus they are virtually invisible except for those few spring days when their blooms push through. While researchers are studying both plants' lack of eagerness to spread to similar and seemingly hospitable habitats, the chief threat to all rare cacti is human collectors. The cacti are easy to collect, transport and sell, and avid collectors will pay hundreds of dollars for some species. *Status: Endangered.*

Navasota ladies' tresses *(Spiranthes parksii)*: The spiraling flower spike of this wild orchid gives the plant its common name; first collected in 1945, it was identified as a distinct species two years later.

CORRELL'S FALSE DRAGON HEAD

The plant wasn't seen again for more than 30 years, and a Smithsonian survey listed it as extinct. Two University of Toronto botanists found more than a dozen specimens north of Navasota in 1978, and federal agencies designated the plant an endangered species in 1982. Protection efforts are proceeding, primarily on land belonging to the Texas Municipal Power Authority. *Status: Endangered.*

Hinckley oak *(Quercus hinckleyi)*: A shrubby artifact of the Pleistocene era, this tree may hold valuable clues about the effects of climate change. It feels at home on the limestones slopes of arid West Texas. *Status: Threatened.*

Correll's false dragon head *(Physostegia correllii)*: This purple-flowered beauty was once prolific in the rice-growing areas of coastal Texas. But this plant has no tolerance for herbicides, and over time rice farming all but wiped it out. Once ranging from Louisiana to northern Mexico, its only known population today waves less than 100 stems from a roadside ditch. "There are probably more of these at Mercer than there are in the wild," says Wieland. If it can be reintroduced in substantial num bers, expect nursery growers to go wild, too. *Status: Threatened.*

Large-fruited sand verbena *(Abronia macrocarpa)*: This broad-leaved perennial grows to 20 inches and has terrific home-garden potential. It poops out in South Texas summers, but returns with rosettes of new flowers each fall. Long, tubular flowers of pinkish purple have more evening perfume than Diamond Lil's Parlour of Delight. Expect visiting parties of hummingbirds and bees. Biologists at Southwest Texas State University have taken this plant under wing: less than 3,000 individuals remain in the wild. *Status: Threatened.*

Prairie dawn *(Hymenoxys texana)*: This is the Rodney Dangerfield of Texas native plants, tagged with the common name "bitterweed" until conservationists rallied behind a more appealing moniker for this unprepossessing plant. "A cause without a rebel," Wieland says of this Houston-area native; in 1988, its discovery thwarted construction of a Harris County golf course. Why not trade it for a golf course? For one thing, this plant seems unfazed by saline soil and harsh weather, so it may offer good genes for related plants we value highly, such as sunflowers. *H. texana* was presumed extinct until living plants were found in Houston in 1982. *Status: Endangered.*

COMPANION PLANTING

For years, vegetable growers have arranged their gardens to take advantage of plants that naturally like each other. "Sometimes these plant friendships are a bit one-sided," notes Louise Riotte, author of the classic *Carrots Love Tomatoes*. Carrots help beans, but beans don't reciprocate — though they do help nearby cucumbers.

Sometimes there is confusion because plants are considered good "companions" for different reasons. A small amount of chamomile planted among peppermints, for example, will increase the mints' essential oils. Most other good companions either change the soil fertility to the other plant's advantage, or they repel pests that would otherwise beseige the companion plant.

These strategies change over time and differ from region to region. Example: Marigolds have traditionally been planted with tomatoes to repel nematodes, and up north it may still be a good idea. In the South, however, marigolds are magnets for spider mites, which will move on to the tomatoes after they've destroyed the marigolds. Both plants may be gone before nematodes can do much damage! (Asparagus, on the other hand, controls some nematode pests, and tomatoes planted with it will repel asparagus beetles. And garlic planted near tomatoes helps repel red spider mites.)

ENEMIES – 'TIL DEATH DO US PART'

Don't Plant . . .	With . . .
Basil	Rue
Beans	Garlic, shallots, chives, onions, gladiolus, fennel
Pole Beans	Beets, kohlrabi, sunflowers
Broccoli	Pole beans, tomatoes, strawberries
Cabbage	Pole beans, tomatoes, strawberries
Carrots	Dill
Cauliflower	Tomatoes, strawberries
Celeriac	Winter vetch (planted before celeriac), leek, scarlet runner beans
Coriander	Fennel
Dill	Carrots

Don't Plant . . .	With . . .
Fennel	Most plants, especially bush beans and tomatoes
Garlic	Beans, peas
Kohlrabi	Pole beans, strawberries, tomatoes
Melon	Potatoes
Onions	Beans, peas
Peas	Garlic, onions, gladiolus
Potatoes	Cucumber, pumpkin, raspberry, squash, tomatoes
Pumpkin	Potato
Radish	Hyssop
Rue	Basil
Sunflowers	Pole beans
Tomato	Any member of the Brassica family, corn, potatoes

COMPANION PLANTING

FRIENDS – 'FOREVER'

Plant . . .	With . . .	Plant . . .	With . . .
Alfalfa	Plants with high-nitrogen demands, cotton	Eggplant	Green beans, redroot pigweed
Alliums	Roses	Garlic	Fruit trees, tomatoes
Amaranth	Potatoes, onions, corn		Jerusalem artichoke
Anise	Coriander	Kohlrabi	Onions, beets, aromatic
Asparagus	Parsley, tomatoes		plants, cucumbers, mustard
Basil	Tomatoes	Lettuce	Carrots, cucumbers,
All Beans	Cabbage, carrots, cauliflower, cucumbers, corn		radishes, strawberries
Bush Beans	Potatoes (alternate rows), beets, cucumbers, strawberries, summer savory	Marigold	Beans
		Melon	Corn, sunflowers
		Mint	Cabbage, tomatoes
		Nasturtium	Squash (give nasturtium a head start)
Pole Beans	Radishes		
Beets	Bush beans, kohlrabi, onions	Okra	Sweet bell peppers, eggplant, melons, cucumbers
Borage	Fruit trees, strawberries		
Broccoli	Aromatic herbs, potatoes, beets, onions	Onions	Cabbage, beets, strawberries, tomatoes, lettuce, summer savory
Cabbage	Hyssop, thyme, southernwood, aromatic herbs with many blossoms (such as dill), onions, potatoes		
		Oregano	Broccoli
		Peas	Beans, carrots, cucumbers, corn, potatoes, radishes, turnips
Carrots	Onions, leeks, leaf lettuce, tomatoes, black salsify, rosemary, wormwood, sage		
		Pennyroyal	Broccoli
		Petunia	Beans
Cauliflower	Celery	Potatoes	Beans, cabbage, corn, horseradish (plant at corners of potato patch), marigold, eggplant
Celery	Bush beans, cauliflower, cabbage, celery, leeks, tomatoes		
Chervil	Radishes	Pumpkin	Corn, datura
Chives	Carrots	Radish	Bush and pole beans, kohlrabi
Citrus	Guava, live oak	Rue	Figs, roses, raspberries
Collards	Tomatoes	Sage	Cabbages
Coriander	Anise	Salsify	Mustard greens, watermelons (plant melons later)
Corn	Beans, cucumbers (raccoons don't like it), Jerusalem artichoke, peas, potatoes, pumpkins, squash		
		Southernwood	Cabbages, fruit trees
		Squash	Radishes, nasturtium
		Tansy	Fruit trees, blackberries, grapes
Cucumbers	Beans, corn, peas, radishes, sunflowers		
		Thyme	Cabbage, most vegetables and herbs
Datura	Pumpkins		
Dill	Cabbage	Tomato	Asparagus, chives, onion, parsley, nasturtium, carrots

HOW
HARVEST THE BEST VEGETABLES
TO...

Some tips on getting the most from your vegetable garden:

Cucumbers: Pick when immature to avoid hard seeds (and cucumbers the size of the Goodyear blimp). Pickling types can be collected tiny (4"-6"), while slicers are better at 8"-10", about an inch and a half thick. Soo Yoh Long will taste fine even if you let it grow larger.

Keep overripe fruit off the vine or production will stop.

Eggplant: Pick before fruits lose glossy look. Heat stress makes eggplants bitter.

Muskmelons: Don't pick until ripe; these fruits will not mature after picking. 'Ambrosia' muskmelons will fall off the plant when ripe.

Okra: Wear gloves when you pick, even Clemson Spineless (the pods are smooth, but the plant is prickly). Most varieties are tastiest when the pods are no more than 6" long, though Zee Best will hold flavor even at 9" or so.

Peppers: Peppers will have more color and (generally) more nutritional value when you leave them on the plant longer, but this also slows down production of new fruits.

Pumpkins: Pick only when completely ripe. Cure for about a week after picking (85-90 degrees) before storing long term (50-60 degrees).

Squash: Pick summer types young, but let winter types mature until the rind has toughened. Most winter squashes, such as 'Tahitian,' get sweeter in storage.

Sweet Corn: Pick when the juice in the kernels is milky (puncture a few kernels with your thumbnail to test it). Clear liquid means you're too early; a gummy ooze means you're too late.

Tomatoes: Pick at first blush (or even when still green but after the tomatoes turn shiny), and let them ripen inside where the birds and other vandals can't get them. They will taste exactly the same as "vine-ripened" as long as you don't refrigerate them.

Watermelons: Pick when ripe; they won't ripen any more once they've been weaned. A ripe melon has a hollow sound when you thump it with your knuckles. "The melon sounds more like your chest when it is ripe," says JoAnna La Force of Santa Barbara Heirloom Seedling Nursery, "when green, it sounds more like your head; when overripe, it sounds more like your stomach." Mark Twain once said a ripe melon says "punk" when thumped, a green one says "pink" or "pank."

HOW TO...

1997 VEGETABLE OF THE YEAR
MESCLUN

Mesclun, declared this year's Vegetable of the Year by the National Garden Bureau, is actually not a vegetable but a mix of greens picked young for salads. Mesclun is dear to the hearts of today's trendiest chefs, who create leafy works of art that combine greens ranging from tart to sweet, subtle to spicy.

So what's in mesclun? Typically a gourmet-quality green lettuce such as 'Oakleaf' and a rosy-colored one such as 'Red Sails.' Then add other greens to create a range of flavors from subtle to snappy: endive, chervil, arugula, cress, chickory, Chinese chrysanthemum and even dandelion.

Both catalogs and retail racks offer seed mixes of mesclun. While they generally work fine in a small patch, extension agents Bill Adams and Tom LeRoy advise against using such mixes if you want to grow these expensive greens on a larger scale. "Plant the ingredients separately and mix them at harvest time," they write in their book, "Commonsense Vegetable Gardening For the South." "The problem with the seed mixes is that some ingredients like arugula grow fast enough to be weedy, and your mesculin may end up tasting strongly of arugula and completely absent of chervil, for example."

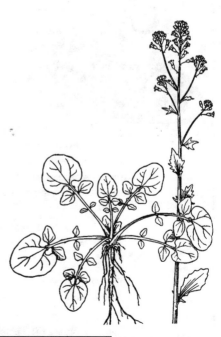

1997 VEGETABLE OF THE YEAR

EGGPLANT PANCAKES

Ingredients:
3 cups grated eggplant
1/2 cup flour
1 tsp. baking soda
2 eggs, lightly beaten
1 tsp. molasses

To make:

Mix the dry ingredients together; combine with zucchini and eggs. Drop by spoonfuls onto a hot, buttered skillet to make 2-3 inch pancakes. Brown on both sides, and eat hot.

Zucchini may be substituted for eggplant in this recipe, but squeeze out excess water from zucchini.

Some fans like to sprinkle these small pancakes with fresh-grated parmesan cheese.

CORN RELISH

Ingredients:
2 quarts cooked corn kernels
    (approx. 2 dozen ears' worth)
2 cups chopped onions
2 cups chopped green bell peppers
2 cups chopped red bell or pimiento
    peppers
2-3 fresh hot peppers
1-1/2 cup sugar
2 TBS. dry mustard
1 TBS. celery seeds
1 TBS. mustard seeds
1 TBS. salt
1 TBS. turmeric
3 cups vinegar
1 cup water

To make:

Combine all ingredients in a heavy enamel kettle and simmer for about 45 minutes. Adjust seasonings to taste. Jar and process as usual.

MUSHROOM-STUFFED TOMATOES

Ingredients:
12 medium tomatoes
Salt
1 pound mushrooms
1/4 cup chopped scallions
1 cup olive oil
1/4 cup chopped parsley
1 cup unflavored bread crumbs
2 TBS. finely minced chives
Black pepper, oregano to taste

To make:

Preheat oven to 350°. Wash tomatoes. With stem end down, cut off tops (this will allow them to stand evenly). Scoop out flesh with a grapefruit knife and discard seeds, but chop and reserve pulp. Sprinkle with salt and invert to drain while preparing filling.

Mince mushrooms and scallions and sauté in 1/2 cup olive oil for about 5 minutes or until mushrooms are soft and lightly browned. Add parsley, crumbs chives and seasonings and blend thoroughly with the tomato pulp.

Fill the shells and arrange in an oiled baking dish. Drizzle additional oil over the tops. Bake for 15 minutes. Serve hot or at room temperature; avoid refrigerating.

HERBAL VINEGAR

Ingredients:

Fresh herbs (enough to fill the jar)
1 quart apple cider vinegar

To make:

For best flavor, chop the herb of your choice (see right) into small pieces and fill jar (up to 1-quart size). Pour room-temperature apple-cider vinegar into the jar until it is full. Seal jar with a plastic screw-on lid, several layers of wax paper held on with a rubber band, or a cork. (Vinegar will disintegrate a metal lid!)

Label jar with the name of the herb and the date. Set jar out of direct sunlight and away from both heat and cold. (A kitchen cupboard is fine.) Let it sit for six weeks, and then enjoy.

If your goal is a decorative bottle, strain the vinegar after six weeks and return the liquid to the bottle with a large sprig or two of the fresh herb (below).

Good herbs for vinegar-making:

Apple mint (leaves, stalks)
Bergamot (flowers, leaves, stalks)
Chicory (leaves, roots)
Chives (greens, blossoms)
Dandelion (flower buds, leaves, roots)
Dill (herb, seeds)
Fennel (herb, seeds)
Garlic
Garlic and mustard
Ginger (roots of *Zingiber officinalis* and *Asarum canadensis*)
Lavender (flowers, leaves)
Mugwort (new leaves, roots)
Orange mint (leaves, stalks)
Orange peel (organically grown only!!)
Peppermint (leaves, stalks)
Perilla (leaves, stalks)
Rosemary (leaves, stalks)
Spearmint (leaves, stalks)
Thyme (leaves, stalks)
Yarrow (flowers, leaves)
Note: Rosehips, raspberries and blackberries are popular in herb vinegars for the color they lend, but they add little flavor.

HARVEST TIME Recipes

GINGERED EGGPLANT

Ingredients:

4 medium-sized Asian-variety eggplants*
  (approx. 2 lbs. total)
1 TBS. vegetable oil
2 TBS. shredded basil, mint or mint
  marigold
2 TBS. toasted sesame seeds

Dressing:

1-1/2 TBS. peeled and minced fresh
  ginger
2 tsp. minced garlic
1 tsp. Chinese five-spice powder
1-1/2 TBS. dark sesame oil
1-1/2 TBS. soy sauce
2 TBS. rice wine vinegar
1 TBS. rice wine
1 TBS. honey
Dash of hot chili oil

To make:

Preheat oven to 450°. Slice eggplant lengthwise in 1/4" pieces. Brush a cookie sheet thinly with vegetable oil. Place eggplant on oiled surface, rubbing into oil and then turning over. Cook in oven 10-12 minutes, turning once midway when bottom begins to brown, until eggplant is soft and lightly browned.

While eggplant bakes, combine ingredients for dressing in a small bowl. Stir well until honey dissolves. When eggplants are cooked, remove to a large shallow dish, spooning some of the dressing in between the layers. Let stand at least 1/2 hour, spooning dressing over eggplant several times. Sprinkle with shredded herbs and toasted sesame seeds. Serves 4-6.

* *Louisiana Long Green, Thai Long Green and other Asian-style eggplants don't need to be peeled; big black eggplants do.*

LIMA BEAN BREAD

Ingredients:

2 cups fresh lima beans
1 TBS. yeast
1/4 cup lukewarm water
1/3 c. vegetable oil
1 tsp. grated orange peel
1/3 c. powdered dry milk
1 tsp. salt
1/2 c. cinnamon
1-1/2 tsp. caraway seed
1/3 cup pumpkin seeds
2 large eggs
1/4 cup sugar
2 cups whole wheat bread flour
1-2 cups unbleached flour

To make:

Dissolve yeast in the lukewarm water. Cook lima beans; drain and retain the water. Add water, if necessary, to make 1/2 cup. Purée beans and liquid in a blender, and dump in large bowl. Add oil, orange peel, powdered milk, salt, cinnamon, caraway seed and pumpkin seeds. Mix well. When lukewarm, add eggs, yeast and sugar. Beat at high speed for one minute. Add flour, 1 cup at a time, to make a soft dough that doesn't stick.

Turn out on a floured board and knead slightly (do not knead as much as most yeast breads). Let rise in greased bowl until double in bulk; punch down, turn our on board and knead lightly. Shape into loaves and let rise in well-greased loaf pans until double in bulk. Bake at 350° for about 50 minutes. Brush tops with butter and cool on a rack.

GNOCCHI
Ingredients:
2 lbs. white potatoes
2-3/4 cups all-purpose flour
1 tsp. salt
1 egg
To make:
Cook potatoes in salted, boiling water until tender. Drain and peel, then put through potato ricer while still hot. Fill large pot with salted water and bring to a boil. Place potatoes in a bowl and allow to cool a bit. Stir in flour, salt and egg, and knead until flour is absorbed.

Roll small pieces of dough quickly on a well-floured board into rolls about the thickness of a finger. Cut into 1-inch lengths and drop into boiling water, a few pieces at a time. When the come to the surface, remove them with a slotted spoon to a large platter.

TOMATO SAUCE FOR GNOCCHI
Ingredients:
1 can (2 lbs. 3 oz.) whole, peeled Italian tomatoes
1 TBS. sweet basil
2 TBS. vegetable oil
1 tsp. salt
1/2 tsp. pepper
1 clove garlic
To make:
Blend tomatoes and basil in a food processor. Put oil and garlic in a skillet and simmer over low heat until garlic turns light brown. Remove garlic. Pour tomatoes and basil in skillet, and add salt and pepper. Bring to a boil, then lower flame and cook for approximately 10 minutes, stirring frequently with a wooden spoon. Raise the heat slightly until liquid has evaporated and sauce as thickened.

Pour over gnocchi and serve.

CILANTRO PESTO
Ingredients:
2 cups cilantro leaves, tightly packed
1/2 cup freshly grated Parmesan cheese
1/3 cup chopped toasted pecans or pumpkin seeds
1/4 cup olive oil
2 TBS. minced garlic
2 TBS. fresh lime juice
1/2 tsp. salt
To make:
Place all ingredients except oil in a food processor and mix well. Stop occasionally to scrape down the sides of the bowl. Add oil slowly and blend well. Place in an air-tight container, and refrigerate to blend flavors. Makes about 3/4 cup.

SWEET TATER SMOOTHIE
Ingredients:
2 medium-sized sweet potatoes
1 tsp. molasses
1-1/2 TBS. brown sugar
1 TBS. sesame tahini
1 teaspoon vanilla
2 cups water or malted vanilla soy milk (adjust as desired)
To make:
Bake sweet potatoes in a hot oven until tender. Let cool for 15 minutes. Peel skins and scoop contents into a blender. Add remaining ingredients except water; blend on high speed until creamy and smooth. Add water as desired to achieve desired consistency. Serves 2-4.

HARVEST TIME RECIPES

CARROT LOAF CAKE
Ingredients:
2 cups sugar
4 eggs
1-1/2 cups vegetable oil
3 cups flour
2 tsp. baking soda
2 tsp. ground cinnamon
Pinch salt
1/3 cup buttermilk or sour milk
3 cups grated carrots
1 teaspoon lemon extract

To make:
Beat together sugar and eggs. Blend in oil, mixing well. Sift together the flour, baking soda, cinnamon and salt. Add alternatively with buttermilk and mix well. Stir in grated carrots and lemon extract. Pour into 2 well-greased loaf pans (9x5 inches). Bake at 300° for about 1-1/2 hours, or until a wooden pick inserted in middle comes out clean. (Cake may be baked in a 10-inch tube pan, well greased and sugared or floured. It will take a little longer to bake.) When cake is nearly ready, prepare the orange syrup recipe (below) on the stovetop.

Remove cake from oven and immediately pour over it, while still in pan, the following syrup:

Orange syrup:
Mix 1 cup sugar, 1/2 cup orange juice and 1 teaspoon grated orange rind over medium heat until sugar dissolves.

SPICED PEARS
Ingredients:
4 cups small pears
3 cups apple juice
1/4 c. packed light brown sugar
1 TBS. grated lemon peel
6 3-inch cinnamon sticks
6 whole cloves
Chocolate sauce
1/2 pt. vanilla ice cream

To make:
A day ahead of serving, peel the pears. Use an apple corer to remove cores from the *bottom* of the pear, but do not remove the stems. In a 2-quart saucepan, heat pears, apple juice, brown sugar, lemon peel, cinnamon sticks and cloves to boiling. Reduce heat to low; cover and simmer until pears are tender, turning occasionally. Spoon pears and liquid into a bowl; cover and refrigerate overnight to chill and blend flavors. Turn pears 2-3 times.

About 10 minutes before serving, remove pears from liquid. Put 1/4 cup ice cream in each of four dessert dishes. Set pears in ice cream, and drizzle chocolate sauce over each pear. Serve immediately. Serves 4.

How To... Start An Organic Garden

By Howard Garrett

Howard Garrett writes about garden-ing for the Dallas Morning News, and is the author of several books on organic gardening. His radio show can be heard on WBAP, news/talk 820 on Saturdays, 11 a.m.-noon and Sundays, 8 a.m.-noon.

Organics is controversial. Organiphobes still exist today and they want organics to fail. The pressures are great from chemical companies, people who make their living recommending chemicals, advertisers with truckloads of money, and people who simply don't undertand what we are talking about. I have attempted to uncover some of those issues in my books, while at the same time explaining in detail how easy it its to be successful using organic techniques.

An organic landscape maintenance pro-gram is not primarily about which pesti-cides to use. Its goal is to eliminate pesti-cides completely. While that is a lofty long-term goal, the organic program uses the lowest-toxicity pesticides possible and, when available, those that are bio-logical and harmful only to the targeted pest. A true organic program isn an entirely different philosophy and attitude. Tradi-tional chemical programs are built around a "force-feeding" philosophy of plant fer-tility and a "kill" philosophy of pest con-trol. A truly organic program, on the other hand, is built around a "health" philoso-phy and; has the primary goal of establishing a natural balance of soil, water, air and biology. Looked at in the simplest terms, an organic program increases the air and the organic matter in the soil, uses naturally balanced fertil-izers, keeps all bare soil mulched, and in-creases soil life and insect life. Healthy soil produces healthy plants that have very powerful resistance to insects and dis-eases. Organic pesticides are used, but only as a last resort; whenever possible, beneficial insects are used instead, and if the rest of the program is done correctly, the pesticides are rarely if ever needed.

Although the picture is starting to change now, organic gardeners don't have as much support from land-grant univer-sities as the chemical people do. We have to learn from the real "old-timers" and increase our knowledge as we go along — often by trial and error.

I learn something new every day. It would frustrate some people to tears, but I love to learn new things — new con-cepts, new science and new techniques — and when I learn that I've been wrong, I'm delighted to be the first to admit it and pass along the new information. In some past columns for the Dallas Morn-ing News, for example, I recommended the use of gypsum on all soils, instead of just those deficient in sulfur and calcium, as I recommend now. In the past I recom-mended spraying soaps regularly; I don't recommend soaps much at all anymore. I know now that they are harmful to soil life if overused. I don't recom-mend organic pesticides nearly as much anymore, either — except as a last resort. I now advise gardeners to spray once if needed and to stop the use as soon as possible. I recommend different soil testing than I did before, and tomorrow I may make some other changes; in fact, I'm sure I will.

However, our way is, itself, pure science. It is the integration of chemistry, physics and biology. This holistic, scientific approach has a name — not a new name — simply one that has been ignored by those specializing in limited areas.

It's called the natural way.

SOIL TESTING

Have soil tested by a lab that gives organic recommendations to learn the total and available levels of organic matter, nitrogen, calcium, magnesium, sulfur, phosphate, potassium, sodium, chloride, boron, iron, manganese, copper and zinc. Check for life by counting the earthworms in a square foot of soil - there should be at least ten.

PLANTING

Prepare new planting beds by scraping away existing grass and weeds, adding 4-6" of compost and tilling the mix 3" into the native soil. Good additions include rock powders such as granite sand, Texas greensand, lava sand, zeolite or colloidal phosphate at 40-80 lbs/1,000 sq. ft. and organic fertilizer and sugar at 20 lbs/1,000 sq. ft. Do not use pine bark, peat moss, concrete sand, artificial fertilizers, or artificial weed block fabrics.

FERTILIZING

Apply a 100% natural organic fertilizer to all turf and planting beds in early spring at 10-20 lbs./1000 sq. ft. Repeat every 60 to 90 days during the growing season if greater response is needed. Three applications per year is normal. Apply rock powder annually at

about 40-80 lbs./1,000 sq. ft. The best choices include lava sand, granite dust, zeolite and other volcanic materials. Add bat guano, fish meal, kelp meal or earthworm castings at 10-20 lbs./1,000 sq. ft. to annuals and perennials in the spring and every 60-90 days if needed during the growing season. Add a small handful of earthworm castings or colloidal phosphate to each hole when planting bulbs or small transplants. Mist or soak bulbs or seeds before planting in a 1%-5% solution of seaweed or some other biostimulant.

FOLIAR FEEDING

Foliar feed all plants with a liquid mixture of fish emulsion, seaweed, natural apple-cider vinegar and blackstrap molasses each at 1 tablespoon per gallon of water. Add commercial biostimulant for greater response. For iron deficiency, add chelated iron and Epsom salts at 1 tablespoon per gallon. Spray during the cool part of the day.

MOWING/TRIMMING

Mow higher than the organiphobes recommend. Start the season at no lower than 2" and raise to at least 3" by mid summer. Mow weekly or more often if necessary, leaving the clippings on the lawn. Put occasional excess clippings in the compost pile. Do not send clippings to the dump. Do not use weed eaters around trees. **Do not scalp the lawn in the spring**. Scalping is hard on equipment, exposes the soil to sunlight and weed germination, and wastes organic matter.

WATERING

Adjust schedule seasonally to allow for deep, infrequent waterings in order to maintain an even moisture level. About 1 inch of water per week in the summer is a good starting point. When possible add 1 tablespoon of natural apple-cider vinegar per gallon of water. Use a siphon attachment and include a light

HOW TO...

7 STEPS TO A NATURAL GARDEN

1. SELECT ADAPTED PLANTS — Plant annuals in the proper season and use diversity in your perennial plantings. If you don't use the most well-adapted plants for specific environments, the rest of the rules will do little good.

2. AERATE THE SOIL — Increase the air in the soil through mechanical aeration when needed. Punch holes in the ground. Deep penetration and ripping with hand or power tools is the most effective technique. Use deeply rooted cover crops, encourage earthworms, add compost and mulch all bare soil. Do mechanical aeration when necessary. All life needs oxygen. The sticky substance given off by microbes as they break down organic materials glues the soil into a crumb structure creating the perfect air-to-soil ratios.

3. BUILD SOIL ORGANIC CONTENT — Use compost to prepare beds and gardens; apply 100% organic fertilizers. Nature has built and maintained fertile soil since the beginning of time in the forest and on prairies, using a constant supply of dead plant and animal life as a mulch protecting and composting the soil. Stimulating microbiotic activity in the soil is critical to build soil organic matter.

4. BUILD MINERAL CONTENT — Add finely crushed volcanic rock to all planting beds, lawns and gardens. Nature has maintained the mineral balance through volcanic eruptions, glacial movement and bed-rock erosion. When a balance of natural materials is used, pH will move to the correct level.

5. MULCH — Nature doesn't allow bare soil and neither should we. For shrubs, trees and ground covers use at least 1" of compost and 3" of shredded native wood chips or shredded hardwood bark. Mulch vegetable gardens with 8" of wheat straw, or better still, alfalfa hay. Partially completed compost is also an excellent topdressing material. Mulch preserves moisture, eliminates weeds and keeps the soil surface cooler, which benefits earthworms, microorganisms and plant roots.

6. DON'T USE POISONS — Do nothing to harm the soil life - the microbes and insects in the soil and those living above. There are millions of types of insects and microbes. Only about 1 percent of the species are considered harmful, the other 99 percent are known to be beneficial. Pesticides and harsh synthetic fertilizers kill both. Why kill all your friends to attack a suspected enemy? A true student of nature soon learns that even the little creatures called pests have a most important role to plants.

7. ENCOURAGE BIODIVERSITY — Promote life in your landscape by introducing beneficial insects and protecting those that already exist. Plant cover crops and hedgerows. Purchase and release ladybugs, green lacewings, and trichogramma wasps. You'll need to buy less every year because natural populations will establish. Troublesome insects, diseases and weeds are symptoms of one of the above rules being violated. Pesticides only treat the symptoms, but pests are the effects of deeper problems. However, most research time and money have been foolishly spent on treating the symptoms and ignoring the cause. Don't be one of the foolish.

HOW TO...

application of fish and seaweed when possible also. Don't use vinegar with acidic water or soil.

WEEDING
Hand-pull large weeds, mulch all bare soil and work on soil health for overall control. **Avoid chemical herbicides**, especially pre-emergent types and those that contain 2,4-D. Use 10% (100 grain) vinegar at full strength or soap herbicides as effective organic herbicides on hot days. Be sure to clean vinegar thoroughly out of metal spray parts, it is very corrosive. Use "The Weeder" or "Lawn Claw" for mechanical weed removal.

PRUNING
Remove dead, diseased and conflicting limbs. Don't overprune. Don't make flush cuts and don't paint cuts. Pruning paint slows the natural healing process and harbors pathogens. If you must paint cuts to be able to sleep nights, use natural shellac or better still, Lac Balsam. These are good to use on oaks in the spring.

PESTS
Aphids and other small insects: build soil health, release ladybugs, green lacewings and trichogramma wasps. Spray garlic tea as a preventative. Spray garlic/pepper tea if needed.

Spider mites: spray liquid seaweed and garlic/pepper tea regularly and release green lacewings. Spray horticultural oil for heavy infestations.

Caterpillars and bagworms: Release trichogramma wasps. *Bacillus thuringiensis* (Bt), Bti 'Israelensis' for mosquitoes. Release trichogramma wasps.

Slugs, snails, fleas, ticks, chinch bugs, roaches, crickets: diatomaceous earth/pyrethrum, hot pepper and beneficial nematodes.

Whiteflies: a mix of liquid seaweed and garlic/pepper tea.

Fire Ants: Logic or *Award* fire ant baits for large areas, pyrethrum/diatomaceous earth powder or drench on individual mounds. Soapy water is also effective. Compost tea with pyrethrum is the most effective all natural mound control.

Grubworms: beneficial nematodes are effective, but maintaining healthy soil biology is the primary control.

Squash bugs, stink bugs and other hard-to-kill pests: sabadilla dust, rotenone or pyrethrum.

Roaches: create bait stations using 50% Arm & Hammer detergent and 50% sugar. Dust indoors with mixture of 40% DE, 40% boric acid, 10% pyrethrum.

Black spot, brown patch, powdery mildew: best control is prevention through soil improvement and avoidance of high nitrogen fertilizers. Baking soda and liquid copper sprays are effective. Natural apple cider vinegar at 3 tbs/gallon of water is also effective.

MAKING COMPOST
A compost pile can be started in sun or shade at any time of the year. Good ingredients include leaves, hay, grass clippings, tree trimmings, non-greasy food scraps, bark, sawdust, rice hulls, weeds, nut hulls and animal manure. Mix the ingredients together in a container of wood, hay bales, hog wire, concrete blocks or simply pile the material on the ground. The best mixture is 75-80% vegetative matter and 20-25% animal waste, although any mix will compost. The ingredients should be a mix of coarse and fine-textured material. Avoid having all the pieces of material the same size since the variety of sizes will help air to move through the pile. Oxygen is a critical ingredient. Turn the pile at least once a month; more often speeds up the process. Keep the pile moist, roughly the moisture of a squeezed-out

sponge, to help the living microorganisms thrive and work their magic. Compost is ready to use when the ingredients are no longer identifiable. The color will be dark brown, the texture soft and crumbly and the aroma that of a forest floor. Use compost in all bed preparation and as a high quality mulch around annuals and perennials.

COMPOST TEA

Compost tea is effective on many pests because of certain microorganisms that exist in it naturally. Here's how to make compost tea at home:

Use any container, but a plastic bucket is easy for most homeowners. Fill the 5-15 gallon bucket half full of compost and finish filling with water. Let the mix sit for 10-14 days and then dilute the leachate down to one part compost liquid to four to ten parts water, depend-

ing on the compost used. It should look like iced tea. Be sure to strain the solids out with old pantyhose, cheese cloth or row-cover material.

Spray compost tea on the foliage of any and all plants including fruit trees, perennials, annuals, vegetables, roses, and other plants that are regularly attacked by insect and fungal pests. It's very effective, for example, on black spot on roses and early blight on tomatoes.

FLEA CONTROL

There are still no silver bullets - here's the comprehensive program.

Diet: Feed pets a balanced, nutritious diet of your own cooking or an organic pet food that does not contain chemical preservatives. Cooking millet and adding chicken makes an excellent dog food.

Sprinkle a small amount of food-grade diatomaceous earth (1%-

HOW TO...

2% of the food volume) on the pet food daily. Add an additional small amount of brewer's yeast, bee pollen, garlic powder or food-grade seaweed. Excellent commercial products include *Natural Animal Herbal Formula* from Eco-Zone and *The Missing Link* from Petscriptions.

Cleaning: Vacuum frequently, rake and sweep dog runs and sleeping areas regularly, pick up and compost pet waste. If the pets don't get natural exercise from running and playing, walk them regularly. It's good for the animals and for you.

Grooming: Bathe pets as needed but only with mild non-toxic soaps. Avoid soaps that contain ammonium laurel sulfate. Herbal shampoos are good. Leave shampoo on pets for 5 minutes before rinsing thoroughly. Brush pets regularly and use a flea comb to remove pests. Drown them in soapy water or alcohol - the fleas, not the pets.

Outdoor treatment: Dust or spray diatomaceous earth and pyrethrum on highly infested areas. Use only as needed to avoid killing beneficial insects. A better choice is to apply beneficial nematodes to problem areas.

Indoor treatment: Treat infested carpets with diatomaceous earth or boric-acid products. For heavy infestations use citrus-oil products and growth regulators on carpets and furniture. Dirty, infested carpets should be hot-water-extraction cleaned or completely removed from the house. Blackmon-Mooring Steamatic, I my view the best system on the market, uses no soaps or chemicals—just hot water which kills and removes fleas, larvae and eggs.

Pet treatment: Apply herbal powders of pennyroyal, eucalyptus, or rosemary and other herbs. Avoid using pennyroyal on cats. Treat heavy infestations with diatomaceous earth/pyre-

thrum products; ready-to-use growth regulator products are available for serious problems. Flea combs are very effective and the least toxic choice.

Note: Remember, DE (diatomaceous earth) for pets and pests is not the same as swimming pool DE. Buy DE only from your local organic retailer. Use all products, including organic choices, carefully. Overuse is dangerous and less effective.

BUILDING BENEFICIAL INSECT POPULATIONS

Building biodiversity in the garden is a critical part of an organic program. By simply ceasing the use of toxic chemical sprays and by releasing a few beneficial insects, you will see a remarkable transformation of your garden.

March - May — Release trichogramma wasps @ 10,000 eggs per acre weekly. First release at leaf emergence.

April — Release green lacewings @ 2,000 eggs per acre weekly for four weeks.

May - September — Release green lacewings @ 1,000 eggs per acre every two weeks.

Note: Release ladybugs (2,000 per 1,000 sq. ft.) directly on plants infested with aphids. Adjust as needed depending on the troublesome insect populations. **Note #2:** Fewer releases are needed each year. **Note #3:** Don't spray pesticides.

RIDDING SKUNK ODOR

If your dog or cat has tangled with the wrong end of a skunk here's an effective way to get rid of the odor: 1 quart of hydrogen peroxide, 1/4 cup of baking soda, 1 teaspoon liquid soap.

HUMATES AND ROCK POWDERS

Humate is one of those magical organic products. Basically it's millions of years old compost formed in swamps, deltas and streams covering most of the West. In some cases they were salt water, and in some cases, fresh wa

How To...

ter. In all cases organic material, dead plants and animals, was deposited and covered by either clay or sand. Over the years these layers of organic material were slowly compressed in the earth to form oils, coal, and humate. As mountains lifted, some areas were exposed to the air. This exposure increased oxidation thereby freeing and concentrating the humic acids.

Humates are a salt form of humic acids. Humates regulate water-holding capacity of the soil and have extremely high ion exchange capacities. Humates reduce soil erosion by increasing the cohesive forces of the very fine soil particles. Very low concentrations of humates have been shown to stimulate seed germination and root growth. They also stimulate beneficial soil microorganisms. The recommended rates of applica-

How To...

tion vary depending on the level of humic acid. Check the rates on the bags - it will be somewhere between 6-10 lbs./1,000 sq. ft. or 300-500 lbs./acre.

Good choices include GreenSmith's Humic Acid, Earthgreen and Desert Peat. Humates can be applied to the garden or farm any time of the year but spring time is an excellent time. The second group of soil additives that also don't contain much nitrogen, phosphorus or potassium are the rocks. Adding rock to the soil should be high on your priorities. Timing again isn't critical but now is a good time to add granite, lava, DE, zeolite, or greensand. The best form of rock to add to farm land, gardens or turf is finely ground powder - the finer the better. What you can usually find easily is a sand texture of these high-energy, high-exchange capacity materials.

Granite sand is the least expensive and most available rock material. It's the least effective of these rocks I mentioned but much better than native sand.

Zeolite is a Texas native rock material with a very high exchange capacity. That means it can hold moisture and nutrients and make those nutrients available to plant roots. It is especially good at holding nitrogen (so it isn't leached away) and making it available when needed by plants.

Lava sand has now taken over the position of most popular rock material. It is highly energetic, high in exchange capacity, and it's pretty. Home gardeners and professional growers of crops from roses to turf farms have discovered how powerful this stuff is - especially in an organic program. Use it in beds of all plants on grass and in potting soil at the rate of anywhere from 40 lbs./1,000 sq. ft. to one-half the volume of the soil. The pH of lava sand is more than 8.0. Use some around a chlorotic plant and you'll see how irrelevant it is to worry about pH. Lava sand or powder, if you can get it, makes nutrients more available to plant roots. And maybe more importantly, lava holds water just at the right level and reduces the irrigation requirements and that saves lots of money.

Diatomaceous earth. Yes, it's an excellent organic insecticide and animal-food supplement but it's also an excellent mineral boost for the soil that's loaded with trace minerals—some that are very rare.

There's a new product in stores, and this may be my best recommendation so far: *Texas greensand*, brought to the market by Living Earth Technology and Garden-Ville. Like other rock materials, it is also loaded with trace minerals. Luckily for those of us in th black and white soils, it contains lots of natural iron. That's a big deal. It really is green

so it looks good, it's nice to the touch and your plants will love it.

Which of these rock materials would be best to use — humate, granite, lava, DE or greensand? Use some of each. The soil will love it and so will your garden and landscape plants.

GARLIC SPRAYS

To make garlic/pepper tea, liquefy 2 bulbs of garlic and 2 hot peppers in a blender 1/2 to 2/3 full of water. Strain the solids and add enough water to the garlic/pepper juice to make 1 gallon of concentrate. Use 1/4 cup of concentrate per gallon of spray. For added strength, add 2 tablespoons of vegetable oil or horticultural oil to each gallon of water in the sprayer. To make garlic tea, simply omit the pepper and add another bulb of garlic.

BAKING SODA FUNGICIDE

Mix 4 teaspoons (about 1 rounded tablespoon) of baking soda and 1 tablespoon of horticultural oil into one gallon of water. Spray lightly on foliage of plants afflicted with black spot, powdery mildew, brown patch and other fungal diseases. Avoid over-using or pouring on the soil.

VINEGAR FUNGICIDE

Mix 3 tablespoons of natural apple-cider vinegar in one gallon of water. Spray during the cool part of the day for black spot on roses and other fungal diseases.

PESTICIDES - THEY'RE ALL BAD

A recent editorial I read proved that we are still a long way away from an overall understanding that pesticides are bad. Pesticides are designed to kill animals. If a small amount of a pesticide will kill a small animal such as an insect or mite, why wouldn't a larger amount or a prolonged exposure to the same pesticide kill a larger animal - like for example a cat or dog or a human?

The debate goes on about which pesticides are the safest and

HOW TO...

Garden Marketplace

whether insects and diseases are more of a threat to human health than small exposures of toxic pesticides, but that's beside the point.

The editorial writer I mentioned earlier suggested that eliminating DDT led to the introduction of more toxic agricultural chemicals. He suggested strongly that DDT wasn't very dangerous and should not have been taken off the market. This reminded me why I don't usually argue about the dangers of toxic pesticides. It's a waste of time. DDT almost wiped out the bald eagle, the peregrine falcon and several other magnificent raptors. You can't change the mind of someone who doesn't see that as a problem.

When the chemical spider-mite product called Kelthane was taken off the market some years back (it contained DDT as an inert ingredient), chemical proponents said, and still say, that they don't understand the concern. Rather than try to change these organiphobe's minds, I have found it better to simply point out how much better the organic approach and its products work.

For example, one of the toughest crowds I've ever addressed was the local rose society in Dallas, a group of people fairly well addicted to chemical fungicides and fertilizers. I gave them my usual explanation of using aeration, rock powder and compost to build the beds and how to fertilize with cottonseed meal and alfalfa meal and spray with fish, seaweed and Epsom salts. During my talk, I noticed one guy right in the middle of the audience near the front. His arms were crossed, his hand was the first to shoot up. His question was something like "OK, smart guy, how do you control spider mites without chemical pesticides?" He smirked, sat back, gave his cohorts on both sides a quick wink

and eagerly waited. "Well sir, uh, that's a good question," I responded. "I'm not sure because you see, using the organic program, I've never had any spider mites on my roses or any other plants in my garden." He was crushed.

Truth is, the pests that organiphobes consider the most troublesome (spider mites and whiteflies) are among the easiest to control with fish, seaweed, garlic tea, healthy soil and beneficial insects.

Almost irrelevant: arguments as to which pesticides have the highest LD50 (that's the # that relates to how much product it takes to kill a rat), which ones break down quickest, and which ones have the worst side effects. None of them are good choices because *none of them* work long term. Here are some helpful guidelines to consider when shopping for pesticides. 1) If you can smell the product before the lid is opened, don't buy it. 2) If the product contains diazinon, don't buy it, 3) if the product contains 2,4-D, don't buy it, 4) if it contains Sevin, don't buy it, 5) if the product contains any other toxic chemical, don't buy it!

What then are you to use to control all these terrible pests? Well, how about a little common sense. If your plants have bugs, the plants are sick. Troublesome insects don't indiscriminately attack plants. Nature put the pest insects here to take out unadapted plants, plants planted in the wrong place, and plants glutted with high-nitrogen, synthetic fertilizer. Bad bugs also prevail where the use of pesticides has killed off their natural enemies.

I agree that dangerous insecticides have been developed since the departure of DDT. There's a simple solution. Those products should be removed from the market also. There is no clear understanding of their long term effects and they aren't needed.

HOW
TO...

PETUNIA

In 1996, the grand high pooh-bahs of the All-America Selections bestowed the "Winner" tag on 'Fantasy Pink Morn,' a milliflora petunia with small but multitudinous flowers. 'Purple Wave,' another new petunia, was such a success that 'Pink Wave' is ... the next wave. In short, the nursery trade has gone wild over petunias — so have Bob and Bobbette Gardener — and it was just a matter of time before this popular bedding plant was promoted as the Flower of the Year.

Many new petunias have appeared in the past five years, offering new forms and more heat tolerance than some of the older garden-center varieties. With a little luck, the Petunia Mania will inspire both growers and home gardeners to look backward as well as forward: to the old-fashioned petunias that are perennial in Zone 8 and 9.

Hard to find except in native-plant specialty nurseries, the old petunias remain popular in gardens and are frequent "passalongs" at plant swaps and garden-club meetings. Why bother when a 4-pack of new hybrids is so cheap? The old-fashioned petunias are both delicately pretty and fragrant, and they come back in the garden bed year after year, whether you want them to or not. Reaching 24-30 inches, most are taller than modern petunias and they can get a little floppy without tending and occasional staking. Planted in creamy pastel drifts, these flowers give a nostalgic flavor to gardens at Peaceable Kingdom near Brenham, Zilker Gardens in Austin, and other display gardens around Texas.

"Once breeders get started on 'improving a plant,'" says author and heirloom plant enthusiast Greg Grant, "they often go too far. That's just what they've done, in my opinion, with the petunia. Despite all the hoopla we hear each spring about heat-tolerant "miracle petunias" and "perennial petunias," it's time that people realize we already have such flowers — and we've had them for a long time."

One of the old petunia's parents, *Petunia axillaris*, is a white-flowered species with a lovely fragrance at night. (You may find it at native specialty nurseries with one of it's old names, *P. nyctanginiflora* or *Nicotiana axillaris*.) The other parent is *P. violacea*, purple-flowered, familiar in form and usually easier to find. Both were introduced from South America in the early 1800s.

1997 ALL-AMERICA SELECTIONS WINNERS

All-America Selections has designated three vegetable varieties, two flowers and one bedding plant as 1997 award winners. These new introductions will be available in many 1997 catalogs and as spring bedding plants in garden centers.

Trial gardens all over the country test candidates for All-America designation, including Extension Service gardens and arboreta across Texas.

ZINNIA ANGUSTIFOLIA 'CRYSTAL WHITE' —

This variety looks like other Mexican zinnia cultivars that have been popular re-seeding annuals in Texas for some time. The daisy-like flowers have pure white petals and yellow-orange centers; the plants form 10-inch mounds of color that do not require pinching or deadheading to keep blooming or to hold their shape. Flowering is continuous from mid-spring to frost; plants are heat-tolerant in summer, but should be well mulched so they do not dry out. Rich organic soil and regular watering will keep this low-maintenance border plant happy.

Highly tolerant of powdery mildew, 'Crystal White' should perform well from the Gulf Coast to the high plains.

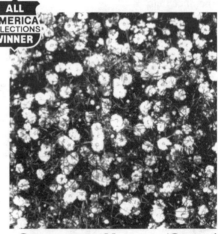

ZINNIA ANGUSTIFOLIA 'CRYSTAL WHITE'

GYPSOPHILA MURALIS 'GYPSY' —

Not usually found on lists of "Texas plants," this All-America winner got surprisingly good reviews in Texas gardens. In one Zone 9 Extension Service display garden, 'Gypsy' put on a beautiful show in spring 1996, but it quickly got a stir-fried crispy look when summer arrived for good. But, in late August, one clump was stolidly pushing up new shoots and

GYPSOPHILA MURALIS 'GYPSY'

1997 ALL-AMERICA SELECTIONS

blooming, the start of a new show for fall. (The culture sheet recommends full sun, but remember these advisories are written several hundred miles north of the Red River — in places where they think winter is miserable and summer is pleasant. Afternoon shade might extend gypsophilia's season here.) 'Gypsy' has the light, airy growth habit of traditional baby's breath, but this variety only grows about 14 inches tall, making it a good candidate for bed edging or containers.

CABBAGE
'DYNAMO'

CABBAGE 'DYNAMO' –

A cabbage that makes compact heads even in unseasonable heat is worth trying in our climate, and 'Dynamo' has delivered in Southern trials both in spring and fall plantings. These F1 hybrids are dense, small-cored and mildly flavored. 'Dynamo' is resistant to Fusarium yellowing. Cabbages are not as popular in Texas vegetable gardens as they should be, partly because of their reputation as a "northern plant." But choose suitable varieties and plant 2-4 weeks before the average last spring freeze, and *voilá*! You get a low-fat, low-calorie food that, eaten raw, has more calcium and ascorbic acid than tomatoes.

OKRA
'CAJUN DELIGHT'

OKRA 'CAJUN DELIGHT' –

Just about any plant in the hibiscus family (from mallow to cotton) feels right at home here, and okras are no exception. 'Cajun Delight' features tender, immature pods that can be harvested earlier and longer than most varieties. This will be more apparent in Zone 6 and 7 than in South Texas, where the only problem with okra production is what to do with it all.

1997 ALL-AMERICA SELECTIONS

'Cajun Delight' is easily grown from seed or bedding plants. Its published mature size is 4 feet tall and about 2 feet across; Texas growers should expect it to grow a little larger. The dark green pods are ready to harvest in about 50 days; pick about twice a week, when pods are 3 to 5 inches long.

BASIL 'SIAM QUEEN' –

Larger leaves, thicker stems and later flowering are the attributes that make this variety an "improved" tropical basil, and a what a worthy addition to the kitchen garden it is! Thai and Vietnamese dishes include Thai basil for the aroma as well as the flavor; when lightly crushed, the leaves of 'Siam Queen' explode with an intense fragrance of licorice basil.

The plants have a symmetrical branching habit and square stems. Once soil and air temperatures stay warm, 'Siam Queen' reaches 3 feet tall and 2 feet across. The purple calyxes and pink-violet corollas of the compact flowers contrast beautifully with the bright green leaves.

BASIL 'SIAM QUEEN'

CELOSIA CRISTATA 'PRESTIGE SCARLET' –

Petunias with more but smaller blossoms have been wildly popular in the nursery trade, and growers are hoping for the same success with cockscombs. 'Prestige Scarlet' is a multiflora type with deep red, velvety blooms about 3-1/2 inches across, suitable for cut flowers or "everlastings" when dried. The plants grow to about 20 inches and generally do not need staking unless situated in too much shade. These heat-tolerant plants can cope with both wet and dry conditions, and grow easily from seed.

CELOSIA CRISTATA 'PRESTIGE SCARLET'

1997 ALL-AMERICA SELECTIONS

'MAY NIGHT'

Originally introduced to the trade in 1956 and already somewhat familiar to the public, the rich purple salvia 'May Night' will ride the current wave of enthusiasm for hardy perennials. Promoted as Perennial of the Year for 1997 by the Perennial Plant Association, 'May Night' will be grown and distributed in much greater quantities than in the past. (It is often called 'Mainacht' — the cultivar was introduced by German horticulturist Karl Foerster.)

'May Night' makes a beautiful border plant in a full sun location with well-drained soil. It looks superb planted with other perennials such as coreopsis, rudbeckia and yellow-blooming yarrow. The mature height is 18 inches, about a third of the potential height of the parent species. 'May Night' is one of the earliest blooming salvias; spring shoppers are more likely to pick up a 'May Night' in color while other cultivars are still green. The blooming season lasts through summer until frost, and frequent pinching will help maintain the plant's shape and promote a new cycle of flowering.

Like most ornamental salvias of this type, 'May Night' can handle Texas heat and a fair amount of drought. Scale and whitefly may appear, especially if plants are stressed or have poor air circulation, but pest and disease problems are generally minor.

Scientifically, this member of the Labitae family is *Salvia x superba* 'May Night' or *S. nemorosa* 'May Night.'

RESOURCE DIRECTORY

WHERE ! TO FIND IT

The following resources will be useful to home gardeners and plant enthusiasts statewide. For regional listings, including your local county extension agent, please refer to the appropriate regional section in the back of this almanac. (See "Table of Contents," page 5.)

Bat Conservation International
P.O. Box 162603
Austin, TX 78716
(512) 327-9721

Botanical Research Institute of Texas
509 Pecan St.
Fort Worth, TX 76102-4060
(817) 332-4441
FAX: (817) 332-4112

Holistic Resources Management
P.O. Box 7128
Albuquerque, NM 87194
(800) 654-3619

Kerr Center for Sustainable Agriculture, Inc.
Hwy. 271 S.
P.O. Box 588
Poteau, OK 74953
(913) 647-9123

National Wildflower Research Center
2600 FM 973 North
Austin, TX 78725
(512) 929-3600

Native Plant Society of Texas
Box 891
Georgetown, TX 78627
(512) 863-9685

Natural Food Associates
P.O. Box 210
Atlanta, TX 75551
(800) 594-2136

Pesticide Hotline
(800) 858-7378
For information on specific pesticides, not which one to use for a problem.

Rachel Carson Council, Inc.
8940 Jones Mill Road
Chevy Chase, MD 20815
(301) 652-1877

Texas A&M University Horticulture Dept.
Dr. Sam Cotner, chairman
225 Hort/Forestry Bldg.
College Station, TX 77843-2134
(409) 845-7341
FAX: (409) 845-8906

Texas Association of Landscape Contractors
1033 La Posada Dr., #220
Austin, TX 78752-3816

Texas Association of Nurserymen
7730 South IH-35
Austin, TX 78745-6698
(512) 280-5182

WHERE !
TO FIND IT •

Texas Botanical Garden Society
P.O. Box 5642
Austin, TX 78763
Contact: Sol Steinberg

Texas Department of Agriculture
Organic Certification Program
P.O. Box 12847
Austin, TX 78711
(512) 475-1641
Contact: Brent Wiseman

Texas Forest Service
Texas A&M University/Research Park
College Station, TX 77843-2136
(409) 845-2641

Texas Natural Resource
Conservation Commission
12100 Park 35 Circle
P.O. Box 13087
Austin, TX 78753
(512) 239-1000

Texas Organic Grower's Association
P.O. Box 15211
Austin, TX 78761
(512) 454-5467

GRAFTWOOD (SCIONS)

Mize Pecan Co.
12005 Eucalyptus
San Antonio, TX 78245
(512) 679-7165

Southwest Fertilizer
5828 Bissonnet
Houston, TX 77081
(713) 666-1744

Stockbauer Nursery
P.O. Box 3426
Victoria, TX 77903
(512) 573-9992

VEGETABLE SEED CATALOGS

Baxter Seed Co.
416 S. Missouri Ave.
Weslaco, TX 78596-6018
Free list. Many melons, oranges and commercial vegetable varieties recommended for Texas. Bulk orders only.

Burpee & Co.
300 Park Ave.
Warminster, PA 18991-0001
Free catalog.

The Cook's Garden
Box 65
Londonderry, VT 05148
Catalog: $1. Gourmet varieties with recipes.

Evergreen Y.H. Enterprises
P.O. Box 17538
Anaheim, CA 92817
Asian varieties, growing manuals cookbooks, etc.

Field's Seed & Nursery Co.
Shenandoah, IA 51602
Free catalog.

Filaree Farm
Rt. 2, Box 162
Okanogan, WA 98840-9774
Catalog: $2. Garlic specialist.

WHERE TO FIND IT!

Fox Hollow Herb & Heirloom Seed Co.
P.O. Box 148
McGrann, PA 16236
Catalog: $1.

Gurney's Seed & Nursery Co.
110 Capital St.
Yankton, SD 57079
Free catalog; lots of usual varieties good for the South, including short-day onions.

Horticultural Enterprises
P.O. Box 810082
Dallas, TX 75381
Free illustrated list. Mexican, South American and Asian varieties are their specialty.

J.L. Hudson, Seedsman
P.O. Box 1058
Redwood City, CA 94064
Catalog: $1. Heirlooms, Mexican varieties and medicinals.

Johnny's Selected Seeds
Foss Hill Rd.
Albion, ME 04910-9731
Free catalog. Many heirloom and exotic varieties.

Kilgore Seed Co.
1400 W. First St.
Sanford, FL 32771
Catalog: $1. Southern variety specialist.

Kitawaza Seed Co.
1111 Chapman St.
San Jose, CA 95126
Free catalog. Soo Yoh Long cucumbers plus other mostly Asian vegetables.

Le Jardin de Gourmet
West Danville, VT 05873
Catalog: 50 cents. Gourmet foods, French seeds, shallots.

Native Seeds/SEARCH
2509 N. Campbell Ave. #325
Tucson, AZ 85719
Seed list: $1. Chiles, squashes, corn, Southwest/Indian vegetable varieties. Quarterly newslwetter and seed list $10.

Nichols Garden Nursery
1190 N. Pacific Highway
Albany, OR 97321
Free catalog. Asian, European varieties, herbs.

Ornamental Edibles
3622 Weedin Ct.
San Jose, CA 95132
Free catalog; many exotics.

Park Seed Co.
Colesbury Rd.
Greenwood, SC 29647-0001
Free catalog. Many exclusive varities.

Peaceful Valley Farm Supply
P.O. Box 2209
Grass Valley, CA 95945
Catalog: $2. Organic supplies and seed.

Pickle's Seeds
345 Curtis
Jasper, TX 75951
Free list. Southern peas and other regional favorites.

WHERE TO FIND IT !

Pinetree Garden Seeds
Box 300
New Gloucester, ME 04260
Free catalog. Gourmet, unusual varieties.

Plants of the Southwest
1812 Second St.
Santa Fe, NM 87501
Catalog: $1. Chiles and Southwest plants.

Porter & Son, Seedsmen
P.O. Box 104
Stephenville, TX 76401-0104
Free catalog. Old faves like the Porter tomato; offer small packages of commercial varieties.

Redwood City Seed Co.
P.O. Box 361
Redwood City, CA 94064
Chiles, Asian vegetables, other exotics.

Ronninger's Seed Potatoes
Star Route
Moyie Springs, ID 83845
Catalog: $2. Wide potato and sunroot selection. Shipping time can be a problem.

Santa Barbara Heirloom Nursery
P.O. Box 4235
Santa Barbara, CA 93140
Free catalog. Certified organically grown seedlings; gourmet varieties.

Shepherd's Garden Seeds
30 Irene St.
Torrington, CT 06790
Catalog: $1. Gourmet varieties, must-read catalog.

Southern Exposure Seed Exchange
P.O. Box 170
Earlysville, VA 22936
Catalog: $3. Unusual, hard-to-find tomatoes, eggplants (including Listada de Gandia) and more.

Thompson & Morgan
P.O. Box 1308
Jackson, NJ 08527-0308
Free catalog.

Tomato Growers Supply Co.
P.O. Box 2237
Fort Myers, FL 33902
Free catalog. Tomatoes plus sweet and hot peppers.

Vermont Bean Seed Co.
Garden Lane
Fair Haven, VT 05743
Free catalog. Beans and gourmet veggies.

Willhite Seed Co.
P.O. Box 23
Poolville, TX 76487
Free catalog. Melons, gourmet veggies, French and Asian varieties.

BOTANY TEXAS STYLE

The Botanical Research Institute of Texas (BRIT) is an international resource that includes impressive collections, a small scientific press and research programs.

The heart of BRIT's collection was originally the herbarium of Southern Methodist University, the personal collection of Dr. Lloyd H. Shinners. Begun in 1944, it was transferred to BRIT in 1987 after Shinners' death. There are now more than 500,000 plant specimens in the collection, which is worldwide with special emphasis on plants of Texas and adjacent states. Both cultivated and naturally occuring species are well-represented, and the carefully documented dried plants will support a future publication of the Flora of Texas and other research projects.

The BRIT library boasts a fascinating collection of botanical and horticultural titles of the 18th and 19th century. Early editions by Carl Linnaeus are just one of the thrills in store for BRIT members and other visitors. The library includes journals, encyclopedic works, floras, horticultural titles, monographs and reprints.

Publications from the BRIT press include a well-respected and peer-reviewed scientific journal, *SIDA: Contributions to Botany*, published semi-annually.

There are three primary research programs at BRIT:

• **Floras:** the mission is to discover, document, inventory and describe elements of some of the world's floras. BRIT is part of a collaborative project to produce a new Flora of Texas. In a joint program with the Phillipine National Museum, BRIT is in the middle of the Phillipine Plant Inventory, attempting to document plants in the last remaining forests in the Phillipines. Many of the 8,000 species of Phillipine plants are threatened by extinction as the natural vegetation rapidly disappears.

• **Landscape Ecology:** This program focuses ecological knowledge and skills on the complex interactions of species, particularly human interactions. BRIT helps resource managers make conservation decisions and provides objective expertise for environmental assessments.

• **Plants & Peoples:** BRIT seeks to document and preserve knowledge of the world's indigenous people about using regional plants for food, fiber, shelter and medicine. A key objective is the scientific documentation of herbal medicine.

Educational programs for the general public target both adults and children, primarily in the nearby Fort Worth area. Students of all ages visit the Learning Center at BRIT, complete with a high-powered dissecting microscope linked to a television monitor. BRIT offers field trips for public, private and home-school students. A popular program with the Fort Worth Botanic Gardens, children become botanists in the field, collecting and pressing plant specimens which they later mount, identify and study at BRIT.

BRIT has also developed lessons for independent classroom use on pollination, leaf identification, grasses, scientific classification and other topics. Pepe's Family, a delightful book about a pumpkin who meet his family (that wacky curcurbit clan!) at the Weatherford market, and learns his true worth. To order any of BRIT's Books on Botany for Children, call the education department at (817) 332-4441.

EXTENSION | A HELPING HAND

By Mike Peters

Formed in 1914 to make the resources of land-grant universities available to solve problems that people faced daily, the Texas Agricultural Extension Service continues to be the largest extension service in the nation.

In 1955, an agreement with the USDA classified extension work as "cooperative," which allowed extension personnel to receive joint state and federal appointments. In the 1960s, TAES established agricultural research and extension centers throughout the state, with agricultural and research personnel housed together. The scientists played an important role in reviving cotton production in the blacklands area of Texas, and they continue important research in crops such as pecans, onions, carrots and peppers. The CEMAP program, based in Dallas, evaluates lantana, verbena and other ornamentals to determine the best varieties for Texas landscapers and home gardeners.

Since World War II, TAES programs have emphasized increased food production, both for commercial and home growers. Extension offices provide information on harvesting, canning, drying and storage as well as growing vegetables and fruits. Bulletins on hundreds of subjects are available free by writing or calling your nearest extension office. Among the most valuable discuss fruit production, since books and articles targeted to national audiences are almost useless here in Texas. About 25 percent of TAES bulletins are currently available on the Internet *(http: aggie-horticulture.tamu. edu)*.

While some critics see the service as a traditional ally of the chemical industry, TAES recently has been more visible promoting low-toxic and organic methods. "We always have," one county agent insisted at a recent Master Gardener training program. "The problem is, most people don't call us and say, 'Help me with a long-term plan for natural pest management.' They say, 'What can I spray this morning so that all of these bugs will be gone by this afternoon?' "

Recent Extension Service achievements include integrated pest management programs, the "Don't Bag It" lawn care program (which received the EPA's 1990 Solid Waste Award), "Partners for Parenting" in 215 counties and 4-H programs that reached one out of every eleven Texas youth between the ages of 9 and 19. TAES officials believe their programs benefit more than 13 million Texans annually.

For the extension office nearest you, refer to the regional sections within this almanac:

- Gulf Coast, page 189
- South Texas, page 198
- East Texas, page 209
- Hill Country & West Texas, page 223
- North Central Texas, page 235
- Panhandle, page 243

SEX IN THE GARDEN

By Mike Peters

Getting the most production from the vegetable garden sometimes takes a little sex education. Does the variety you planted need another pollinator? Does it produce only female flowers? Knowing the answer can be the difference between having several zucchinis or, well, several thousand.

Many plants set fruit with little or no outside help: they are either self pollinating, or pollen is ready at hand and the wind can be trusted to deliver it. Pecan trees belong to this group, while pears not only need a nearby pollinator but one that flowers at the same time. Honeybees are critical for pollination of many vegetables, and the widely reported shortage of honeybees in 1996 — caused by a combination of freezes, mite infestations and chemical pesticides — should make any thinking gardener more solicitous of these creatures than we might have been in the past.

Bee shortages and the general cussedness of some plants have inspired some growers to intervene in the sex lives of some vegetables. Home gardeners can use a Q-tip to manually spread the pollen among flowers of cucumbers, melons, tomatoes, squashes and pumpkins. It's best to do this before 10 a.m. I once had a neighbor in Houston who would rent a bee suit from Frankel's Costume Shop to wear when she pollinated her cukes. It was cute but it probably didn't make much difference (unless you count the effect on another neighbor, who we're convinced gave up gin after she saw Georgina buzzing around her curcurbits).

On the following page are some notes on specific vegetables and their pollination needs.

CUCUMBERS: Monoecious varieties produce male and female flowers on the same plant. Gynoecious types, including Slice Master and Dasher II, only make female flowers. Seed packets of gynoecious varieties will contain a few seeds of a monoecious variety to ensure germination, but if you start from bedding plants *you* have to provide that insurance.

Then there are parthenocarpic varieties such as Sweet Success, which don't need pollination to set fruit (developed for honeybee-less culture in greenhouses). The cukes will be seedless unless they are pollinated. Parthenocarpic varieties are not the heaviest producers.

MUSKMELONS: Female and "perfect" flowers, with small immature fruit directly behind the flower petals, are usually singular. Male flowers don't have fruit and appear in clusters of three to five; they usually bloom first. The problem is typical of a singles bar: male flowers outnumber females by about 20-to-1, so it's important to get a high percentage of female/perfect to set. Bees are essential for pollination.

"Many folks believe poor flavor is caused by cantaloupes crossing with cucumbers or some other members of the curcurbit family," writes Sam Cotner in "The Vegetable Book: A Texan's Guide to Gardening." "But this simply cannot occur." Poor flavor, he adds, is caused by too much soil moisture or planting an inappropriate variety.

POTATOES will sometimes flower and even set fruit. No problem; this is triggered by cool weather and doesn't affect tuber growth significantly. (If you've grown ornamental *Solanum* plants, the flowers will be very familiar-looking.)

PUMPKINS and **SQUASHES** need a pollen transfer from male to female flowers before they will set fruit. Some varieties have many more male than female blossoms, so it's important to be sweet to honeybees.

TOMATOES may inspire more cotton-swab pollinating by hand than any other veggie. That's because tomato growers in Texas are among the world's most determined creatures. But there are easier and better ways. Poor blossom set may be a lack of calcium, not libido; try a blossom-set spray if you suspect a mineral deficiency. If your tomatoes are staked or caged, grab the support and give it a good shake every few days during the flowering season. It's a lot less hassle than Q-tips (or a bee costume!), and it works just as well.

FEAR & LOATHING OF CROSS POLLINATION

Most gardeners have an exaggerated fear of cross-pollination. Even when it occurs, the existing fruit is not affected — only the seed inside and, of course, any fruit that seed later produces. Most of us don't collect and save seed — which is a shame, but that's another story.

In the case of **CORN**, however, cross pollination has a dramatic effect on the current crop. "The seed is actually what we eat," notes Urban Harvest director Bob Randall. "So if you have two different varieties of corn, and they both pollinate at the same time, it will affect the ears you'll eat later."

If you want two different corns in the same season, he suggests, stagger the plantings — and plant the one that matures fastest first.

WATER - WISE GARDENING

You've made a commitment to the landscape: a line of new shrubs here, a fine shade tree over there, a little kitchen garden by the patio, and you're going to build up the soil all over while you're at it. But can you afford... the water?

As gardening becomes more popular, conserving water in the landscape has become an issue in many parts of Texas. It's more than a question of dollars, it's simple availability. In the San Antonio area, the problem is already acute, and aggressive conservation is under way. On the Gulf Coast there is more water to go around, but public works officials in Houston point out that nearly one-half of Houston's household water is used on lawns and gardens.

That jabs the green conscience of some, and the pocketbooks of others. And all over Texas, urban planners and home gardeners are learning about "xeriscaping."

The word is widely misunderstood. Xeriscaping is not about cactus, yucca and gravel in an expanse of green concrete. It simply means planning and planting a water-efficient landscape.

Xeriscaping means getting serious about getting lazy. "When I add any plant to *my* yard," says landscape contractor Gary Patrick, "I ask myself, 'If I do this, can I tend it from the comfort of my porch swing?'" Patrick is hardly afraid of yard work, but he says wasting money on big water bills is silly. "And gardening should be fun. Hauling hoses and sprinklers around for an hour at a time is not fun."

Plan: Make a sketch of your yard, showing the existing trees, shrubs, grass and other plants. Make notes about naturally occurring water, and then draw the landscape you want, grouping plants with similar water needs where they will be happiest.

Work slowly if you wish. If you implement the plan gradually, you can make adjustments as you go.

Analyze the soil: Should your soil be holding more water? Either your favorite nursery or your county extension center can make an analysis and suggest how to improve your plot.

Choose suitable plants: The ideal trees and ground covers for any garden are either native or adapted to that climate and soil. Once again, local nurseries and your extension center are good sources for specific information. (Houston, San Antonio and some other cities offer free guides through the public works department.) Books and articles about Texas native plants are useful, too, but read them carefully. The term "Texas native" is not a blank check: Plants that are native to San Angelo may get the willies in Houston, and vice versa.

Select plants carefully, and situate them with their preferred growing conditions in mind: bog plants for low, wet areas and drought-tolerant trees, shrubs and perennials where it's high and dry.

Look for turf alternatives: Grass needs more water and routine maintenance than almost any other plant. Restrict grass to functional areas that can be efficiently watered. Try something else in areas that are narrow, small, sloping, odd-shaped or close to pavement — there are many attractive ground covers that will save both watering and mowing time.

Treat water like it costs money: Water only when and where needed. Adjust sprinklers so you water grass and plants, not pavement. Water early in the morn

WATER - WISE GARDENING

ing or late in the afternoon. Try to minimize evaporation: drip irrigation works well except in turf areas.

Sprinkler systems can save water and money if they are well designed and monitored by a human brain. "Automatic" settings waste water.

Use mulch: It holds water, reduces evaporation, cools soil and limits weeds and soil erosion. It looks neat, too.

Be vigilant: Pull up weeds when they appear — they will rob your plants of valuable water. Make sure your irrigation system doesn't leak. Keep turf and other plants healthy and pest free.

Mow long: Top St. Augustine at 3", Zoysia and Centipede at 2" and Bermuda at 1". You'll have to mow a little more often, but scalped grass is thirsty grass. (Try "mowing by the moon," mowing on the lunar cycle that's said to retard growth. See the monthly calendar section in the center of this almanac.)

Protect your veggies: When vegetable gardens are planted in the summertime for fall production, water is critical to transplant survival, says Jerry Parsons, the San Antonio vegetable specialist for the Texas Agricultural Extension Service. "For several weeks after transplanting occurs, each plant will be producing a root system which will be capable of absorbing the necessary water and nutrients which the plants need to grow.

"If a transplant is ever without adequate soil moisture, it will die," says Parsons. "Forget the heat; it is the lack of moisture that causes fall transplanting failures." How can a gardener ensure that each and every transplant has adequate moisture every day when temperatures are over 90°? "The answer is simple," he says.

"Lightly water each transplant every day until all are well established."

A drip irrigation system makes that easy to do. Drip irrigation is the controlled application of water at a very low flow rate over a prolonged period of time. If differs from conventional watering systems in that the soil is not supersaturated with water. When the rate of drip is adjusted correctly, there is no puddling of water and no runoff. "If puddling occurs," he adds, "the rate should be slowed down." The drip irrigation tube has small holes which allow the water to come out in small amounts. Before you plant, start by placing the tube along the row where you intend to plant, so that the root zone will be moistened by the dripping water. The holes are pre-punched at 12-inch intervals so that adequate water is made available for all vegetable crops.

Spots of water will appear at each emitting orifice. Transplants should be planted in the spots of water at the proper spacing, i.e., tomato plants should be planted 36 inches apart, so plant in every third spot of water. (Set pepper plants in every second spot of water.)

How long should the drip irrigation be on? Large plants growing in hot temperatures require two to three hours of dripping two or three times a week. Seedlings require more; these water-sensitive plants should be dripped for an hour every day until they are well established. Transplants should receive this frequent watering for at least three weeks after you set them out.

A good rule for established plants, says Parsons, is to operate the system three hours a day three times a week. Make it routine (such as Monday-Wednesday-Friday) so it's easy to remember.

SOIL PREPARATION FOR VEGGIES

Is your garden ready for vegetable planting? Here's a psychological test: Do you call the black stuff you plan to dig up "soil" or "dirt"? If you call it soil, you're probably already paying attention to what's in it, so you're ahead of the game.

Garden soil does much more than give plants a place to put their feet. Properly prepared, it's a high-voltage battery for your veggies, providing organic matter, nutrients, air and water. Texas gardeners start with many different soils from sticky clay to rocky, shallow stuff you might call... dirt.

Sandy soils generally do not hold enough water — and in windy areas, blowing sand actually damages vegetables. Clays, on the other hand, hold too much water and they don't allow enough air to enter the soil. Problem soils are usually improved by adding organic matter, says extension horticulturist Dean McCraw, because it:

• loosens tight clay;
• helps sand hold more water;
• makes soil easier to dig;
• adds nutrients.

There are two primary ways to add organic matter to the garden bed: compost it first and add it to the garden bed, or put it in the garden bed first, way ahead of your planting date, and let it "compost" there. There are two drawbacks to the latter approach. First, you can't grow anything in the bed until your additives have decayed satisfactorily. Second, most advocates of this method sug-

gest adding "hot" organic matter during the winter, when you are (they presume) giving the garden a rest. But our biggest volume of yard waste — grass clippings, tree trimmings, etc. — is produced in the spring and summer. So go ahead and make a backyard compost bin. (It's a hip thing to do now; nobody will call you an environmental wacko.)

Tough clay soils will also benefit from a soil additive called gypsum. It adds a little nutrition, but the main benefit is the way it loosens the soil structure. "Spread three or four pounds of gypsum per 100 square feet over garden soil after it has been dug up in the winter," McCraw writes in an extension-service bulletin. "Then work it into the soil."

Adding sand makes clay more workable, too; add organic matter at the same time and you get soil that is more friable, better draining and more nutrient-rich — all at once. Put 2 inches of clean sand and 3 inches of composted organic matter on top of the soil, and till to a depth of 8 or 10 inches.

In most areas of Texas, planting vegetables in raised beds is the way to go. Most of the plants you'll want to grow need a depth of at least 8 inches (two landscape timbers minimum), while carrots, sweet potatoes and some other root crops need 12 inches (three timbers). Raised beds are especially useful on the Gulf Coast and other areas that get periods of heavy rain during the growing season.

GREEN MANURE

Many growers who let their gardens go fallow for a season like to recharge the soil with a "green manure." This is simply a nitrogen-fixing crop — elbon rye, vetch, red clover and oats are common choices — that is generally planted in the fall and tilled under in early spring.

DIAL UP...

Mike Peters' TEXAS GARDEN HOTLINE

Before you put on your gloves and head out to the garden, "dial up" **Mike Peters' TEXAS GARDEN HOTLINE** to receive tips on . . .
- VEGETABLES — what and when to plant.
- FLOWERS — for a new and beautiful garden.
- HOW-TO HINTS — for an earth-friendly garden.
- SECRETS — that only our gardening experts will tell you.

Call for the latest news from Mike Peters, editor of *Texas Garden Almanac* ... Find out how current weather affects your garden, plus what to plant, prune and fertilize *RIGHT NOW*.

1·900·990·2900

$1.59 per minute. Service available for both rotary and touchtone phones. Under 18 must have permission before calling.

...DIG IN!

How COMPOST To...

Composting is the art of using garbage to its best advantage. And why throw away good organic matter today, and then go to the nursery tomorrow and by sacks of "soil amendment"?

The "recipes" here are flexible; there's probably no need to mow twice this week or eat an extra 30 potatoes to keep a ratio exact. Adjust them to your own taste, the speed you want to produce compost and the success you're having within a pile or bin. More nitrogen materials means more heat and faster compost. In the lists below, N = nitrogen, NN = higher nitrogen content, NNN = highest nitrogen. C = carbon, CC = more carbon, CCC = most carbon. Notice that the ratio of "browns" to "greens" stays the same from recipe to recipe. All of the recipes given on this page will work; they just work a little slower as you go down the list.

To avoid anaerobic conditions, especially when you are trying to make compost quickly, the materials in your pile should be:
- as varied as possible
- well mixed, not layered
- sliced and diced (many cuts and scratches in stems and leaves will provide entry for microorganisms)
- turned frequently
- kept moist.

Compost bins and piles work best when the bottom of the pile makes contact with the ground. You get great traffic of microorganisms between the working compost

THE FAST COOK
2 parts dry leaves	CC	Browns
2 parts hay or wood shavings	CCC	Browns
1 part manure	NNN	Greens
1 part grass clippings	NN	Greens
1 part fresh garden weeds	NN	Greens
1 part food scraps	N	Greens

THE MEDIUM COOK
3 parts dry leaves	CC	Browns
1 part fresh garden weeds	NN	Greens
1 part fresh grass clippings	NN	Greens
1 part food scraps	N	Greens

— or —

6 parts dry leaves	CC	Browns
3 parts food scraps	N	Greens
3 parts fresh grass clippings	NN	Greens

THE SLOW COOK
3 parts dry leaves	CC	Browns
3 parts fresh grass clippings	NN	Greens

— or —

2 parts dry grass clippings	CC	Browns
1 part shredded newspaper	C	Browns
3 parts fresh grass clippings	NN	Greens

and the outside soil. If your compost doesn't have a floor that blocks such microbial traffic, you probably don't need "compost starter." (Though it won't hurt.)

The following are good supplements to any compost pile. Add a shovelful of one (or all!)

- Garden Soil
  High in microorganisms
- Finished Compost
  Very high in microorganisms
- Bone Meal
  High in nitrogen
- Blood Meal
  High in nitrogen
- Fireplace Ashes (cooled!)
  High in potash and carbon
- Crushed Fertilizer Rock Dust
  Rich in minerals

ROCKET SCIENCE?

"Scientists have taken compost and made it so complicated, instead of just telling people how to let things rot. Nothing lives forever. When it dies it's going to rot whether you want it to or not. And composting is an art not a science. It's the art of working with that rotting process in an economical way - that's really important. I see big operations put more energy into making compost than it contains when they get through with it."
— *Malcolm Beck, founder of Garden-Ville*

EARTHWORMS In The Garden

By Mike Peters

You grow vegetables. You have kitchen scraps. You put them in the worm bin. Worms take in old cabbage leaves at one end and put out black, magical compost at the other. You put it out in the garden, and you grow more vegetables.

Sounds like a beautiful system, eh?

It's almost that easy, and even more beneficial. Some test kitchens have reduced their kitchen waste by as much as 75 percent, and the "black gold" residue you get from worm composting has few equals as a soil builder and plant food.

Worm composting is so simple kids can do it. In fact, your kids may be doing it at school right now. Mary Appelhof, author of the humorously readable "Worms Eat My Garbage," has adapted that book into a classroom workbook for teachers and kids, and worm composting has become a popular science project for grade schoolers.

CONTAINERS for worm composting should be shallow — 8" to 12" — because worms are generally surface feeders. Deep containers invite compaction and the anaerobic

conditions that kill both worms and compost. ("Anaerobic" is a word scientists use when they mean "get yucky.")

What size? Depends. Are you a vegetarian, or an enthusiastic veggie eater? (Bigger!) Do you eat out all the time? (Smaller; you'll probably want to ask your neighbors to save their peels, too.) To decide, monitor your kitchen garbage: Appelhof's formula is to build or buy a bin with about 1 square foot of surface area for every pound of waste you generate per week.

Example: A non-vegetarian couple is likely to produce 3.5 pounds of potato peels, citrus rinds, outer leaves of lettuce and cabbage, tea bags, moldy leftovers, cucumber rinds pulverized egg shells and onion skins. Ideal bin: 2-foot x 2-foot x 8-inches.

Karen Overgaard, who teaches Master Composter classes in Montgomery County, likes 20-quart Rubbermaid bins for home worm-composting. (You'll have to punch holes for ventilation.) But any chemical-free opaque container will do; if you build it

Illustration by Joan Peters

with plywood, use exterior grade panels so they won't come apart from the constant damp. Place the bin indoors (the smell won't be bad unless you let it get yucky) or in a shaded area outdoors.

BEDDING MATERIAL comes next: 2 to 3 inches of soilless potting mix, finely shredded cardboard or paper, or hardwood sawdust. Some gardeners like to use manures, but this can make the medium too hot for the worms. Commercial growers often use peat moss, but this provides no nutrients for earthworms and should be leached in a water bath overnight to neutralize acid content. Both Appelhof and Texas organic gardening guru Howard Garret have recommended bedding that is one-third manure, one-third peat moss and one-third shredded paper.

Dampen the bedding until it's about as moist as a wrung sponge. Keep the bedding misted but don't pour water on it. The worm media should stay damp but never be soggy.

FOOD for worms can be most any vegetable matter that isn't salty or oily; many composters don't like to add meat (though the worms will cope with it fine), and you should avoid putting in fish, meat bones and dairy products. Cat feces are a no-no; do not let the worm bin double as a litter box. (You laugh.) Chop up large items to speed up their eventual consumption. Two pounds of worms will consume about 7 pounds of food scraps per week, though temperature and worm activity will make this vary some.

If fruit flies appear, sprinkle a little cold fireplace ash or soft rock phosphate on top of the food material. If your food and bedding look too wet, loosen it with a trowel and add more paper or dry leaves.

HARVESTING OPTIONS: After a few weeks, when the worm compost has the look and fragrance of the forest floor, you have some choices. Appelhof likes to push the vermicompost and worms to one side and add new bedding and food; the worms will move to the new material and in a few weeks you can take out wormless compost and fill in more bedding stuff. In another technique, "divide and dump," you take all but one-third of the vermicompost, worms and all, and dump it straight into the garden. (You should have enough worms and cocoons left in the bin to service another cycle.) Garrett has an aggressive version of Method No. 1: "Place the bin under a bright light. Earthworms like the dark and will move under the top layer. Remove the top layer and fill the bin with fresh layers of moist bedding material and food."

Children (and some adults) should be told that cutting a worm in half is not a good way to double your worms. Worms do have remarkable regenerative powers, but while a front end may grow a new tail, a back end never grows a new head. If you want more worms, provide a good home and put your trust in invertebrate lust. (Harvesting your compost more frequently tends to promote breeding, but the resulting compost is less finished.)

1997 THE YEAR AHEAD

1997 — A whole year of gardening just waiting to happen! The following pages are designed as a daily resource: you'll find propitious dates for planting and feeding, special notes on the seasons, and reference tables for sun and moon rising and setting times. Those tables are calculated from data provided by the U.S. Naval Observatory.

GLOSSARY OF TERMS

Aphelion — Point at which a planet's orbit is farthest from the sun.

Apogee — Point of the moon's orbit farthest from the earth.

Perihelion — Point at which a planet's orbit is nearest the sun.

Perigree — Point of the moon's orbit nearest the earth.

KEY TO ASTRONOMICAL SYMBOLS

Sun — ☉
Moon — ☾
Mercury — ☿
Venus — ♀
Earth — ●
Mars — ♂
Jupiter — ♃
Saturn — ♄
Uranus — ⛢
Neptune — ♆
Pluto — ♇
Half Moon — ◑

ASPECTS

The aspect of a planet refers to its apparent situation in relation to another heavenly body.

♂ "In conjunction" — When this symbol appears between two symbols for heavenly bodies, it means they have the same longtitude in the sky and appear near each other.

♂ "In opposition" — This symbol indicates that the two heavenly bodies differ by 180 degrees of longtitude.

PLANNING FOR SPRING VEGETABLE PLANTING

VEGETABLE	Row Spacing	Seed Spacing	Thin To	Depth To Plant	Days To Mature
Beans (Bush)	18-36"	2-4"	4-6"	.5-1"	45-60
Beans (Pole)	36-48"	2-4"	6"	.5-1.5"	50-60
Beans (Lima)	30-36"	1-2"	4-6"	1.5"	65-75
Beets	14-24"	1"	3-5"	.25-.5"	50-65
Broccoli	24-36"	4-6"/trans.	8"	.25-.5"	55-80
Brussels Sprouts	24-36"	transplants	2-18"	.25-.5"	85-110
Cabbage	24-48"	3-4"	8-24"	.25-.5"	60-120
Cabbage (Chinese)	24-36"	3-4"	8-12"	.25-.5"	90
Carrots	14-24"	.25-.5"	1-2"	scratch in	70-80
Cucumbers	48-72"	6"	2-18"	1-1.5"	50-70
Eggplant	24-36"	transplants	8-24"	.25-.5"	90
Endive	12-24"	.5-1"	8-12"	scratch in	40-90
Kale	24-36"	3-4"	8-12"	.25-.5"	50-75
Kohlrabi	18-30"	3-4"	8-12"	.25-.5"	50-75
Lettuce (Leaf)	12-24"	.5-1"	8-12"	scratch in	40-90
Lettuce (Head)	12-24"	.5-1"	8-12"	scratch in	40-90
Melons (Honeydew)	48-72"	6-12"	8-24"	.5-1"	60-90
Muskmelons	48-72"	6-12"	8-24"	.5-1"	60-90
Mustard Greens	18-24"	1"	3-4"	.25-.5"	30-55

AVERAGE LAST FREEZE DATES

Amarillo	Apr. 17	Kerrville	Apr. 6
Austin	Mar. 3	Lubbock	Apr. 9
Corpus Christi	Feb. 9	McAllen	Feb. 7
Dallas	Mar. 23	Port Arthur	Mar. 11
El Paso	Mar. 9	San Antonio	Mar. 6
Galveston	Jan. 24	Texarkana	Mar. 21
Houston	Feb. 14	Wichita Falls	Mar. 27

PLANNING FOR SPRING VEGETABLE PLANTING

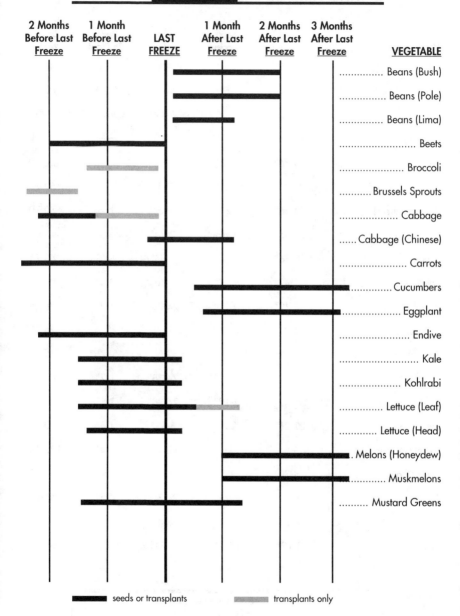

2 Months Before Last Freeze	1 Month Before Last Freeze	LAST FREEZE	1 Month After Last Freeze	2 Months After Last Freeze	3 Months After Last Freeze	VEGETABLE
						Beans (Bush)
						Beans (Pole)
						Beans (Lima)
						Beets
						Broccoli
						Brussels Sprouts
						Cabbage
						Cabbage (Chinese)
						Carrots
						Cucumbers
						Eggplant
						Endive
						Kale
						Kohlrabi
						Lettuce (Leaf)
						Lettuce (Head)
						Melons (Honeydew)
						Muskmelons
						Mustard Greens

seeds or transplants   transplants only

PLANNING FOR SPRING VEGETABLE PLANTING

VEGETABLE	Row Spacing	Seed Spacing	Thin To	Depth To Plant	Days To Mature
Okra	36-42"	4-6"	5-24"	.5-1"	48-60
Onions (Plants)	12-24"	.5"	4-6"	.25-.5"	95-160
Parsley	18-24"	1-2"	8-12"	scratch in	90
Parsnips	14-24"	.25-.5"	3"	scratch in	100+
Peas (English)	24-36"	1-2"	2-3"	1"	50-70
Peas (Edible Pod)	24-36"	1-2"	2-3"	1"	50-70
Peas (Southern)	24-36"	2"	4-6"	1-2"	60-70
Peppers (Bell)	20-35"	transplants	2-24"	.25"	60-100
Peppers (Hot)	20-36"	transplants	2-25"	.25"	60-75
Potatoes	36-42"	8-12"	n/a	3-4"	85-110
Pumpkins	48-72"	6-12"	24-36"	1-2"	45-120
Radishes	18-24"	.5"	1-2"	.25-.5"	25-30
Spinach	14-18"	1"	3-5"	.5-.75"	45-60
Squash (Summer)	24-36"*	6-12"	24-36"	1-2"	45-120
Squash (Winter)	24-36"*	6-12"	24-36"	1-2"	45-120
Sweet Corn	22-26"	2-4"	8-12"	.5-1"	70-95
Sweet Potatoes (Slips)	48-54"	slips	12-14"	3-4"	120-140
Swiss Chard	18-30"	2-3"	6-8"	.5"	50-60
Tomatoes	36-48"	transplants	24-36"	.25"	65-90
Turnips	18-24"	1"	3-4"	.25-.5"	30-55
Watermelons	8-12"	6-12"	8-24"	.5-1"	65-90

* for bush types; trailing and vining types should be spaced 48-72" apart

AVERAGE LAST FREEZE DATES

Amarillo	Apr. 17	Kerrville	Apr. 6
Austin	Mar. 3	Lubbock	Apr. 9
Corpus Christi	Feb. 9	McAllen	Feb. 7
Dallas	Mar. 23	Port Arthur	Mar. 11
El Paso	Mar. 9	San Antonio	Mar. 6
Galveston	Jan. 24	Texarkana	Mar. 21
Houston	Feb. 14	Wichita Falls	Mar. 27

PLANNING FOR SPRING VEGETABLE PLANTING

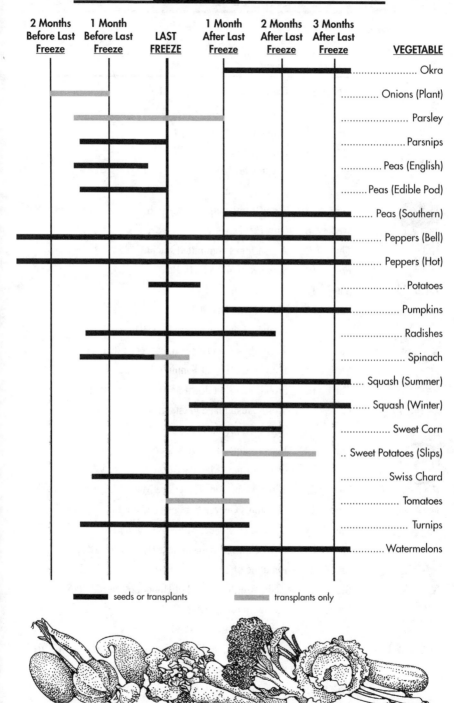

2 Months Before Last Freeze	1 Month Before Last Freeze	LAST FREEZE	1 Month After Last Freeze	2 Months After Last Freeze	3 Months After Last Freeze	VEGETABLE
						Okra
						Onions (Plant)
						Parsley
						Parsnips
						Peas (English)
						Peas (Edible Pod)
						Peas (Southern)
						Peppers (Bell)
						Peppers (Hot)
						Potatoes
						Pumpkins
						Radishes
						Spinach
						Squash (Summer)
						Squash (Winter)
						Sweet Corn
						Sweet Potatoes (Slips)
						Swiss Chard
						Tomatoes
						Turnips
						Watermelons

▬▬▬ seeds or transplants   ▬▬▬ transplants only

$\mathfrak{J}$ANUARY 1997

Day		Event
Wed	1	Battle of Galveston ends, 1863
Thu	2	"Tex" Rickard b., 1871
Fri	3	Slanton water well, 1911
Sat	4	Alford No. 1 oil well, 1948
Sun	5	Alvin Ailey b. in Rogers, TX, 1931
Mon	6	Sam Rayburn b., 1882
Tue	7	Texas frontiersman W.A.A. "Blackfoot" Wallace d., 1899
Wed	8	Gov. E.J. Davis sworn in, 1870
Thu	9	Anson Jones committed suicide, 1858
Fri	10	Spindletop oil well, 1901
Sat	11	Gail Borden d., 1874
Sun	12	"Tex" Ritter b., 1905
Mon	13	Chemist Louis Weisberg b., 1891
Tue	14	Texas shrank 630 acres in border settlement, 1963
Wed	15	John Duval, last of Fannin's Army, d., 1897
Thu	16	Prohibition shut down 13 Texas breweries, 1919
Fri	17	Moses Austin land grant, 1821
Sat	18	SEC sued Frank Sharp, 1971
Sun	19	Janis Joplin b. in Port Arthur, 1943
Mon	20	Gov. Miriam "Ma" Ferguson sworn in, 1925
Tue	21	Thomas Munson, The Grape Man of Denison, d., 1913
Wed	22	Houston's George Foreman defeated Joe Frazier, 1973
Thu	23	Optometry pioneer Molly Wright b., 1875
Fri	24	Jared Groce settlement near Hempstead, 1822
Sat	25	Republic of Texas adopted flag, 1839
Sun	26	Audie Murphy Medal of Honor bestowed, 1945
Mon	27	Matagorda settlement, 1829
Tue	28	Dallas Cowboys b., 1960
Wed	29	Texas Agricultural Extension Service formally est., 1915
Thu	30	State Fair of Texas originally chartered, 1886
Fri	31	Mockingbird declared state bird, 1927

LAST
QUARTER
JAN. 1

NEW
MOON
JAN. 8

FIRST
QUARTER
JAN. 15

FULL
MOON
JAN. 23

LAST
QUARTER
JAN. 31

Sun Rise	Sun Set	Moon Rise	Moon Set	Moon's Place	Astronomy
6:53	**5:29**	**11:46**	**11:58**	Libra	● at Perihelion
6:53	**5:30**	12:39	**12:32**	Libra	
6:54	**5:31**	1:35	**1:09**	Libra	
6:54	**5:31**	2:32	**1:50**	Scorpio	
6:54	**5:32**	3:31	**2:36**	Scorpio	
6:54	**5:33**	4:33	**3:27**	Sagittarius	
6:54	**5:34**	5:34	**4:25**	Sagittarius	♀σ☾
6:54	**5:35**	6:34	**5:28**	Capricorn	
6:54	**5:35**	7:31	**6:35**	Capricorn	
6:54	**5:36**	8:23	**7:43**	Aquarius	☾ at Perihelion
6:54	**5:37**	9:11	**8:51**	Aquarius	
6:54	**5:38**	9:55	**9:57**	Pisces	☿σ♀; ☿ Stationary
6:54	**5:39**	10:36	**11:01**	Pisces	♄σ☾
6:54	**5:40**	11:16	—	Aries	
6:54	**5:41**	11:55	12:04	Aries	
6:54	**5:41**	**12:36**	1:04	Taurus	
6:54	**5:42**	**1:18**	2:03	Taurus	♆σ☉
6:53	**5:43**	**2:02**	3:00	Gemini	
6:53	**5:44**	**3:48**	4:55	Gemini	♃σ☉
6:53	**5:45**	**3:36**	4:47	Gemini	
6:53	**5:46**	**4:26**	5:36	Cancer	
6:52	**5:47**	**5:18**	6:21	Cancer	
6:52	**5:48**	**6:10**	7:03	Leo	☿ Greatest Elong. W.
6:52	**5:49**	**7:03**	7:42	Leo	⚵σ☉
6:51	**5:50**	**7:55**	8:18	Virgo	☾ at Apogee
6:51	**5:50**	**8:47**	8:53	Virgo	
6:50	**5:51**	**9:39**	9:26	Libra	
6:50	**5:52**	**10:32**	10:59	Libra	♂σ☾
6:49	**5:53**	**11:25**	10:32	Libra	
6:49	**5:54**	—	11:08	Scorpio	
6:48	**5:55**	12:20	11:46	Scorpio	

Boldface times indicate p.m.

Sunday	Monday	Tuesday	Wednesday	Thursday	Friday	Saturday
			1 New Year's Day — LAST QUARTER	2	3	4
5	6	7	8 — NEW MOON	9	10	11
12	13	14	15 — FIRST QUARTER	16	17	18
19	20	21	22	23 — FULL MOON	24	25
26	27	28	29	30	31 — LAST QUARTER	

> " *The wonder is that*
> *we can see trees and*
> *not wonder more.* "
> — *Ralph Waldo Emerson*

BEST ...
PLANTING DATES & MAINTENANCE DATES

Plant

Leafy Vegetables, Flowers, Grains
.... Jan. 8-14
.... *Best Time: Jan. 12-13*

Fruiting Vegetables
.... Jan. 15-22
.... *Best Time: Jan. 21-22*

Root Corps, Permanent Plants
.... Jan. 23-30
.... *Best Time: Jan. 28-30*

Mow Lawns

To increase growth
.... Jan. 4-5, 12-13, 21-22, 31
To retard growth
.... Jan. 6-7, 10-11, 14-15,
.... 18-20, 23-27

Cultivate, Spray & Weed

.... Jan. 1-7; 31
.... *Best Time: Jan. 1-3, 6-7*

Fertilize

.... Use any ONE of these dates:
.... Jan. 4, 5, 8, 9, 12, 13,
.... 16, 17, 21, 22, 31

JANUARY   *Gardener's Diary*

Your Personal Journal Of Planning & Planting

Wed	1	_____
Thu	2	_____
Fri	3	_____
Sat	4	_____
Sun	5	_____
Mon	6	_____
Tue	7	_____
Wed	8	_____
Thu	9	_____
Fri	10	_____
Sat	11	_____
Sun	12	_____
Mon	13	_____
Tue	14	_____
Wed	15	_____
Thu	16	_____
Fri	17	_____
Sat	18	_____
Sun	19	_____
Mon	20	_____
Tue	21	_____
Wed	22	_____
Thu	23	_____
Fri	24	_____
Sat	25	_____
Sun	26	_____
Mon	27	_____
Tue	28	_____
Wed	29	_____
Thu	30	_____
Fri	31	_____

FEBRUARY 1997

NEW MOON

FEB. 7

FIRST QUARTER

FEB. 13

FULL MOON

FEB. 21

Day		Event
Sat	1	Menger Hotel opened in San Antonio, 1859
Sun	2	Mexican War ended, 1848
Mon	3	Buddy Holly d., 1959
Tue	4	Fletcher Stockdale d., 1890
Wed	5	Gov. W.P. Hobby signed women's right to vote, 1919
Thu	6	End of Dalton Gang, 1897
Fri	7	Fred Gipson, author of 'Old Yeller,' b., 1908
Sat	8	Crockett arrived at Alamo, 1836
Sun	9	Weather Bureau est. 1891
Mon	10	1st Texas train run (Harrisburg), 1850
Tue	11	Crew of the *San Antonio* mutinied, 1842
Wed	12	Temp. in Seminole, TX was 23 below, 1933
Thu	13	1st American magazine, 1740
Fri	14	20" snowfall in Houston, Orange, 1895
Sat	15	Astronomer Galileo b. 1564
Sun	16	Resolution to divide Texas into two states failed, 1852
Mon	17	H.L. Hunt b., 1889
Tue	18	Planet Pluto disc. 1930
Wed	19	U.S. annexes Texas, 1846
Thu	20	1st U.S. manned space flight, 1962
Fri	21	Santa Anna b., 1794
Sat	22	Yankee soldiers failed to take Aransas Pass, 1862
Sun	23	Texas voted to secede, 1861
Mon	24	Siege of The Alamo began, 1836
Tue	25	Income Tax became law, 1913
Wed	26	Rip Collins b., 1896
Thu	27	John Connally b., 1917
Fri	28	Texas legislature adopted 18th Amendment, 1918

Sun Rise	Sun Set	Moon Rise	Moon Set	Moon's Place	Astronomy
6:48	**5:56**	1:17	**12:27**	Scorpio	♀☌♇
6:47	**5:57**	2:15	**1:14**	Sagittarius	
6:46	**5:58**	3:15	**2:07**	Sagittarius	
6:46	**5:59**	4:14	**3:06**	Capricorn	
6:45	**5:59**	5:12	**4:10**	Capricorn	♀☌♃; ☿☌☾
6:44	**6:00**	6:06	**5:17**	Aquarius	♆☌☾; ♂ Stationary
6:44	**6:01**	6:57	**6:27**	Aquarius	☾ at Perigee; ♀☌☊
6:43	**6:02**	7:45	**7:59**	Pisces	
6:42	**6:03**	8:29	**8:43**	Pisces	
6:41	**6:04**	9:12	**9:49**	Aries	♄☌☾
6:41	**6:05**	9:53	**10:53**	Aries	
6:40	**6:06**	10:35	—	Taurus	☿☌♃
6:39	**6:06**	11:17	11:54	Taurus	
6:38	**6:07**	**12:01**	12:54	Taurus	
6:37	**6:08**	**12:46**	1:50	Gemini	
6:36	**6:09**	**1:34**	2:43	Gemini	♃☌☊
6:35	**6:10**	**2:23**	3:33	Cancer	
6:34	**6:11**	**3:14**	4:19	Cancer	
6:33	**6:11**	**4:06**	5:02	Cancer	
6:32	**6:12**	**4:58**	5:42	Leo	
6:31	**6:13**	**5:50**	6:19	Leo	
6:30	**6:14**	**6:42**	6:54	Virgo	
6:29	**6:14**	**7:34**	7:28	Virgo	
6:28	**6:15**	**8:27**	8:01	Virgo	♂☌☾
6:27	**6:16**	**9:20**	8:34	Libra	
6:26	**6:17**	**10:14**	9:09	Libra	
6:25	**6:18**	**11:09**	9:46	Scorpio	
6:04	**6:18**	—	10:25	Scorpio	

Boldface times indicate p.m.

Sunday	Monday	Tuesday	Wednesday	Thursday	Friday	Saturday
						1
2	3	4	5	6	7 ● NEW MOON	8
9	10	11	12 Ash Wednesday	13 ◗ FIRST QUARTER	14	15
16	17 Washington's Birthday	18	19	20	21 ○ FULL MOON	22
23	24	25	26	27	28	

"

Gardening is the only unquestionably useful job.
— *George Bernard Shaw*

"

BEST ...
PLANTING DATES & MAINTENANCE DATES

Plant

Leafy Vegetables, Flowers, Grains
.... Feb. 7-12
.... *Best Time: Feb. 8-9*

Fruiting Vegetables
.... Feb. 13-20
.... *Best Time: Feb. 17-19*

Root Corps, Permanent Plants
.... Feb. 21-28
.... *Best Time: Feb. 27-28*

Mow Lawns

To increase growth
.... Feb. 1, 8-9, 17-19, 21, 28
To retard growth
.... Feb. 2-3, 6-7, 10-11,
.... 15-16, 20-24

Cultivate, Spray & Weed

.... Feb. 1-6
.... *Best Time: Feb. 6*

Fertilize

.... Use any ONE of these dates:
.... Feb. 1, 8, 9, 12, 13, 14,
.... 17, 18, 19, 27, 28

ℱEBRUARY Gardener's Diary
Your Personal Journal Of Planning & Planting

Sat   1 _____

Sun   2 _____

Mon   3 _____

Tue   4 _____

Wed   5 _____

Thu   6 _____

Fri   7 _____

Sat   8 _____

Sun   9 _____

Mon 10 _____

Tue 11 _____

Wed 12 _____

Thu 13 _____

Fri 14 _____

Sat 15 _____

Sun 16 _____

Mon 17 _____

Tue 18 _____

Wed 19 _____

Thu 20 _____

Fri 21 _____

Sat 22 _____

Sun 23 _____

Mon 24 _____

Tue 25 _____

Wed 26 _____

Thu 27 _____

Fri 28 _____

SPRING

Spring begins when the days and nights are

exactly equal: the spring equinox.

On this day, the sun is exactly half-way

between its north and south extremes.

SPRING EQUINOX

March 20

7:55 a.m.

Ash Wednesday is on the first Wednesday after the moon of Spring.

· · · · ·

English Folklore: Daffodils were not to be brought into the house as long as the goose was hatching; the narcissus did not bring good luck. "She (mother goose) might, on account of their color, think that the goslings had come out of the eggs and leave the nest. This was the explanation given by the old people in my younger days," writes Archdeacon Kewley in one account. This may explain why "goose" and "silly" have become synonyms.

· · · · ·

"When April sounds aloud his horn,
Great crops will be of hay and corn."
— a saying from the Isle of Man,
meaning that a dry April is good for crops

· · · · ·

And you thought snails were useless! In the folkore of the Isle of Man, a maiden who placed a snail between two pewter dishes on May Day Eve (April 30) could expect to wake the next morning and find the name of her future husband in visible characters on a dish. (This didn't work unless she watched until midnight, having first purified her hands and face by washing them in the dew of wheat.)

· · · · ·

In several parts of Europe, May Day Eve was a time to dress the house with flowers, particularly to strew primroses in every doorway. Crosses made of mountain ash were fastened to cattle and to people's clothing. All to ward off witches, believed to be active on this day.

ꟿARCH 1997

Day		Event
Sat	1	Peace Corps est., 1961
Sun	2	Sam Houston b., 1793
Mon	3	Moses Rose left the Alamo, 1836
Tue	4	Jesse Chisholm d., 1868
Wed	5	Mission San Francisco moved to San Antonio, 1731
Thu	6	Fall of the Alamo, 1836
Fri	7	Bluebonnet named state flower, 1901
Sat	8	Preston Smith b., 1912
Sun	9	"Old Fifty-Six" settled in San Antonio, 1731
Mon	10	Salvation Army founded, 1880
Tue	11	Sam Houston takes command of Texas Army, 1836
Wed	12	Oilman Columbus Marion "Dad" Joiner b., 1860
Thu	13	Standard Time adopted, 1884
Fri	14	Lindbergh began pilot training in San Antonio, 1924
Sat	15	Lightnin' Hopkins b., 1912
Sun	16	Gov. Jim Hogg pardoned John Wesley Hardin, 1894
Mon	17	Shamrock Hotel opened in Houston, 1949
Tue	18	New London school explosion, 1937
Wed	19	Swallows return to Capistrano
Thu	20	La Salle shot at Navasota River, 1687
Fri	21	Shoot-out at Tascosa, 1886
Sat	22	Robert F. Flagg b., 1924
Sun	23	Lucille Leseur (Joan Crawford) b. in San Antonio, 1908
Mon	24	Czech Catholic Union of Texas est., 1889
Tue	25	Ralph Waldo Emerson b., 1803
Wed	26	Sandra Day O'Connor b. in El Paso, 1930
Thu	27	300 Texans executed at Goliad, 1836
Fri	28	Antonio Zapata convicted in Mexico, 1840
Sat	29	Earl Campbell b., 1955
Sun	30	Dallas County created, 1846
Mon	31	Daylight Savings Time est., 1918

LAST QUARTER
MAR. 1

NEW MOON
MAR. 8

FIRST QUARTER
MAR. 15

FULL MOON
MAR. 23

LAST QUARTER
MAR. 31

Sun Rise	Sun Set	Moon Rise	Moon Set	Moon's Place	Astronomy
6:23	**6:19**	12:06	11:09	Scorpio	
6:22	**6:20**	1:03	11:57	Sagittarius	
6:21	**6:21**	2:00	**12:51**	Sagittarius	
6:20	**6:21**	2:56	**1:50**	Capricorn	
6:18	**6:22**	3:51	**2:54**	Capricorn	♆☌☾
6:17	**6:23**	4:42	**4:01**	Aquarius	☊☌☾; ♃☌☾
6:16	**6:23**	5:31	**5:09**	Aquarius	
6:15	**6:24**	6:17	**6:18**	Pisces	Eclipse ☉; ☾ at Perigee
6:14	**6:25**	7:01	**7:26**	Pisces	
6:13	**6:26**	7:44	**8:33**	Aries	♄☌☾
6:11	**6:26**	8:27	**9:38**	Aries	☿ Superior
6:10	**6:27**	9:10	**10:40**	Taurus	
	6:28	9:55	**11:40**	Taurus	
6:08	**6:28**	10:41	—	Gemini	
6:06	**6:29**	11:29	12:36	Gemini	
6:05	**6:30**	**12:19**	1:28	Cancer	
6:04	**6:30**	**1:09**	2:16	Cancer	
6:03	**6:31**	**2:01**	3:00	Cancer	
6:01	**6:32**	**3:53**	3:41	Leo	
6:00	**6:32**	**3:45**	4:19	Leo	Spring Begins
5:59	**6:33**	**4:37**	4:55	Virgo	
5:58	**6:34**	**5:29**	5:29	Virgo	
5:56	**6:34**	**6:22**	6:02	Virgo	♂☌☾
5:55	**6:35**	**7:15**	6:36	Libra	Eclipse ☾
5:54	**6:36**	**8:09**	7:10	Libra	
5:52	**6:36**	**9:05**	7:47	Scorpio	
5:51	**6:37**	**10:01**	8:25	Scorpio	
5:50	**6:38**	**10:57**	9:07	Scorpio	
5:49	**6:39**	—	9:54	Sagittarius	
5:47	**6:40**	**11:54**	10:45	Sagittarius	♄☌☉
5:46	**6:40**	12:49	11:41	Capricorn	

NOTE:
All times are calculated in Central Standard Time (CST) for HOUSTON, TYLER and other Texas communities located at approximately 95 degrees longitude. To recalculate times for other locations, add (+) or subtract (-) minutes as shown:

Abilene .... +17
Amarillo .... +26
Austin .... +10
Beaumont .... -5
Brownsville ..... +8
Corpus Christi . +8
Dallas .... +6
El Paso .... +44
(adjust for Mountain Time)
Galveston .... -2
Laredo .... +16
Lubbock .... +26
Odessa .... +28
San Angelo .... +20
San Antonio ... +12
Sherman .... +6
Texarkana .... -4
Waco .... +7
Wichita Falls .. +12

Boldface times indicate p.m.

Sunday	Monday	Tuesday	Wednesday	Thursday	Friday	Saturday
						1 ◗ LAST QUARTER
2	3	4	5	6	7	8 ● NEW MOON
9	10	11	12	13	14	15 ◗ FIRST QUARTER
16	17	18	19	20 First Day Of Spring	21	22
23 Palm Sunday ○ FULL MOON	24	25	26	27	28 Good Friday	29
30 Easter	31 ◗ LAST QUARTER					

> **All Nature seems at work,**
> **Slugs leave their lair —**
> **The bees are stirring —**
> **Birds are on the wing —**
> **And Winter, slumbering in the open air,**
> **Wears on his smiling face a dream of Spring!**
> — *Samuel Taylor Coleridge*

ᗷEST ...
PLANTING DATES & MAINTENANCE DATES

Plant

Leafy Vegetables, Flowers, Grains
.... Mar. 8-14
.... *Best Time: Mar. 8-9*

Fruiting Vegetables
.... Mar. 15-22
.... *Best Time: Mar. 16-18*

Root Corps, Permanent Plants
.... Mar. 23-30
.... *Best Time: Mar. 26-28*

Mow Lawns

To increase growth
.... Mar. 1, 8-9, 16-18, 26-27
To retard growth
.... Mar. 2-3, 6-7, 10-11,
.... 14-15, 19-23, 30

Cultivate, Spray & Weed

.... Mar. 1-7, 31
.... *Best Time: Mar. 2-3*

Fertilize

.... Use any ONE of these dates:
.... Mar. 1, 5, 6, 8, 9, 12, 13, 16,
.... 17, 18, 26, 27, 28, 31

ᶆARCH   *Gardener's Diary*

Your Personal Journal Of Planning & Planting

Sat	1	_____
Sun	2	_____
Mon	3	_____
Tue	4	_____
Wed	5	_____
Thu	6	_____
Fri	7	_____
Sat	8	_____
Sun	9	_____
Mon	10	_____
Tue	11	_____
Wed	12	_____
Thu	13	_____
Fri	14	_____
Sat	15	_____
Sun	16	_____
Mon	17	_____
Tue	18	_____
Wed	19	_____
Thu	20	_____
Fri	21	_____
Sat	22	_____
Sun	23	_____
Mon	24	_____
Tue	25	_____
Wed	26	_____
Thu	27	_____
Fri	28	_____
Sat	29	_____
Sun	30	_____
Mon	31	_____

Day		Event
Tue	1	All Fools' Day until noon
Wed	2	1st Texas junior college awarded to Amarillo, 1929
Thu	3	Horse trainer Max Hirsch d., 1969
Fri	4	Former Sen. John Tower killed in plane crash, 1991
Sat	5	Jesse Jones b. in Tennessee, 1874
Sun	* 6	Mexico bans American immigration to Texas, 1830
Mon	7	Sarah Berhnardt performed as Camille in Galveston, 1911
Tue	8	Friendswood became "dry," 1963
Wed	9	Astrodome opened, 1965
Thu	10	1st major league baseball in Texas, 1962
Fri	11	U.S. Apollo 13 flight, 1970
Sat	12	Yuri Gagarin 1st man in space, 1961
Sun	13	Architect John Staub d., 1981
Mon	14	Van Cliburn won Tchaikovsky Competition, 1958
Tue	15	Sam Houston's army marched to San Jacinto, 1836
Wed	16	576 killed in Texas City chemical fires, 1947
Thu	17	LULAC founded in Corpus Christi, 1929
Fri	18	Santa Anna's wooden leg captured in Mex. War, 1847
Sat	19	Battle of Lexington, 1775
Sun	20	Indian battle at Howard's Well, 1872
Mon	21	Battle of San Jacinto, 1836
Tue	22	UTMB graduated first class, 1892
Wed	23	William Shakespeare b., 1564
Thu	24	Library of Congress est., 1800
Fri	25	Brownsville skirmish ignited Mexican War, 1846
Sat	26	John James Audubon b., 1785
Sun	27	Rogers Hornsby b., 1896
Mon	28	1st mass parachute drop, San Antonio, 1929
Tue	29	John Tyler b., 1790
Wed	30	Willie Nelson b. in Abbott, 1933

NEW
MOON

APR. 7

FIRST
QUARTER

APR. 14

FULL
MOON

APR. 22

LAST
QUARTER

APR. 29

*Daylight Savings
Time begins at 2 a.m..*

Sun Rise	Sun Set	Moon Rise	Moon Set	Moon's Place	Astronomy
5:45	**6:40**	1:43	**12:40**	Sagittarius	♆☌☾
5:43	**6:41**	2:33	**1:44**	Aquarius	♀ Superior
5:42	**6:42**	3:21	**2:49**	Aquarius	♃☌☾
5:41	**6:42**	4:07	**3:56**	Pisces	
5:40	**6:43**	4:50	**5:03**	Pisces	☾ at Perigee
6:38	**7:43**	6:33	**7:10**	Aries	
6:37	**7:44**	7:16	**8:16**	Aries	
6:36	**7:45**	7:59	**9:21**	Taurus	☿☌☾
6:35	**7:45**	8:44	**10:23**	Taurus	
6:33	**7:46**	9:31	**11:23**	Gemini	
6:32	**7:47**	10:20	—	Gemini	
6:31	**7:47**	11:10	12:18	Gemini	
6:30	**7:48**	**12:01**	1:10	Cancer	
6:29	**7:49**	**12:54**	1:56	Cancer	
6:27	**7:49**	**1:46**	2:39	Cancer	
6:26	**7:50**	**2:38**	3:18	Leo	
6:25	**7:51**	**3:30**	3:54	Leo	☾ at Apogee
6:24	**7:51**	**4:22**	4:29	Leo	
6:23	**7:52**	**5:15**	5:03	Virgo	♂☌☾
6:22	**7:53**	**6:08**	5:36	Virgo	
6:20	**7:53**	**7:02**	6:10	Libra	
6:19	**7:54**	**7:58**	6:46	Libra	
6:18	**7:55**	**8:55**	7:24	Scorpio	
6:17	**7:55**	**9:52**	8:06	Scorpio	
6:16	**7:56**	**10:50**	8:51	Sagittarius	☿ Inferior
6:15	**7:57**	—	9:41	Sagittarius	
6:14	**7:58**	11:46	10:36	Capricorn	
6:13	**7:58**	12:40	11:34	Capricorn	
6:12	**7:59**	1:31	**12:35**	Aquarius	♂ Stationary; ♆☌☾
6:11	**8:00**	2:18	**1:38**	Aquarius	♃☌☾

Boldface times indicate p.m.

Sunday	Monday	Tuesday	Wednesday	Thursday	Friday	Saturday
		1	*2*	*3*	*4*	*5*
6	*7* NEW MOON	*8*	*9*	*10*	*11*	*12*
13	*14* FIRST QUARTER	*15*	*16*	*17*	*18*	*19*
20	*21*	*22* Passover Begins FULL MOON	*23*	*24*	*25*	*26*
27	*28*	*29* LAST QUARTER	*30*			

" **The bees like plum blossoms
and so do I.
They smell exactly like
cherry Lifesavers taste.**
— *Sue Hubbell* "

BEST ...
PLANTING DATES & MAINTENANCE DATES

Plant

Leafy Vegetables, Flowers, Grains
.... Apr. 7-13
.... *Best Time: Apr. 13*

Fruiting Vegetables
.... Apr. 14-21
.... *Best Time: Apr. 14*

Root Corps, Permanent Plants
.... Apr. 22-28
.... *Best Time: Apr. 23-24*

Mow Lawns

To increase growth
.... Apr. 4-5, 13-14, 23-24
To retard growth
.... Apr. 2-3, 6-7, 10-12,
.... 15-19, 25-26, 29-30

Cultivate, Spray & Weed

.... Apr. 1-6, 29-30
.... *Best Time: Apr. 2-3, 29-30*

Fertilize

.... Use any ONE of these dates:
.... Apr. 1, 4, 5, 8, 9, 13, 14,
.... 23, 24, 27, 28

APRIL   *Gardener's Diary*

Your Personal Journal Of Planning & Planting

Tue 1 _____

Wed 2 _____

Thu 3 _____

Fri 4 _____

Sat 5 _____

Sun 6 _____

Mon 7 _____

Tue 8 _____

Wed 9 _____

Thu 10 _____

Fri 11 _____

Sat 12 _____

Sun 13 _____

Mon 14 _____

Tue 15 _____

Wed 16 _____

Thu 17 _____

Fri 18 _____

Sat 19 _____

Sun 20 _____

Mon 21 _____

Tue 22 _____

Wed 23 _____

Thu 24 _____

Fri 25 _____

Sat 26 _____

Sun 27 _____

Mon 28 _____

Tue 29 _____

Wed 30 _____

AY   1997

Day		Event
Thu	1	San Antonio de Valero, a.k.a. The Alamo, founded, 1718
Fri	2	Childress Army Air Field est., 1942
Sat	3	Henderson Co. Junior College est, 1946
Sun	4	Jean Lafitte forced to leave Galveston, 1821
Mon	5	Mexican Army defeated the French at Puebla, 1862
Tue	6	Scattered tornadoes in Texas kill at least 82, 1930
Wed	7	Julius Real b., 1860
Thu	8	Zachary Taylor engaged Mex. army near Brownsville, 1846
Fri	9	Sam Houston married Margaret Lea, 1846
Sat	10	Transcontinental railroad completed, 1869
Sun	11	114 killed by tornado in Waco, 1953
Mon	12	Norris Wright Cuney b., 1846
Tue	13	Bob Wills d., 1975
Wed	14	Gabriel Farenheit b. 1686
Thu	15	Katherine Anne Porter b., 1890
Fri	16	Sen. Temple Houston dedicates state capitol building, 1888
Sat	17	Bell clapper returned to Texas A&M, 1975
Sun	18	114 killed by tornado at Goliad, 1902
Mon	19	Cynthia Ann Parker captured by Comanches, 1836
Tue	20	Homestead Act approved, 1862
Wed	21	Naturalist Ferdinand Jacob Lindheimer b., 1801
Thu	22	Tidelands bill gave State of Texas right to offshore oil, 1953
Fri	23	Bonnie and Clyde ambushed in Louisiana, 1934
Sat	24	Mission San Francisco de los Tejas est., 1690
Sun	25	Texas chapter, Daughters of the Confederacy founded, 1896
Mon	26	Samuel Pepys d., 1703
Tue	27	Michael Francis "Pinky" Higgins b. in Red Oak, 1909
Wed	28	Texon oil well, 1923
Thu	29	Texas Spring Palace opened in Ft. Worth, 1889
Fri	30	T. Roosevelt's Rough Riders departed San Antonio, 1898
Sat	31	Texas-born war hero Audie Murphy killed, 1971

NEW MOON

MAY 6

FIRST QUARTER

MAY 13

FULL MOON

MAY 21

LAST QUARTER

MAY 28

Sun Rise	Sun Set	Moon Rise	Moon Set	Moon's Place	Astronomy
6:10	**8:00**	3:03	**2:43**	Aquarius	♆ Stationary
6:09	**8:01**	3:46	**3:47**	Pisces	
6:08	**8:02**	4:27	**4:52**	Pisces	☾ at Perigee
6:07	**8:02**	5:08	**5:57**	Aries	♄☌♄; ☿☌☾
6:06	**8:03**	5:50	**7:02**	Aries	
6:05	**8:04**	6:34	**8:05**	Taurus	
6:04	**8:04**	7:19	**9:07**	Taurus	☿ Stationary
6:03	**8:05**	8:08	**10:05**	Gemini	
6:02	**8:06**	8:58	**10:59**	Gemini	
6:02	**8:07**	9:50	—	Cancer	
6:01	**8:07**	10:43	**11:49**	Cancer	
6:00	**8:08**	11:36	12:34	Leo	
5:59	**8:09**	**12:29**	1:15	Leo	⚷ Stationary
5:59	**8:09**	**1:22**	1:53	Leo	
5:58	**8:10**	**2:14**	2:28	Virgo	☾ at Apogee
5:57	**8:11**	**3:06**	3:02	Virgo	♂☌☾
5:56	**8:11**	**3:59**	3:35	Virgo	
5:56	**8:12**	**4:53**	4:09	Libra	
5:55	**8:13**	**5:48**	4:44	Libra	
5:55	**8:13**	**6:45**	5:21	Scorpio	
5:54	**8:14**	**7:43**	6:01	Scorpio	
5:53	**8:15**	**8:41**	6:46	Sagittarius	☿ Greatest Elong W.
5:53	**8:15**	**9:39**	7:35	Sagittarius	
5:52	**8:16**	**10:35**	8:29	Capricorn	
5:52	**8:16**	**11:28**	9:27	Capricorn	♇☍
5:51	**8:17**	—	10:29	Capricorn	♆☌☾
5:51	**8:18**	12:18	11:32	Aquarius	⚷☌☾
5:51	**8:18**	1:03	**12:36**	Aquarius	♃☌☾
5:50	**8:19**	1:46	**1:39**	Pisces	☾ at Perigee
5:50	**8:19**	2:27	**2:43**	Pisces	
5:49	**8:20**	3:07	**3:46**	Aries	♄☌☾

NOTE:
All times are calculated in Central Standard Time (CST) for HOUSTON, TYLER and other Texas communities located at approximately 95 degrees longitude.
To recalculate times for other locations, add (+) or subtract (-) minutes as shown:
Abilene .... +17
Amarillo .... +26
Austin .... +10
Beaumont .... -5
Brownsville ..... +8
Corpus Christi . +8
Dallas .... +6
El Paso .... +44
(adjust for Mountain Time)
Galveston .... -2
Laredo .... +16
Lubbock .... +26
Odessa ....: +28
San Angelo .... +20
San Antonio ... +12
Sherman .... +6
Texarkana .... -4
Waco .... +7
Wichita Falls .. +12

Boldface times indicate p.m.

MAY _____ 1997

Sunday	Monday	Tuesday	Wednesday	Thursday	Friday	Saturday
				1	2	3
4	5	6 ● NEW MOON	7	8	9 Islamic New Year	10
11 Mother's Day	12	13 ☾ FIRST QUARTER	14	15	16	17
18 Pentecost Armed Forces Day	19	20	21 ○ FULL MOON	22	23	24
25	26 Memorial Day	27	28 ☽ LAST QUARTER	29	30	31

" *In the spring,*
at the end of the day,
you should smell like dirt.
— *Margaret Atwood* "

BEST ...
PLANTING DATES & MAINTENANCE DATES

Plant

Leafy Vegetables, Flowers, Grains
.... May 6-12
.... *Best Time: May 10-11*

Fruiting Vegetables
.... May 13-20
.... *Best Time: May 13*

Root Corps, Permanent Plants
.... May 21-27
.... *Best Time: May 21*

Mow Lawns

To increase growth
...... May 2-3, 10-11, 20-21, 29-30
To retard growth
.... May 1, 4-5, 8-9, 12-17,
.... 22-23, 27-28, 31

Cultivate, Spray & Weed
.... May 1-5, 28-31
.... *Best Time: May 4-5, 28*

Fertilize
.... Use any ONE of these dates:
.... May 2, 3, 6, 7, 10, 11, 20,
.... 21, 24, 25, 26, 29, 30

AY   *Gardener's Diary*

Your Personal Journal Of Planning & Planting

Thu	1	_____
Fri	2	_____
Sat	3	_____
Sun	4	_____
Mon	5	_____
Tue	6	_____
Wed	7	_____
Thu	8	_____
Fri	9	_____
Sat	10	_____
Sun	11	_____
Mon	12	_____
Tue	13	_____
Wed	14	_____
Thu	15	_____
Fri	16	_____
Sat	17	_____
Sun	18	_____
Mon	19	_____
Tue	20	_____
Wed	21	_____
Thu	22	_____
Fri	23	_____
Sat	24	_____
Sun	25	_____
Mon	26	_____
Tue	27	_____
Wed	28	_____
Thu	29	_____
Fri	30	_____
Sat	31	_____

SUMMER

Summer begins with the longest day and the

shortest night: the summer solstice.

On this day, the sun is as far north

as it will appear.

SUMMER SOLSTICE

June 21

3:20 a.m.

SUMMER NOTES

On July 4, we get up in the morning eager for picnics and fireworks, humming "Stars and Stripes Forever" as we wish away the rainclouds. What a difference 500 years makes! Back then, Europeans celebrated July 4 and 5 with a Midsummer Day fair they hoped would be rained out. They believed a good shower on those days was essential (and an omen) for productive summer crops.

· · · · ·

Because heat and drought are trademarks of summer in much of Texas, many growers slow down and use the hot days to gear up for a second growing season in the fall. Dr. Bob Randall, director of the Urban Harvest community gardens program in Houston, likes to surprise listeners by saying that July is his favorite month in the garden. Why? Because there is not much to do except enjoy the harvest from his extensive edible landscape.

· · · · ·

Hot-weather crops that offer good backyard production include chiles, okra and sweet potatoes in most parts of Texas.

· · · · ·

Mulch is a gardener's best friend at this time, retaining moisture as it keeps surface soil and root zones cool. Coarse-ground native mulches offer the most benefit.

JUNE   1997

	Day		Event

NEW MOON

JUNE 4

FIRST QUARTER

JUNE 12

FULL MOON

JUNE 20

LAST QUARTER

JUNE 27

Day		Event
Sun	1	1st women in class at Texas A&M, 1963
Mon	2	Andrew Jackson Houston sworn in as U.S. Senator, 1941
Tue	3	1st professional theater in Dallas, 1947
Wed	4	Lone Star Gas chartered, 1909
Thu	5	UT diver and Olympic champ David Browning b., 1931
Fri	6	Raid closed gambling in Galveston, 1957
Sat	7	William P. Hobby d., 1964
Sun	8	Ralph Yarborough b., 1903
Mon	9	1st commercial Texas oil field at Corsicana, 1894
Tue	10	Moses Austin d., 1821
Wed	11	Bandits strike state treasury in Austin, 1865
Thu	12	Rabbi Henry Cohen d., 1952
Fri	13	Miriam "Ma" Ferguson b., 1875
Sat	14	Jefferson Davis offered presidency of Texas A&M, 1875
Sun	15	Waylon Jennings b. in West Texas, 1937
Mon	16	Texan Edward White made Gemini 4 space walk, 1965
Tue	17	Gov. Pendleton Murrah fled to Mexico, 1865
Wed	18	J.A. Ranch founded, Palo Duro Canyon (approx. date), 1877
Thu	19	Slaves freed in Galveston, 1865
Fri	20	Great Brazos River flood, 1899
Sat	21	Berlin airlift began, 1948
Sun	22	Santa Anna d., 1876
Mon	23	Wiley Post began airplane trip around the world, 1931
Tue	24	Ramón Expedition soldiers staged Texas' 1st horse race, 1716
Wed	25	Korean War began, 1950
Thu	26	Democratic National Convention in Houston, 1928
Fri	27	2nd battle of Adobe Walls, Hutchinson Co., 1874
Sat	28	1st battleship *Texas* launched, 1892
Sun	29	Sculptor Elisabet Ney d., 1907
Mon	30	Mexican troops abandon Fort Anahuac, 1835

Sun Rise	Sun Set	Moon Rise	Moon Set	Moon's Place	Astronomy
5:49	**8:20**	3:47	**4:49**	Aries	
5:49	**8:21**	4:29	**5:51**	Taurus	
5:49	**8:22**	5:12	**6:53**	Taurus	☿☌☾
5:48	**8:22**	5:58	**7:42**	Gemini	
5:48	**8:23**	6:47	**8:48**	Gemini	
5:48	**8:23**	7:39	**9:40**	Cancer	♀☌☾
5:48	**8:24**	8:32	**10:28**	Cancer	
5:48	**8:24**	9:25	**11:11**	Cancer	
5:48	**8:24**	10:19	—	Leo	
5:48	**8:25**	11:12	11:51	Leo	♃ Stationary
5:48	**8:25**	**12:37**	12:27	Virgo	
5:48	**8:26**	**12:57**	1:02	Virgo	☾ at Apogee
5:48	**8:26**	**1:49**	1:35	Virgo	♂☌☾
5:48	**8:26**	**2:42**	2:08	Libra	
5:48	**8:27**	**3:36**	2:42	Libra	
5:48	**8:27**	**4:31**	3:17	Scorpio	
5:48	**8:27**	**5:29**	3:55	Scorpio	
5:48	**8:28**	**6:27**	4:38	Scorpio	
5:48	**8:28**	**7:27**	5:25	Sagittarius	
5:48	**8:28**	**8:25**	6:18	Sagittarius	
5:49	**8:28**	**9:21**	7:15	Capricorn	Summer Begins
5:49	**8:28**	**10:13**	8:17	Capricorn	♆☌☾
5:49	**8:29**	**11:02**	9:22	Aquarius	♅☌☾
5:49	**8:29**	—	10:27	Aquarius	☾ at Perigee; ♃☌☾
5:50	**8:29**	**11:47**	11:32	Pisces	☿ Superior
5:50	**8:29**	12:29	**12:36**	Pisces	
5:50	**8:29**	1:09	**1:40**	Aries	
5:51	**8:29**	1:49	**2:42**	Aries	♄☌☾
5:51	**8:29**	2:29	**3:44**	Taurus	
5:51	**8:29**	3:11	**4:44**	Taurus	

Boldface times indicate p.m.

JUNE   1997

Sunday	Monday	Tuesday	Wednesday	Thursday	Friday	Saturday
1	2	3	4 NEW MOON	5	6	7
8	9	10	11 Feast of Weeks	12 FIRST QUARTER	13	14 Flag Day
15 Father's Day	16	17	18	19 Emancipation Day	20 FULL MOON	21 First Day Of Summer
22	23	24	25	26	27 LAST QUARTER	28
29	30					

> **"** *What I enjoy is*
> *not the fruits alone,*
> *but the soil itself,*
> *its nature and its power.* **"**
> *— Cicero*

BEST . . .
PLANTING DATES & MAINTENANCE DATES

Plant
Leafy Vegetables, Flowers, Grains
......................................June 4-11
.... *Best Time: June 6-8*

Fruiting Vegetables
.... June 12-19
.... *Best Time: June 16-18*

Root Corps, Permanent Plants
.... June 20-26
.... *Best Time: June 25-26*

Mow Lawns
To increase growth
..... June 6-8, 16-18, 25-26, 29-30
To retard growth
.... June 1, 4-5, 9-13,
.... 22-23, 27-28, 31
Cultivate, Spray & Weed
.... June 1-3, 27-30
.... *Best Time: June 1, 27-28*
Fertilize
.... Use any ONE of these dates:
.... June 2, 3, 6, 7, 8, 16, 17, 18,
.... 21, 22, 25, 26, 29, 30

JUNE

Gardener's Diary

Your Personal Journal Of Planning & Planting

Sun	1	_____
Mon	2	_____
Tue	3	_____
Wed	4	_____
Thu	5	_____
Fri	6	_____
Sat	7	_____
Sun	8	_____
Mon	9	_____
Tue	10	_____
Wed	11	_____
Thu	12	_____
Fri	13	_____
Sat	14	_____
Sun	15	_____
Mon	16	_____
Tue	17	_____
Wed	18	_____
Thu	19	_____
Fri	20	_____
Sat	21	_____
Sun	22	_____
Mon	23	_____
Tue	24	_____
Wed	25	_____
Thu	26	_____
Fri	27	_____
Sat	28	_____
Sun	29	_____
Mon	30	_____

ULY   1997

NEW MOON

JULY 4

FIRST QUARTER

JULY 12

FULL MOON

JULY 19

LAST QUARTER

JULY 26

Day		Event
Tue	1	Civil War battle at Round Top, 1863
Wed	2	Beginning of continuous settlement of Texas, 1716
Thu	3	Blind Lemon Jefferson b. near Wortham, 1897
Fri	4	1st Indian indoor rodeo in Ft. Worth, 1883
Sat	5	Kirby Lumber Co. chartered, 1901
Sun	6	City of Uvalde incorporated, 1886
Mon	7	Arthur Conan Doyle d., 1930
Tue	8	C.W. Post d. in Garza Co., 1907
Wed	9	San Antonio-San Diego mail route est., 1857
Thu	10	Richard King, founder of King Ranch, b., 1824
Fri	11	Gov. Beauford Jester d. in office, 1949
Sat	12	Oscar Hammerstein b., 1895
Sun	13	Start of Cortina Wars on Mexico border, 1859
Mon	14	Baritone Jules Bledsoe d., 1943
Tue	15	Battle of the Neches, 1839
Wed	16	Chief Bowles killed at Battle of the Neches, 1839
Thu	17	Disneyland's opening day, 1955
Fri	18	"Lone Star" 36th Div. organized from Tex. Nat'l Guard, 1917
Sat	19	"Wrong Way" Corrigan flight, New York to Dublin, 1938
Sun	20	Apollo 11 lift off, 1969
Mon	21	Spanish flag last flew over San Antonio, 1821
Tue	22	Great Freeport Flood, 1933
Wed	23	Jane Long b., 1798
Thu	24	Jack Kilby sketches computer chip concept, 1958
Fri	25	Barbara Jordan speech at Nixon impeachment hearings, 1974
Sat	26	San Houston d., 1863
Sun	27	Texas-Oklahoma clash over Red River Bridge, 1931
Mon	28	14th Amendment passed, 1868
Tue	29	Composer Oscar Fox d., 1961
Wed	30	Last public hanging in Texas, at Waco, 1923
Thu	31	Jim Reeves d., 1964

Sun Rise	Sun Set	Moon Rise	Moon Set	Moon's Place	Astronomy
5:52	**8:29**	3:55	**5:43**	Gemini	
5:52	**8:29**	4:42	**6:40**	Gemini	
5:53	**8:29**	5:31	**7:33**	Gemini	
5:53	**8:29**	6:23	**8:22**	Cancer	● at Aphelion
5:54	**8:29**	7:16	**9:07**	Cancer	
5:54	**8:29**	8:10	**9:49**	Leo	♀ ☌ ☾
5:55	**8:29**	9:03	**10:26**	Leo	
5:55	**8:28**	9:56	**11:02**	Leo	
5:56	**8:28**	10:48	**11:35**	Virgo	☾ at Apogee
5:56	**8:28**	11:40	—	Virgo	
5:57	**8:28**	**12:32**	12:08	Libra	♂ ☌ ☾
5:58	**8:27**	**1:25**	12:41	Libra	
5:58	**8:27**	**2:19**	1:15	Libra	
5:59	**8:27**	**3:15**	1:51	Scorpio	
5:59	**8:26**	**4:12**	2:31	Scorpio	
6:00	**8:26**	**5:10**	3:15	Sagittarius	
6:01	**8:25**	**6:09**	4:04	Sagittarius	
6:01	**8:25**	**7:07**	4:59	Capricorn	
6:02	**8:24**	**8:02**	6:00	Capricorn	
6:03	**8:24**	**8:54**	7:04	Aquarius	☿ ☌ ☾
6:03	**8:23**	**9:42**	8:11	Aquarius	♃ ☌ ☾; ☾ at Perigee
6:04	**8:23**	**10:26**	9:19	Pisces	
6:05	**8:22**	**11:08**	10:25	Pisces	
6:05	**8:22**	—	11:31	Aries	
6:06	**8:21**	**11:49**	**12:35**	Aries	♄ ☌ ☾
6:07	**8:21**	12:30	**1:37**	Taurus	
6:07	**8:20**	1:11	**2:38**	Taurus	
6:08	**8:19**	1:55	**3:38**	Taurus	
6:09	**8:18**	2:40	**4:34**	Gemini	
6:09	**8:18**	3:28	**5:28**	Gemini	
6:10	**8:17**	4:18	**6:18**	Cancer	

Boldface times indicate p.m.

Sunday	Monday	Tuesday	Wednesday	Thursday	Friday	Saturday
		1	2	3	4 *Fourth of July* ● NEW MOON	5
6	7	8	9	10	11	12 ◗ FIRST QUARTER
13	14	15	16	17	18	19 ○ FULL MOON
20	21	22	23	24	25	26 ◖ LAST QUARTER
27	28	29	30	31		

> " *Deep in the greens of summer*
> *sing the lives I've come to love.*
> *A vireo whets its bill.*
> *The great day balances upon the leaves;*
> *my ears can hear the bird when all is still.* "
> — *Theodore Roethke*

Best...
Planting Dates & Maintenance Dates

Plant

Leafy Vegetables, Flowers, Grains
.... July 4-11
.... *Best Time: July 4-5*

Fruiting Vegetables
.... July 12-18
.... *Best Time: July 14-15*

Root Corps, Permanent Plants
.... July 19-25
.... *Best Time: July 22-23*

Mow Lawns

To increase growth
.... July 4-5, 14-15, 22-23, 31
To retard growth
.... July 1-3, 6-10, 16-17,
.... 21, 24, 28-30

Cultivate, Spray & Weed

.... July 1-3, 26-31
.... *Best Time: July 29-30*

Fertilize

.... Use any ONE of these dates:
...July 4, 5, 11, 12, 13, 14, 15, 18,
.... 19, 22, 23, 26, 27, 28, 31

JULY

Gardener's Diary

Your Personal Journal Of Planning & Planting

Tue   1 _____

Wed   2 _____

Thu   3 _____

Fri   4 _____

Sat   5 _____

Sun   6 _____

Mon   7 _____

Tue   8 _____

Wed   9 _____

Thu 10 _____

Fri 11 _____

Sat 12 _____

Sun 13 _____

Mon 14 _____

Tue 15 _____

Wed 16 _____

Thu 17 _____

Fri 18 _____

Sat 19 _____

Sun 20 _____

Mon 21 _____

Tue 22 _____

Wed 23 _____

Thu 24 _____

Fri 25 _____

Sat 26 _____

Sun 27 _____

Mon 28 _____

Tue 29 _____

Wed 30 _____

Thu 31 _____

⚀UGUST 1997

Day		Event
Fri	1	Sniper killed 17 people from UT tower, 1966
Sat	2	Chicken Ranch closed in La Grange, 1973
Sun	3	Columbus sailed from Spain, 1492
Mon	4	Gov. "Pappy" O'Daniel resigned to be U.S. Senator, 1941
Tue	5	Neil Armstrong b.,1940
Wed	6	H-bomb on Hiroshima, 1945
Thu	7	Coach Blair Cherry, creator of T-formation at UT, d., 1907
Fri	8	Gen. Custer came to Texas to command cavalry, 1865
Sat	9	Thoreau's *Walden* published, 1954
Sun	10	Union sympathizers killed on banks of Neches River, 1862
Mon	11	1st radio S.O.S., 1909
Tue	12	Hottest day recorded in Texas, 120 degrees at Seymour, 1936
Wed	13	Golfer Ben Hogan b. at Dublin, Texas, 1912
Thu	14	Gulf Frwy. between Houston and Galveston dedicated, 1952
Fri	15	Pres. Sam Houston ended bloody feud in Shelby Co., 1844
Sat	16	Mirabeau B. Lamar b., 1798
Sun	17	Davy Crockett b., 1786
Mon	18	Texas' 1st billion-dollar hurricane, Alicia, hit coast, 1983
Tue	19	John Wesley Hardin d. in El Paso, 1895
Wed	20	Trombonist Jack Teagarden b. in Vernon, 1905
Thu	21	One Texas Ranger, one riot, 1906
Fri	22	Fitch steamboat demo., 1787
Sat	23	Camp Logan riots in Houston, 1917
Sun	24	Mt. Vesuvius erupted, A.D. 79
Mon	25	National Park Service est., 1916
Tue	26	Allen brothers bought land that became Houston, 1836
Wed	27	Lyndon Baines Johnson b., 1908
Thu	28	LBJ won Senate primary runoff by 87 votes, 1948
Fri	29	Colt revolver patented, 1839
Sat	30	First battle of Red River Indian War, 1874
Sun	31	Norway caught 1st live giant squid, 1962

NEW MOON

AUG. 2

FIRST QUARTER

AUG. 10

FULL MOON

AUG. 17

LAST QUARTER

AUG. 24

Sun Rise	Sun Set	Moon Rise	Moon Set	Moon's Place	Astronomy
6:11	**8:16**	5:10	**7:04**	Cancer	
6:12	**8:15**	6:03	**7:47**	Leo	♄ Stationary
6:12	**8:15**	6:56	**8:26**	Leo	☿ Greatest Elong E.
6:13	**8:14**	7:49	**9:02**	Leo	
6:14	**8:13**	8:42	**9:36**	Virgo	☿ ☌ ☾
6:14	**8:12**	9:34	**10:09**	Virgo	♀ ☌ ☾; ☾ at Apogee
6:15	**8:11**	9:26	**10:42**	Libra	
6:16	**8:10**	10:18	**11:15**	Libra	
6:16	**8:09**	11:10	—	Libra	♃ ☍ ●☌ ♂ ☌ ☾
6:17	**8:08**	**12:04**	11:50	Scorpio	
6:18	**8:07**	**1:59**	12:27	Scorpio	
6:19	**8:06**	**1:56**	1:08	Sagittarius	
6:19	**8:05**	**3:43**	1:53	Sagittarius	
6:20	**8:04**	**4:50**	2:44	Sagittarius	
6:21	**8:03**	**5:46**	3:41	Capricorn	
6:21	**8:02**	**6:39**	4:43	Capricorn	☿ Stationary; ♆ ☌ ☾
6:22	**8:01**	**7:30**	5:49	Aquarius	♃ ☌ ☾
6:23	**8:00**	**8:17**	6:57	Aquarius	
6:23	**7:59**	**9:02**	8:06	Pisces	☾ at Perigee
6:24	**7:58**	**9:45**	9:14	Pisces	
6:25	**7:57**	**10:27**	10:21	Aries	
6:25	**7:56**	**11:09**	11:27	Aries	
6:26	**7:55**	—	**12:30**	Taurus	
6:27	**7:54**	11:53	**1:31**	Taurus	
6:27	**7:52**	12:38	**2:29**	Gemini	
6:28	**7:51**	1:26	**3:24**	Gemini	
6:29	**7:50**	2:15	**4:16**	Cancer	
6:29	**7:49**	3:07	**5:03**	Cancer	
6:30	**7:48**	3:59	**5:46**	Cancer	
6:31	**7:46**	4:52	**6:26**	Leo	
6:31	**7:45**	5:44	**7:03**	Leo	☿ Inferior

Boldface times indicate p.m.

UGUST   1997

Sunday	Monday	Tuesday	Wednesday	Thursday	Friday	Saturday
					1	2 ● NEW MOON
3	4	5	6	7	8	9
10 ◗ FIRST QUARTER	11	12	13	14	15	16
17 ○ FULL MOON	18	19	20	21	22	23
24 ◖ LAST QUARTER	25	26	27	28	29	30
31						

> **If we persist,**
> **I do not doubt that by age 96 or so**
> **we will all have gardens we are pleased with,**
> **more or less.**
> — Henry Mitchell

Best...
Planting Dates & Maintenance Dates

Plant

Leafy Vegetables, Flowers, Grains
.... Aug. 2-9
.... *Best Time: Aug. 7-9*

Fruiting Vegetables
.... Aug. 10-16
.... *Best Time: Aug. 10-11*

Root Corps, Permanent Plants
.... Aug. 17-23
.... *Best Time: Aug. 19-20*

Mow Lawns

To increase growth
.... Aug. 1, 10-11, 19-20, 27-28
To retard growth
.... Aug. 2-6, 12-14,
.... 17-18, 21-22

Cultivate, Spray & Weed
.... Aug. 1, 24-31
.... *Best Time: Aug. 30-31*

Fertilize
.... Use any ONE of these dates:
.... Aug. 1, 7, 8, 10, 11, 15, 16,
.... 19, 20, 23, 24, 27, 28

₳UGUST   *Gardener's Diary*

Your Personal Journal Of Planning & Planting

Fri	1	_____
Sat	2	_____
Sun	3	_____
Mon	4	_____
Tue	5	_____
Wed	6	_____
Thu	7	_____
Fri	8	_____
Sat	9	_____
Sun	10	_____
Mon	11	_____
Tue	12	_____
Wed	13	_____
Thu	14	_____
Fri	15	_____
Sat	16	_____
Sun	17	_____
Mon	18	_____
Tue	19	_____
Wed	20	_____
Thu	21	_____
Fri	22	_____
Sat	23	_____
Sun	24	_____
Mon	25	_____
Tue	26	_____
Wed	27	_____
Thu	28	_____
Fri	29	_____
Sat	30	_____
Sun	31	_____

PLANNING FOR FALL VEGETABLE PLANTING

VEGETABLE	Row Spacing	Seed Spacing	Thin To	Depth To Plant	Days To Mature
Beans (Bush)	18-36"	2-4"	4-6"	.5-1"	45-60
Beans (Pole)	36-48"	2-4"	6"	.5-1.5"	50-60
Beans (Lima)	30-36"	1-2"	4-6"	1.5"	65-75
Beets	14-24"	1"	3-5"	.25-.5"	50-65
Broccoli	24-36"	4-6"/trans.	8"	.25-.5"	55-80
Brussels Sprouts	24-36"	transplants	2-18"	.25-.5"	85-110
Cabbage	24-48"	3-4"	8-24"	.25-.5"	60-120
Cabbage (Chinese)	24-36"	3-4"	8-12"	.25-.5"	90
Carrots	14-24"	.25-.5"	1-2"	scratch in	70-80
Cauliflower	24-48"	transplants	24"	.25-.5"	50-75
Celery	24-36"	transplants	6-10"	.25"	80-105
Cucumbers	48-72"	6"	2-18"	1-1.5"	50-70
Eggplant	24-36"	transplants	8-24"	.25-.5"	90
Endive	12-24"	.5-1"	8-12"	scratch in	40-90
Garlic	12-24"	2" (cloves)	4-6"	cover tip .5"	120-160
Kale	24-36"	3-4"	8-12"	.25-.5"	50-75
Kohlrabi	18-30"	3-4"	8-12"	.25-.5"	50-75
Leeks	12-24"	.5"	4-6"	.25-.5"	95-160
Lettuce (Leaf)	12-24"	.5-1"	8-12"	scratch in	40-90
Lettuce (Head)	12-24"	.5-1"	8-12"	scratch in	40-90

AVERAGE FIRST FREEZE DATES

Amarillo	Oct. 24	Kerrville	Nov. 6
Austin	Nov. 28	Lubbock	Nov. 3
Corpus Christi	Dec. 15	McAllen	Dec. 8
Dallas	Nov. 13	Port Arthur	Nov. 16
El Paso	Nov. 12	San Antonio	Nov. 26
Galveston	Dec. 25	Texarkana	Nov. 11
Houston	Dec. 11	Wichita Falls	Nov. 11

PLANNING FOR **FALL** VEGETABLE PLANTING

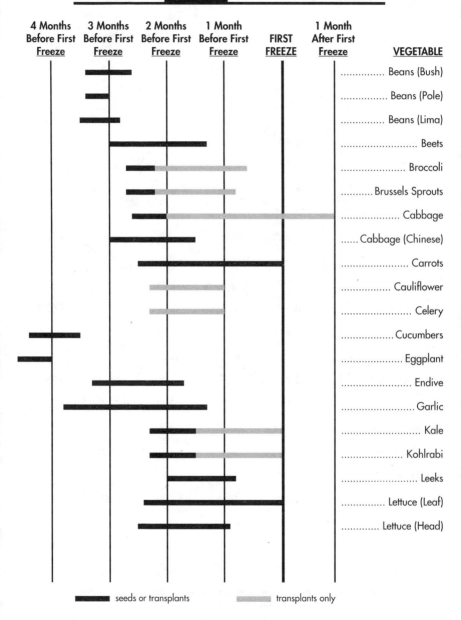

	4 Months Before First Freeze	3 Months Before First Freeze	2 Months Before First Freeze	1 Month Before First Freeze	FIRST FREEZE	1 Month After First Freeze	VEGETABLE
Beans (Bush)		■■■					
Beans (Pole)		■					
Beans (Lima)		■■					
Beets			■■■■				
Broccoli			■▒▒▒				
Brussels Sprouts			■▒▒▒				
Cabbage			■▒▒▒▒▒▒▒				
Cabbage (Chinese)		■■■					
Carrots			■■■■■				
Cauliflower			▒▒▒				
Celery			▒▒▒				
Cucumbers	■■						
Eggplant	■■						
Endive		■■■					
Garlic	■■■■■						
Kale			■▒▒▒				
Kohlrabi			■▒▒▒				
Leeks			■■				
Lettuce (Leaf)			■■■■				
Lettuce (Head)			■■				

■■■ seeds or transplants   ▒▒▒ transplants only

PLANNING FOR FALL VEGETABLE PLANTING

VEGETABLE	Row Spacing	Seed Spacing	Thin To	Depth To Plant	Days To Mature
Melons (Honeydew)	48-72"	6-12"	8-24"	.5-1"	60-90
Muskmelons	48-72"	6-12"	8-24"	.5-1"	60-90
Mustard Greens	18-24"	1"	3-4"	.25-.5"	30-55
Okra	36-42"	4-6"	5-24"	.5-1"	48-60
Onions	12-24"	.5"	4-6"	.25-.5"	95-160
Parsley	18-24"	1-2"	8-12"	scratch in	90
Peas (English)	24-36"	1-2"	2-3"	1"	50-70
Peas (Edible Pod)	24-36"	1-2"	2-3"	1"	50-70
Peas (Southern)	24-36"	2"	4-6"	1-2"	60-70
Peppers (Bell)	20-35"	transplants	2-24"	.25"	60-100
Peppers (Hot)	20-36"	transplants	2-25"	.25"	60-75
Potatoes	36-42"	8-12"	n/a	3-4"	85-110
Pumpkins	48-72"	6-12"	24-36"	1-2"	45-120
Radishes	18-24"	.5"	1-2"	.25-.5"	25-30
Spinach	14-18"	1"	3-5"	.5-.75"	45-60
Squash (Summer)	24-36"*	6-12"	24-36"	1-2"	45-120
Squash (Winter)	24-36"*	6-12"	24-36"	1-2"	45-120
Sweet Corn	22-26"	2-4"	8-12"	.5-1"	70-95
Swiss Chard	18-30"	2-3"	6-8"	.5"	50-60
Tomatoes	36-48"	transplants	24-36"	.25"	65-90
Turnips	18-24"	1"	3-4"	.25-.5"	30-55
Watermelons	8-12"	6-12"	8-24"	.5-1"	65-90

* for bush types; trailing and vining types should be spaced 48-72" apart

AVERAGE FIRST FREEZE DATES

Amarillo	Oct. 24	Kerrville	Nov. 6
Austin	Nov. 28	Lubbock	Nov. 3
Corpus Christi	Dec. 15	McAllen	Dec. 8
Dallas	Nov. 13	Port Arthur	Nov. 16
El Paso	Nov. 12	San Antonio	Nov. 26
Galveston	Dec. 25	Texarkana	Nov. 11
Houston	Dec. 11	Wichita Falls	Nov. 11

PLANNING FOR FALL VEGETABLE PLANTING

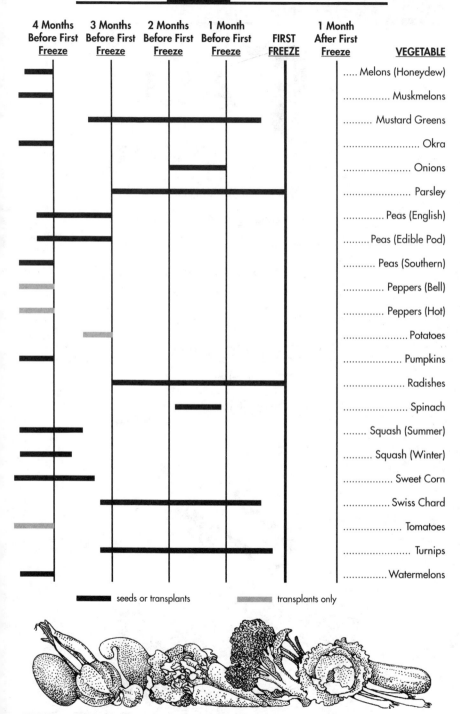

4 Months Before First Freeze	3 Months Before First Freeze	2 Months Before First Freeze	1 Month Before First Freeze	FIRST FREEZE	1 Month After First Freeze	VEGETABLE

..... Melons (Honeydew)
.... Muskmelons
.... Mustard Greens
.... Okra
.... Onions
.... Parsley
.... Peas (English)
.... Peas (Edible Pod)
.... Peas (Southern)
.... Peppers (Bell)
.... Peppers (Hot)
.... Potatoes
.... Pumpkins
.... Radishes
.... Spinach
.... Squash (Summer)
.... Squash (Winter)
.... Sweet Corn
.... Swiss Chard
.... Tomatoes
.... Turnips
.... Watermelons

seeds or transplants   transplants only

FALL

Fall begins when the days and nights

are exactly equal again: the fall equinox.

On this day, the sun returns to the midpoint

of its north and south extremes.

FALL EQUINOX

September 22

6:56 p.m.

One of many traditions European settlers brought to Texas was that blackberries should not be picked after the feast day of Simon and Jude (October 28); children were told that "the club" — now believed to be a mildew — was upon them. Blackberries are hard to find in Texas in late October, but several farm journals from the late 1800s include the dictum that no blackberry jam was to be made or eaten on this day.

· · · · ·

Fall is the most underrated season in the garden: many vegetables perform better now than in spring. One reason: when fall veggies are beginning to mature, the days are getting shorter and cooler. The skins of tomatoes and eggplants, for example, are less likely to scorch. (Spring-planted tomatoes, on the other hand, may be ripening just as it gets really hot.) The fall season's window is tighter as you move away from the Gulf Coast, but every Texas gardener can enjoy a productive fall garden with good timing and well chosen varieties.

· · · · ·

Plant wildflowers in October for a good show next spring. More seed will be available when bluebonnets are blooming, but it's way too late to plant then.

$\mathfrak{S}$EPTEMBER 1997

NEW MOON
SEPT. 1

FIRST QUARTER
SEPT. 9

FULL MOON
SEPT. 16

LAST QUARTER
SEPT. 23

Day		Event
Mon	1	1st La Raza Unida convention, El Paso, 1972
Tue	2	U.S. Treasury Dept. est., 1789
Wed	3	Construction of Castroville begun, 1844
Thu	4	1st reported Texas hurricane hits Galveston, 1766
Fri	5	Sara Emma Edmonds, author, nurse and spy, d. 1898
Sat	6	Erik Jonsson, co-founder Texas Instruments, b., 1901
Sun	7	Union ships arrive at Sabine Pass, 1863
Mon	8	Neiman-Marcus opened in Dallas, 1907
Tue	9	Kilgore Rangerettes debut, 1940
Wed	10	Hurricane Carla hit Texas Coast, 1961
Thu	11	Abilene Christian College opened with 4-yr program, 1906
Fri	12	Kiowa Indian battle in Hemphill County, 1874
Sat	13	Confederate Gen. Joseph Lewis Hogg b., 1806
Sun	14	Corpus Christi demolished by hurricane, 1919
Mon	15	1st session at University of Texas, 1883
Tue	16	Indianola destroyed by hurricane, 1875
Wed	17	Tex. Ranger Roy Aldrich b., 1869
Thu	18	1st issue of *NY Times*, 1851
Fri	19	Leon Jaworski b. in Waco, 1905
Sat	20	Hurricane Beulah hits South Texas, 1967
Sun	21	Battle of Monterrey, 1846
Mon	22	Francisco Vásquez de Coronado d., 1554
Tue	23	William Marsh Rice murdered, 1867
Wed	24	1st issue of the Daily Texan at UT, 1913
Thu	25	Oliver Loving d., 1867
Fri	26	J. Frank Dobie b. in Live Oak County, 1888
Sat	27	Olympic medalist "Babe" Zaharias d., 1956
Sun	28	Indian battle in the Panhandle, 1874
Mon	29	Gene Autry b. in Tioga, 1907
Tue	30	Jim Bowie made a Texas citizen, 1830

Sun Rise	Sun Set	Moon Rise	Moon Set	Moon's Place	Astronomy
6:32	**7:44**	6:37	**7:38**	Virgo	Eclipse ☉
6:32	**7:43**	7:29	**8:11**	Virgo	☽ at Apogee
6:33	**7:41**	8:21	**8:44**	Virgo	
6:34	**7:40**	9:13	**9:17**	Libra	
6:34	**7:39**	10:05	**9:51**	Libra	♀☌☽
6:35	**7:38**	10:58	**10:26**	Scorpio	
6:36	**7:36**	11:52	**11:05**	Scorpio	♂☌☽
6:36	**7:35**	**12:47**	—	Scorpio	
6:37	**7:34**	**1:42**	**11:48**	Sagittarius	☿ Stationary
6:37	**7:33**	**2:37**	12:35	Sagittarius	
6:38	**7:31**	**3:32**	1:27	Capricorn	
6:39	**7:30**	**4:25**	2:25	Capricorn	♆☌☽
6:39	**7:29**	**5:16**	3:27	Aquarius	♃☌♄; ☊☌☽
6:40	**7:27**	**6:04**	4:33	Aquarius	
6:41	**7:26**	**6:50**	5:41	Pisces	
6:41	**7:25**	**7:34**	6:50	Pisces	Eclipse ☽; ☽ at Perigee
6:42	**7:24**	**8:18**	7:59	Aries	
6:42	**7:22**	**9:02**	9:07	Aries	♄☌☽
6:43	**7:21**	**9:46**	10:14	Taurus	
6:44	**7:20**	**10:33**	11:18	Taurus	
6:44	**7:18**	**11:21**	12:20	Gemini	
6:45	**7:17**	—	**1:18**	Gemini	Fall Begins
6:45	**7:16**	12:11	**2:11**	Gemini	
6:46	**7:14**	1:02	**3:00**	Cancer	
6:47	**7:13**	1:55	**3:45**	Cancer	
6:47	**7:12**	2:47	**4:26**	Leo	
6:48	**7:11**	3:40	**5:04**	Leo	
6:48	**7:09**	4:32	**5:39**	Virgo	
6:49	**7:08**	5:25	**6:13**	Virgo	☽ at Apogee
6:50	**7:07**	6:16	**6:46**	Virgo	

Boldface times indicate p.m.

Sunday	Monday	Tuesday	Wednesday	Thursday	Friday	Saturday
	1 Labor Day ● NEW MOON	2	3	4	5	6
7	8	9 ◐ FIRST QUARTER	10	11	12	13
14	15	16 ○ FULL MOON	17	18	19	20
21	22 First Day Of Fall	23 ◑ LAST QUARTER	24	25	26	27
28	29	30				

"

The sun's away
And the bird estranged;
The wind has dropped,
And the sky's deranged;
Summer has stopped.
— *Robert Browning*

"

Best...
Planting Dates & Maintenance Dates

Plant

Leafy Vegetables, Flowers, Grains
.... Sept. 1-8
.... *Best Time: Sept. 6-8*

Fruiting Vegetables
.... Sept. 9-15
.... *Best Time: Sept. 15*

Root Corps, Permanent Plants
.... Sept. 16-22
.... *Best Time: Sept. 15-16*

Mow Lawns

To increase growth
.... Sept.6-8, 15-16, 24-25
To retard growth
.... Sept. 1-3, 9-10, 13-14,
.... 17-18, 21-23, 26-30

Cultivate, Spray & Weed

.... Sept. 23-30
.... *Best Time: Sept. 26-30*

Fertilize

.... Use any ONE of these dates:
.... Sept. 4, 5, 6, 7, 11,12, 15,
.... 16, 19, 20, 24, 25

SEPTEMBER _Gardener's Diary_

Your Personal Journal Of Planning & Planting

Mon	1	
Tue	2	
Wed	3	
Thu	4	
Fri	5	
Sat	6	
Sun	7	
Mon	8	
Tue	9	
Wed	10	
Thu	11	
Fri	12	
Sat	13	
Sun	14	
Mon	15	
Tue	16	
Wed	17	
Thu	18	
Fri	19	
Sat	20	
Sun	21	
Mon	22	
Tue	23	
Wed	24	
Thu	25	
Fri	26	
Sat	27	
Sun	28	
Mon	29	
Tue	30	

Day		Event
Wed	1	Kimbell Art Museum opened in Ft. Worth, 1972
Thu	2	Battle of Gonzalez fought over town cannon, 1835
Fri	3	Daisy Bradford oil well, 1930
Sat	4	Union began blockade of Galveston, 1862
Sun	5	Geo. Washington Carver Museum opened, Austin, 1980
Mon	6	Hemisfair closed in San Antonio, 1968
Tue	7	2nd battle of Saratoga, 1777
Wed	8	Surveyors killed by Kickapoo Indians, 1838
Thu	9	Samuel McCullough wounded at Goliad, 1835
Fri	10	U.S. Naval Academy opened, 1845
Sat	11	William P. Longley hanged at Giddings, 1878
Sun	12	Big Thicket national preserve est., 1974
Mon	13	Aviation pioneer Jacob Brodbeck b., 1821
Tue	14	Dwight Eisenhower b. in Denison, 1890
Wed	15	Land purchased for Angelina Nt'l Forest, 1936
Thu	16	Galveston Bay & Tex. Land Co. founded, 1830
Fri	17	Mex. garrison est. at Ft. Tenoxtitlán on Brazos R., 1830
Sat	18	A&M football star Joe Routt b., 1914
Sun	19	42 Northern sympathizers hanged at Gainesville, 1862
Mon	20	Mickey Mantle b., 1931
Tue	21	Geo. Wilkins Kendall, pioneer sheep farmer, d. 1867
Wed	22	Texas 1st president, Sam Houston, sworn in, 1836
Thu	23	Swallows leave Capistrano
Fri	24	Pony Express ended, 1861
Sat	25	Probable debut of Texas Prison Rodeo, 1931
Sun	* 26	Battle of Indianola, 1862
Mon	27	Construction of Galveston seawall begun, 1902
Tue	28	Juan Seguin b. in San Antonio, 1806
Wed	29	"Black Tuesday" stock market crash, 1929
Thu	30	Saddle-maker Paul Bauer b. in Yorktown, 1855
Fri	31	"Black Jack" Ketchum b. in San Saba, 1863

NEW MOON

OCT. 1

FIRST QUARTER

OCT. 9

FULL MOON

OCT. 15

LAST QUARTER

OCT. 22

NEW MOON

OCT. 30

* Daylight Savings Time ends at 2 a.m..

Sun Rise	Sun Set	Moon Rise	Moon Set	Moon's Place	Astronomy
6:50	**7:05**	7:08	**7:18**	Libra	
6:51	**7:04**	8:01	**7:52**	Libra	
6:52	**7:03**	8:54	**8:27**	Scorpio	
6:52	**7:02**	9:48	**9:05**	Scorpio	
6:53	**7:00**	10:42	**9:46**	Scorpio	♀☌☽
6:53	**6:59**	11:37	**10:31**	Sagittarius	♂☌☽
6:54	**6:58**	**12:31**	**11:21**	Sagittarius	
6:55	**6:57**	**1:25**	—	Capricorn	♃ Stationary
6:55	**6:56**	**2:17**	12:15	Capricorn	
6:56	**6:54**	**3:07**	1:13	Capricorn	♆☌☽; ☿☌☽
6:57	**6:53**	**3:54**	2:15	Aquarius	♃☌☽
6:57	**6:52**	**4:39**	3:20	Aquarius	
6:58	**6:51**	**5:23**	4:26	Pisces	☿ Superior
6:59	**6:50**	**6:06**	5:34	Pisces	☽ at Perigee
6:59	**6:49**	**6:50**	6:42	Aries	♄☌☽
7:00	**6:47**	**7:34**	7:50	Aries	
7:01	**6:46**	**8:21**	8:57	Taurus	
7:01	**6:45**	**9:10**	10:02	Taurus	
7:02	**6:44**	**10:00**	11:04	Gemini	
7:03	**6:43**	**10:53**	**12:02**	Gemini	
7:03	**6:42**	—	**12:54**	Cancer	
7:04	**6:41**	**11:47**	1:42	Cancer	
7:05	**6:40**	12:40	**2:25**	Leo	
7:06	**6:39**	1:34	**3:04**	Leo	
7:06	**6:38**	2:27	**3:40**	Leo	
6:07	**5:37**	2:19	**3:14**	Virgo	♀☌♂
6:08	**5:36**	3:11	**3:47**	Virgo	☽ at Apogee
6:08	**5:35**	4:03	**4:20**	Libra	
6:09	**5:34**	4:55	**4:53**	Libra	
6:10	**5:33**	5:48	**5:28**	Libra	
6:11	**5:32**	6:42	**6:05**	Scorpio	

NOTE:
All times are calculated in Central Standard Time (CST) for HOUSTON, TYLER and other Texas communities located at approximately 95 degrees longitude.
To recalculate times for other locations, add (+) or subtract (-) minutes as shown:
Abilene .... +17
Amarillo .... +26
Austin .... +10
Beaumont .... -5
Brownsville ..... +8
Corpus Christi . +8
Dallas .... +6
El Paso .... +44
(adjust for Mountain Time)
Galveston .... -2
Laredo .... +16
Lubbock .... +26
Odessa .... +28
San Angelo .... +20
San Antonio ... +12
Sherman .... +6
Texarkana .... -4
Waco .... +7
Wichita Falls .. +12

Boldface times
indicate p.m.

OCTOBER 1997

Sunday	Monday	Tuesday	Wednesday	Thursday	Friday	Saturday
			1 NEW MOON	2 Rosh Hashana	3	4
5	6	7	8	9 FIRST QUARTER	10	11 Yom Kippur
12	13 Columbus Day	14	15	16 FULL MOON First Day of Tabernacles	17	18
19	20	21	22 LAST QUARTER	23	24	25
26	27	28	29	30 NEW MOON	31 Halloween	

> " *Among the more effective labor-saving devices is the neighbor who hasn't returned your gardening tools.* — *Anonymous* "

BEST ...
PLANTING DATES & MAINTENANCE DATES

Plant

Leafy Vegetables, Flowers, Grains
.... Oct. 1-8, 30
.... *Best Time: Oct. 3-5*

Fruiting Vegetables
.... Oct. 9-14
.... *Best Time: Oct. 13-14*

Root Corps, Permanent Plants
.... Oct. 15-20
.... *Best Time: Oct. 21*

Mow Lawns

To increase growth
.... Oct. 3-5, 13-14, 21-23
To retard growth
.... Oct. 6-7, 11-12, 15-16,
.... 19-20, 23-27

Cultivate, Spray & Weed

.... Oct. 22-29
.... *Best Time: Oct. 23-27*

Fertilize

.... Use any ONE of these dates:
.... Oct. 1, 2, 3, 4, 5, 9, 10, 13, 14,
.... 17, 18, 21, 22, 28, 29, 30, 31

OCTOBER *Gardener's Diary*

Your Personal Journal Of Planning & Planting

Wed 1 _____

Thu 2 _____

Fri 3 _____

Sat 4 _____

Sun 5 _____

Mon 6 _____

Tue 7 _____

Wed 8 _____

Thu 9 _____

Fri 10 _____

Sat 11 _____

Sun 12 _____

Mon 13 _____

Tue 14 _____

Wed 15 _____

Thu 16 _____

Fri 17 _____

Sat 18 _____

Sun 19 _____

Mon 20 _____

Tue 21 _____

Wed 22 _____

Thu 23 _____

Fri 24 _____

Sat 25 _____

Sun 26 _____

Mon 27 _____

Tue 28 _____

Wed 29 _____

Thu 30 _____

Fri 31 _____

NOVEMBER 1997

FIRST QUARTER

Nov. 7

FULL MOON

Nov. 14

LAST QUARTER

Nov. 21

NEW MOON

Nov. 29

Day		Event
Sat	1	Architect Nicholas Clayton b., 1880
Sun	2	All Souls' Day
Mon	3	Stephen F. Austin b., 1793
Tue	4	Edward House met Woodrow Wilson, 1911
Wed	5	16-month term of Gov. Pendleton Murrah began, 1863
Thu	6	Cabeza de Vaca lands at Galveston, 1528
Fri	7	San Antonio breeders est. Texas Hereford Assn., 1889
Sat	8	Halley's Comet sighted, 1985
Sun	9	John Nance Garner entered Congress, 1903
Mon	10	Houston Ship Channel officially opened, 1914
Tue	11	World War I ended, 1918
Wed	12	U.S. first exported oil, 1861
Thu	13	Chipita Rodríguez only female legally hanged in Texas, 1863
Fri	14	Camp Worth renamed Fort Worth, 1849
Sat	15	Lorenzo de Zavala d., 1836
Sun	16	Sam Rayburn d., 1961
Mon	17	LBJ married Claudia "Lady Bird" Taylor, 1934
Tue	18	Standard Time Zones adopted, 1883
Wed	19	2nd U.S. manned moon landing, 1969
Thu	20	Howard Hughes applied for Rock Bit patent, 1908
Fri	21	William Henry Murray b. in Toadsuck, TX, 1869
Sat	22	Roy Hofheinz d., 1982
Sun	23	James Henderson became governor for 28 days, 1853
Mon	24	Scott Joplin b. in Texarkana, 1868
Tue	25	55 mph speed limit set, 1973
Wed	26	"Kit" Carson in Indian battle at Adobe Walls, 1864
Thu	27	Magellan rounded The Horn, 1520
Fri	28	Grand Ole Opry debut, 1925
Sat	29	Stark Museum of Art opened in Orange, 1978
Sun	30	Erastus "Deaf" Smith d., 1837

Sun Rise	Sun Set	Moon Rise	Moon Set	Moon's Place	Astronomy
6:12	**5:32**	7:37	**6:45**	Scorpio	
6:12	**5:31**	8:33	**7:29**	Sagittarius	
6:13	**5:30**	9:28	**8:17**	Sagittarius	♂☌☽
6:14	**5:29**	10:22	**9:10**	Sagittarius	♀☌☽
6:15	**5:28**	11:14	**10:06**	Capricorn	
6:15	**5:28**	**12:04**	**11:06**	Capricorn	♀ Greatest Elong. E.
6:16	**5:27**	**12:51**	—	Aquarius	♃☌☽
6:17	**5:26**	**1:35**	12:08	Aquarius	
6:18	**5:25**	**2:17**	1:11	Pisces	
6:19	**5:25**	**2:59**	2:16	Pisces	
6:19	**5:24**	**3:40**	3:22	Aries	♄☌☽
6:20	**5:24**	**4:23**	4:28	Aries	☽ at Perigee
6:21	**5:23**	**5:08**	5:35	Taurus	
6:22	**5:22**	**5:55**	6:41	Taurus	
6:23	**5:22**	**6:46**	7:45	Gemini	
6:24	**5:21**	**7:39**	8:46	Gemini	
6:24	**5:21**	**8:33**	9:43	Cancer	
6:25	**5:21**	**9:29**	10:34	Cancer	
6:26	**5:20**	**10:24**	11:20	Cancer	
6:27	**5:20**	**11:18**	**12:01**	Leo	
6:28	**5:19**	—	**12:39**	Leo	
6:28	**5:19**	12:11	**1:14**	Virgo	
6:29	**5:19**	1:03	**1:47**	Virgo	☽ at Apogee
6:30	**5:18**	1:55	**2:20**	Virgo	
6:31	**5:18**	2:47	**2:53**	Libra	
6:32	**5:18**	3:40	**3:27**	Libra	
6:32	**5:18**	4:34	**4:03**	Scorpio	♇☌☉
6:33	**5:18**	5:29	**5:42**	Scorpio	☿ Greatest Elong. E.
6:34	**5:18**	6:25	**5:25**	Sagittarius	
6:35	**5:17**	7:21	**6:12**	Sagittarius	

NOTE:
All times are calculated in Central Standard Time (CST) for HOUSTON, TYLER and other Texas communities located at approximately 95 degrees longitude. To recalculate times for other locations, add (+) or subtract (-) minutes as shown:
Abilene .... +17
Amarillo .... +26
Austin .... +10
Beaumont .... -5
Brownsville ..... +8
Corpus Christi . +8
Dallas .... +6
El Paso .... +44
(adjust for Mountain Time)
Galveston .... -2
Laredo .... +16
Lubbock .... +26
Odessa .... +28
San Angelo .... +20
San Antonio ... +12
Sherman .... +6
Texarkana .... -4
Waco .... +7
Wichita Falls .. +12

Boldface times indicate p.m.

NOVEMBER 1997

Sunday	Monday	Tuesday	Wednesday	Thursday	Friday	Saturday
						1
2	3	4 Election Day	5	6	7 FIRST QUARTER	8
9	10	11 Veteran's Day	12	13	14 FULL MOON	15
16	17	18	19	20	21 LAST QUARTER	22
23	24	25	26	27 Thanksgiving	28	29 NEW MOON
30 First Sunday of Advent						

> " *To get the best results*
> *you must talk to your vegetables.* "
> — *Charles, Prince of Wales*

Best...
Planting Dates & Maintenance Dates

Plant

Leafy Vegetables, Flowers, Grains
.... Nov. 1-6, 29-30
.... *Best Time: Nov. 1*

Fruiting Vegetables
.... Nov. 7-13
.... *Best Time: Nov. 9-10*

Root Corps, Permanent Plants
.... Nov. 14-20
.... *Best Time: Nov. 17-19*

Mow Lawns

To increase growth
.... Nov. 6-7, 15-16, 24-26
To retard growth
.... Nov. 4-5, 8-9, 13-14,
.... 17-21, 27-28, 31

Cultivate, Spray & Weed

.... Nov. 21-28
.... *Best Time: Nov. 21-24*

Fertilize

.... Use any ONE of these dates:
..... Nov. 1, 5, 6, 9, 10, 13, 14, 17,
.... 18, 19, 25, 26, 27, 28

ℜOVEMBER  *Gardener's Diary*
Your Personal Journal Of Planning & Planting

Sat	1	_____
Sun	2	_____
Mon	3	_____
Tue	4	_____
Wed	5	_____
Thu	6	_____
Fri	7	_____
Sat	8	_____
Sun	9	_____
Mon	10	_____
Tue	11	_____
Wed	12	_____
Thu	13	_____
Fri	14	_____
Sat	15	_____
Sun	16	_____
Mon	17	_____
Tue	18	_____
Wed	19	_____
Thu	20	_____
Fri	21	_____
Sat	22	_____
Sun	23	_____
Mon	24	_____
Tue	25	_____
Wed	26	_____
Thu	27	_____
Fri	28	_____
Sat	29	_____
Sun	30	_____

INTER

Winter begins with the shortest day and the

longest night of the year: the winter solstice.

On this day, the sun is as far south

as it will appear.

WINTER SOLSTICE

December 21

2:07 p.m.

In several folkloric traditions, including that of medieval England, the weather on the 12 days after Old Christmas Day (January 5) indicated the weather in each month of the following year.

• • • • •

Take advantage of cool weather to grow greens and other crops that confound Texas gardeners once it warms up. Even Zone 9 gardeners can get several harvests of salad greens, cabbage and lettuce with good timing (see planting dates, page 98 and 138).

• • • • •

In England, St. Paul's feast day (January 25) foretold the weather for the entire coming year:

"Paul's Day stormy and windy,
Famine in the world, and great death of mankind.
Paul's Day fair and clear,
Plenty of corn and meal in the world."

• • • • •

One traditional beverage for Christmas Eve: Hot ale flavored with spice, particularly ginger and pepper.

DECEMBER 1997

FIRST QUARTER

DEC. 6

FULL MOON

DEC. 14

LAST QUARTER

DEC. 21

NEW MOON

DEC. 28

Day		Event
Mon	1	Mary Martin b., 1913
Tue	2	Sam Houston first visited Texas, 1832
Wed	3	Waco Male and Female Academy chartered, 1850
Thu	4	Ty Cobb d., 1961
Fri	5	Pres. Sam Houston's Indian peace policy is law, 1836
Sat	6	Huddie Ledbetter ("Leadbelly") d., 1949
Sun	7	Pearl Harbor attacked, 1941
Mon	8	Architect Nicholas Clayton arrived in Galveston, 1872
Tue	9	Anson Jones sworn in as Texas president, 1844
Wed	10	1st Nobel prizes awarded, 1901
Thu	11	Amon Carter b., 1879
Fri	12	1st Bank of the U.S. est., 1791
Sat	13	George Strake hit oil in Montgomery Co., 1931
Sun	14	Amundsen 1st at S. Pole, 1911
Mon	15	2nd transcontinental railroad linked at Sierra Blanca, 1881
Tue	16	Republic of Fredonia declared in Nacogdoches, 1826
Wed	17	Benjamin Franklin Terry killed in action, 1861
Thu	18	Slavery abolished, 1865
Fri	19	Leonides Cigarroa, physician & civic leader, b., 1922
Sat	20	Goliad Declaration of Independence, 1835
Sun	21	Edith Wilmans, 1st woman elected to Texas House, b., 1882
Mon	22	Claudia Alta Taylor ("Ladybird" Johnson), b., 1912
Tue	23	Fed. Reserve System est., 1913
Wed	24	Mexico gives Texas Shawnees 1 sq. mi. per warrior, 1824
Thu	25	Rev. Jos. Chromcik, Czech missionary, in Fayetteville, 1872
Fri	26	1st commercial buffalo hunt in Texas, 1874
Sat	27	City of Austin incorporated, 1839
Sun	28	Westminster Abbey dedicated, 1065
Mon	29	Texas became 28th state, 1845
Tue	30	Harrisburg municipality (later Houston) est., 1835
Wed	31	End of the "Archives War," 1842

Sun Rise	Sun Set	Moon Rise	Moon Set	Moon's Place	Astronomy
6:36	**5:17**	8:17	**7:05**	Sagittarius	☿☌☾
6:36	**5:17**	9:11	**8:01**	Capricorn	♂☌☾
6:37	**5:17**	10:02	**9:00**	Capricorn	♀☌☾; ♆☌☾
6:38	**5:17**	10:51	**10:02**	Aquarius	♅☌☾
6:39	**5:17**	11:35	**11:04**	Aquarius	♃☌☾
6:39	**5:18**	**12:18**	—	Pisces	
6:40	**5:18**	**12:58**	12:07	Pisces	☿ Stationary; ♀☌♆
6:41	**5:18**	**1:38**	1:11	Aries	
6:42	**5:18**	**2:19**	2:15	Aries	♄☌☾; ☾ at Perigee
6:42	**5:18**	**3:01**	3:19	Taurus	
6:43	**5:18**	**3:46**	4:23	Taurus	♀ Greatest Brillancy
6:44	**5:19**	**4:33**	5:27	Taurus	
6:44	**5:19**	**5:24**	6:29	Gemini	
6:45	**5:19**	**6:18**	7:28	Gemini	
6:46	**5:20**	**7:14**	8:22	Cancer	♂☌♆
6:46	**5:20**	**8:10**	9:12	Cancer	
6:47	**5:20**	**9:05**	9:56	Leo	☿ Inferior; ♄ Stationary
6:47	**5:21**	**10:01**	10:36	Leo	
6:48	**5:21**	**10:53**	11:13	Virgo	
6:48	**5:22**	—	11:47	Virgo	
6:49	**5:22**	**11:46**	**12:20**	Virgo	Winter Begins
6:49	**5:23**	12:38	**12:52**	Libra	♀☌♂
6:50	**5:23**	1:30	**1:25**	Libra	
6:50	**5:24**	2:23	**2:01**	Scorpio	
6:51	**5:24**	3:17	**2:37**	Scorpio	♀ Stationary
6:51	**5:25**	4:12	**3:18**	Scorpio	♂☌♅
6:52	**5:26**	5:09	**4:04**	Sagittarius	☿ Stationary; ☿☌☾
6:52	**5:26**	6:06	**4:54**	Sagittarius	
6:52	**5:27**	7:02	**5:50**	Capricorn	
6:53	**5:28**	7:56	**6:50**	Capricorn	
6:53	**5:28**	8:47	**7:52**	Aquarius	♆☌☾; ♀☌☾; ♅☌☾

NOTE:
All times are calculated in Central Standard Time (CST) for HOUSTON, TYLER and other Texas communities located at approximately 95 degrees longitude. To recalculate times for other locations, add (+) or subtract (-) minutes as shown:

Abilene .... +17
Amarillo .... +26
Austin .... +10
Beaumont .... -5
Brownsville ..... +8
Corpus Christi . +8
Dallas .... +6
El Paso .... +44
(adjust for Mountain Time)
Galveston .... -2
Laredo .... +16
Lubbock .... +26
Odessa .... +28
San Angelo .... +20
San Antonio ... +12
Sherman .... +6
Texarkana .... -4
Waco .... +7
Wichita Falls .. +12

Boldface times indicate p.m.

DECEMBER   1997

Sunday	Monday	Tuesday	Wednesday	Thursday	Friday	Saturday
	1	*2*	*3*	*4*	*5*	*6* Hanukkah Begins FIRST QUARTER
7	*8*	*9*	*10*	*11*	*12*	*13*
14 FULL MOON	*15*	*16*	*17*	*18*	*19*	*20*
21 First Day Of Winter LAST QUARTER	*22*	*23*	*24* Hanukkah	*25* Christmas	*26*	*27*
28 NEW MOON	*29*	*30*	*31*			

" *But make no mistake:*
the weeds will win:
nature bats last.
— Robert Michael Pyle "

BEST...
PLANTING DATES & MAINTENANCE DATES

Plant

Leafy Vegetables, Flowers, Grains
.... Dec. 1-5, 28-31
.... *Best Time: Dec. 2-3, 29-30*

Fruiting Vegetables
.... Dec. 6-13
.... *Best Time: Dec. 6-7*

Root Corps, Permanent Plants
.... Dec. 14-20
.... *Best Time: Dec. 15-16*

Mow Lawns

To increase growth
.... Dec. 6-7, 15-16, 24-26
To retard growth
.... Dec. 1, 4-5, 8-9, 13-14,
.... 17-21, 27-28, 31

Cultivate, Spray & Weed
.... Dec. 21-27
.... *Best Time: Dec. 27*

Fertilize
.... Use any ONE of these dates:
Dec. 2, 3, 6, 7, 10, 11, 12, 15, 16,
.... 22, 23, 24, 25, 26, 29, 30

DECEMBER  Gardener's Diary

Your Personal Journal Of Planning & Planting

Mon 1 _____

Tue 2 _____

Wed 3 _____

Thu 4 _____

Fri 5 _____

Sat 6 _____

Sun 7 _____

Mon 8 _____

Tue 9 _____

Wed 10 _____

Thu 11 _____

Fri 12 _____

Sat 13 _____

Sun 14 _____

Mon 15 _____

Tue 16 _____

Wed 17 _____

Thu 18 _____

Fri 19 _____

Sat 20 _____

Sun 21 _____

Mon 22 _____

Tue 23 _____

Wed 24 _____

Thu 25 _____

Fri 26 _____

Sat 27 _____

Sun 28 _____

Mon 29 _____

Tue 30 _____

Wed 31 _____

THYME

By Madalene Hill & Gwen Barclay

Editor's note: The International Herb Association singles out one herb for celebration and education every year. For 1997, the herb in the spotlight is thyme. To mark the occasion, we've asked Madalene Hill and Gwen Barclay to revisit some of their past writings on this popular plant.

Now as in Shakespeare's day, banks of sweet-blooming thyme sweeten the moors of many parts of England and Scotland. The thyme we grow here has not quite adapted to the wild, but it certainly is one of our most widely used culinary herbs. *Thymus vulgaris* includes both the common thyme and the narrow-leaf French and can be grown from seed. Broad-leaf English thyme *(T. vulgaris x seryphphllum)* must be propagated from cuttings in order to be true. These all have the same basic flavor but different leaf shapes and slightly varying growth habits. Thymes are gray-green plants and do not like to be kept wet. Many types are perennial and do not require winter protection — usually a good mulch is sufficient here.

The word "thyme" is derived from the Greek, meaning incense or to fumigate, and thyme was probably so named because of its clean aroma. Thyme came to our shores with the earliest settlers. The colonists placed it on fats such as lard to keep them more palatable. This was probably effective since thyme has an antioxidant principle that would help to keep fats from becoming rancid. Thyme was used in simple cough syrups and was used by the Spanish to preserve olives. Our great grandmothers used thyme branches, rosemary and powdered cloves to keep the woolens and furs free of moths.

Thyme became a symbol of courage: A sprig of thyme signalled the secret meetings of the French Republicans during the revolution. Soup made of thyme and beer was considered a cure for shyness.

Thyme has a long history of association with the nether world. It was thought our souls inhabited the thyme blossoms. Branches were tossed onto the coffin of a departed one to ensure passage into the next world. (Many herbs that are perennials or biennials, thereby remaining green through a season or two, were thought to be magical, thus giving rise to their usage as "grave plants.")

Some 40 years ago a writer recorded that there were probably 22 varieties of this important herb. We doubt that anyone knows exactly how many varieties there are, certainly more than 22. The figure is probably closer to 400, for thymes are notorious cross-pollinators, like the mints, and new thymes pop up every year.

Thymes fall into three broad groups: upright subshrubs 12-18 inches tall, creeping herbs up to 6 inches, and very flat creepers 1-2 inches tall. The culinary thymes are in the upright category, and many lend themselves to bonsai-type growth.

The creeping thymes, which are generally not suitable for culinary use — only because of the tedious harvesting — are lovely to grow as ground covers for sunny areas. They are not always successful in rock gardens under the hot Southern sun in August, since temperatures will be well over 100° on the rocks or stone, and hot enough to cook the small plants. They do make lovely container and basket plants.

The tiny-leaf low creeping thymes are harder to come by but well worth a try. They are noted on the varieties list with an asterisk(*).

Texas growing conditions can produce a microclimate that gives us very cold winters and, sometimes, extremely dry springs and falls. We grow several dozen varieties of thymes, both upright and creeping, with great success. Our most commonly used culinary thymes are the narrow-leaf French, the broadleaf English and lemon.

The upright varieties of thyme are quite reasonable in their "affairs." They rarely cross-pollinate and thus remain true. The small creepers are quite the opposite. They not only intermingle as they grow, but if allowed to set seed many cross pollinate like mad. Thus, you will have a variety or two of strange seedlings appearing in your thyme beds, but who minds?

CULTURE: Thymes like well-drained soils and ample sunshine. Upright varieties are really woody subshrubs capable of making great hummocks in a couple of years. In Texas, thymes should be kept pruned lightly and regularly. Severe pruning is hard on them and will result in dieback in hot weather. If not kept pruned, thyme branches become very woody and are easily split by wind or pets. Thin the centers of thickly growing plants to open their forms for better air circulation.

Once established in a sunny location, they are relatively carefree, except for weeding. Someone has written, "To know humility, one must weed the Thymes." Because they grow in a tangled mat, it is a tedious job, but once free of weeds, they will almost maintain themselves. If you can plant roots under a stone or brick, this will keep them cool, while the foliage is not bothered to be hot and dry in the summer.

> **66 SOUP MADE OF THYME AND BEER WAS CONSIDERED A CURE FOR SHYNESS."**

The seeds of French and common thymes, while extremely small, can be successfully grown by the home gardener, but they grow slowly. Unless you are in need of a small thyme hedge, it is simpler to begin from a small purchased plant or get a cutting from a friend.

Thymes are among the easiest plants to propagate. Semiwoody cuttings taken in the fall, winter or early spring will root quickly in potting soil, perlite or sphagnum. Because of their branching habits, thymes are well adapted to layering. Peg down a branch with soil or a hairpin; roots will form quickly. The new plant can then be cut away and carefully transplanted.

IN THE KITCHEN: Thyme is one of the basic seasonings in cuisines throughout the world. While its leaves are small, they speak with authority and should be

1997 **HERB OF THE YEAR**

used with a light touch. Generally an upright variety — French, English, winter or lemon thyme — is used, but any of the creepers will do if you have the patience.

Thyme is a must in the stewpot but also lends itself to the strong leafy vegetables. Thyme finds its way into the legumes of the world's cookery, and its influence on beef, lamb, pork, poultry — and especially fish — is unbelievable.

Culpeper wrote that thyme was under the dominion of Venus and, therefore, good for nervous ailments, queasiness of the stomach and "uneasiness" of the brain. Don't know about that, but it is surely good with beef and burgundy; and does nothing but improve green beans and roast chicken. Thyme is one of the three major herbs in a French bouquet garni (the others are usually bay leaf and parsley, although it can vary).

This is one of the herbs that lends itself so well to being preserved in oil to protect its fresh flavor. To do this, blend at least 2 tablespoons of fresh thyme leaves (minus the woody stems) with 2 cups parsley in 1/2 cup of good-quality vegetable oil. Store in refrigerator no more than two weeks, or freeze in small containers for up to two years.

> ❝ OUR MOST COMMONLY USED CULINARY THYMES TEND TO BE THE NARROW-LEAF FRENCH, THE BROADLEAF ENGLISH, LEMON THYME AND WINTER VARIETIES. ❞

To dry thyme for future use, harvest leaves just prior to blooming. Place branches on newspapers or a tray in an air-conditioned room, where drying will be rapid. Do not dry outdoors unless humidity is low. This usually does not include the Gulf Coast area. Drying *must* be rapid. Do not dry in conventional ovens or microwaves. Thyme will dry quickly in a frost-free refrigerator. Once completely dry, gently rub leaves from stems between the hands. Pick out small , broken stems. Store in an air-tight container in a cool, dark place — prefereably the freezer for maximum freshness.

TIPS FOR LEMON THYME...

- Steam a small head of cabbage, very thinly sliced. Sprinkle with chopped, fresh lemon thyme or dried leaves; stir in a small amount of sour cream, butter or margarine. Salt if you like.
- Place a few sprigs of lemon thyme together with chive sprigs in a container. Cover with a good wine or cider vinegar. Use on salads.
- To a hearty pot roast, add good burgundy, a fat clove of garlic (mashed), a chopped onion, a little salt and lots of lemon thyme leaves. You can use the whole branch; just lift out stems before serving.

1997 HERB OF THE YEAR

𝒥ust think what
Kathy Huber's gardening
column could do for you.
Read it every Saturday in the
Houston section.

Houston Chronicle
Houston's leading information source

For home delivery, call (713) 220-7211 or (800) 735-3811.

THYME RECIPES

TANGY SHRIMP & BEAN SALAD

Ingredients:

2 cups cooked fresh pinto beans or frozen lima beans
1 cup sliced celery
1/2 cup green onions, with tops
1/4 cup chopped pimento or red sweet pepper
1/2 cup pitted ripe olives, halved
1/4 cup sliced radishes
3/4 lb. shrimp, cooked and peeled
1 clove garlic, crushed
1 TBS. chopped lemon thyme
1/2 teaspoon paprika
Black pepper to taste
1/2 cup white vinegar or fresh lemon juice
1/2 cup salad oil
1/2 teaspoon Tabasco

To make:

Prepare vegetables and combine with shrimp. Blend until smooth the garlic, thyme, paprika, pepper, vinegar, oil and Tabasco. Pour dressing over salad and chill thoroughly. Serves 8.

TOMATO WINE SOUP

This soup serves as an excellent appetizer.

Ingredients:

2 cups fresh or canned tomatoes
1/4 cup butter
2 TBS flour
1 tsp. salt
1 tsp. lemon thyme
1 TBS. fresh basil or 1 tsp. dried
Pinch pepper
1/4 tsp. baking soda
1/2 cup dry white wine

HILLTOP'S BOURSIN CHEESE

This takeoff on the classic French Boursin evolvd in our kitchen over several years. We form it into logs, then freeze and slice it as needed.

Ingredients:

1 lb. cream cheese, softened
1/2 lb. butter or margarine, softened
1 tsp. mashed garlic
1-1/2 TBS. chopped sweet marjoram
1-1/2 TBS. chopped chives
1 TBS. chopped basil
1 tsp. chopped English or French thyme
1 TBS. chopped parsley
1/2 tsp. salt
1/4 tsp. freshly ground pepper

To make:

Beat cheese and butter together. Add mashed garlic to cheese, mixing well. Add finely chopped herbs, salt and pepper.

Chill slightly and form into ball or logs. Wrap tightly in plastic wrap. Refrigerate or freeze. Serve with toast. Serves 12.

To make:

If using fresh tomatoes, chop and simmer in a saucepan with butter until soft. Cool slightly, then purée or blend. Return to saucepan. If using canned tomatoes, blend, then place in saucepan and add butter.

Stir in flour, salt, lemon thyme, basil and pepper. Bring to a boil. Reduce heat and simmer for 5 minutes. Stir in soda and half-and-half. Cook over low heat sill slightly thickened. Do not boil. Stir in wine and heat to simmer. Cook 15-20 minutes till sharp wine taste is cooked away. Serves 6.

1997 HERB OF THE YEAR

The following list includes thymes grown by Madalene Hill and Gwen Barclay at Hilltop Herb Farm, at Festival Hill in Round Top, and in other gardens in Texas.

Upright

Thyme x *citriodorous*, lemon thyme — The darling of the thymes; a beautiful, dark green, lemon-scented variety that is superb in the kitchen.

T. citriodorous 'Argenteus,' silver thyme — A beautiful plant.

T. x 'Clear Gold' — Low growing; yellow-green leaves; mild lemon fragrance. Creeping variety also available.

T. compactus — Dark green leaves.

T. x 'Golden Lemon' — Another lemon scented variety.

T. hyemalis, winter thyme — Long-lived; gray-green leaves; good flavor.

T. praecox subsp. *skorpilii* (formerly known as *T. jankae*) — Good lemon fragrance.

T. vulgaris, common thyme — The English call it garden thyme; good flavor.

T.v. 'Broadleaf English' — As the name implies, has unusually wide leaves for a thyme; good flavor.

T.v. 'Narrow-leaf French' — Thin, gray leaves; good flavor.

Creeping

Note: The asterisk indicates the tiny-leaf, low creepers. While they can be grown in other parts of Texas with some success, the small, woolly creepers are not recommended for Gulf Coast gardens, where they generally melt.

T. adamovicii — Looks like small savory; 2 to 4 inches tall.

T. balticus — Hardy; gray leaves; good grower.

T. caespititius (formerly *T. azoricus*) — Forms matlike hairy growth 3/4 to 2-1/2 inches high.

T. camphoratus — Hardy, with interesting growth habit.

T. x 'Dr. Blackburn' — Hardy grower.

T. x 'Foster' — Good bloomer; white flower.

T. glabrescens — Low; hairy; mat-forming.

T. 'Golden' — Lovely upright growth but a creeper.

T. herba-barona, sometimes called Corsican thyme, caraway thyme or herb of the barons — According to legend, reserved for cooking with great joints of beef associated with old English cookery; distinct caraway fragrance.

T. lanicaulis — Woolly creeper.

T. x 'Long Blossom' — Good grower; green leaves.

T. occidentalis — Dark green; from Leningrad.

T. praecox cultivars:

'Albus' — Tiny-leaf creeper with small white blossoms.

'Aureus,' golden thyme — Beautiful, with multicolored leaves in cool or cold weather; a delightful plant.

'Britannicus' — Gray leaves; good grower.

'Doone Valley' — Golden-edged leaves.

'Kew' — Green creeper from Kew Gardens

T.p. subsp. *arcticus* — Old mother-of-thyme.

T.p. subsp. *arcticus* cultivars:

'Coccineus' — Crimson-flowered thyme; beautiful.

'Hall's Woolly' — Gray, woolly leaves.

'Nutmeg' — Beautiful grower.

* *T. pseudolanuginosis* — Woolly; matlike; scarecely 1/2 inch high.

T. pulegioides 'Latvia' — Dark green, from its namesake Baltic country.

T. x 'University of Heidelberg' — Dark green.

T. zygis — Good grower; white flower.

Using THYME Wisely...

- Add a small amount of thyme oil when braising or sautéing meats or vegetables to bring out a delightful flavor.
- Combine a little fresh, chopped thyme, chives, basil and dill with 1 cup sour cream. Add a little salt (and paprika if you want a blush). Great for vegetable sticks.

- Add a little thyme to your oil and vinegar dressing.
- Baste the fish with thyme oil and fresh lemon juice.
- Drop thyme branches (not woody stems) into soup, stew or a pot of dried beans. Let cook and the tiny leaves will drop off; remove stems with tongs or a slatted spoon before serving.

1997 HERB OF THE YEAR

HERB TEA

By Howard Garrett

Herbs have many practical uses, but one of the best is making tea. It's good anytime but especially in the evening, particularly at bedtime. Making healthy tea is just another one of the many uses of herbs. My family has been into drinking herb tea for sometime. In fact, It has become a year round ritual. Some of our favorites are lemon verbena, peppermint (especially chocolate peppermint), lemon balm, lemon grass, rosemary, ginkgo, purple coneflower, lavender, thyme, spearmint, sambac jasmine, oregano, lemongrass and chamomile.

Hot tea is good at night in hot and cold weather. Herb teas are relaxing, many will help you breathe easier, and some will help you sleep better. To prepare herb teas, simply pick fresh leaves from herbs, put them in a tea pot and pour in boiling water. Don't boil the leaves. Letting the boiling water cool down slightly before pouring is a good idea. The color is usually a light yellow/green. Let the brew steep from 3 to 10 minutes depending on your taste and then enjoy a nice cup of hot tea. Some people like to let the tea leaves remain in the water longer. If the time is overdone, tannic acid will be released into the tea, making it bitter. A single herb or a mix of various plants can be used. I often use chocolate peppermint as a base and add various other herbs to create a different taste each night. For a nice lemony tea, try lemongrass (my favorite lemon herb), lemon verbena and lemon balm.

These natural teas are great "as is," but lemon juice or honey can be added for taste. Herb tea helps me get on the air sometimes despite sore throats and sinus problems with the following recipe - chocolate peppermint, a squeeze of lemon juice and honey to taste. By the way, it also helps if you use clean, filtered water. Chlorine and other contaminants can ruin the taste of any good drink.

After you have finished drinking the tea, what you have left over in the tea pot has a couple of uses. Even if it has honey it makes a good organic fertilizer. Just pour on the plants after it has cooled. Of course, don't over do it, too much watering is hard on plants. It could also be put into your foliar spray solution. The other use is to drink it cold over ice the next day. Toss a couple of fresh leaves into your iced drink for additional flavor. Don't forget to pick a good supply of leaves, flowers and such to dry and store for wintertime use. You can also plan to grow some of these wonderful plants in pots indoors this winter.

COMMUNITY GARDENS

By Bob Randall, Ph.D.

Most people in cities know little about how food is produced or about the natural life that surrounds them. This is regrettable, because many urban areas have plenty of land which would support gardens and beautiful natural areas if people had inspiration and the appropriate knowledge. As director of a community garden program in Houston, I try to understand why people have forgotton what they once knew, and look for a way to help them recover and enhance their horticultural heritage.

Part of the answer lies in the changing role agriculture has played in everyday life. Urban residents' knowledge of plants, nature and sound land use seems to have been declining. At the turn of the century, Americans were rural, and in closer contact with nature. Because of farming, they were motivated to learn the basics of land use, and had the informal networks and agrarian institutions to do so. As the century progressed, the nation became urban. For a time, the rural heritage guided garden building in the expanding cities and suburbs, but eventually, this heritage became more remote, and more people reached adulthood without even basic horticultural knowledge.

The efforts of Agricultural Extension, landscapers, garden clubs, horticultural educators, environmentalists, schools and media have not been enough to stop this slide, and until recently there have seemed to be no economic reasons for cities to take action to reverse these trends. This growing urban and suburban ignorance about horticulture has, however, severe environmental, medical, economic, and psychological consequences.

• The lack of fresh, locally–grown produce in backyards, markets, and restaurants means that fruits, herbs and vegetables are shipped distances and are usually much less flavorful than they can be. (Reportedly, the average spoon of food in the U.S. travels 1,200 miles.) To ship, a farmer must grow a cultivar with long shelf life, must harvest it well before buyers consume it, and must use costly methods to retard spoilage in shipment. Even so, because a lot spoils before it sells, "fresh" is costly when compared to preserved food. Canned, dried and frozen foods, on the other hand, usually have less flavor, so they are usually served with salt, fat, or sugar. The overall result is that urban people do not eat the 5-9 servings of produce that cancer and heart authorities recommend, and eat a lot more of food products that are bad for them.

• During the last decade, the old view that vegetables and fruits promote good health through "alphabet" vitamins has gradually been replaced by a far more complicated view. Vegetables and fruits contain 500 different carotenes and hundreds of other phytochemicals that promote health in many specific ways. For example, two carotenes in collards help the eyes filter UV rays out, thereby preventing cataracts; sterols in cucumbers help decrease blood cholesterol; and a carotene mainly found in tomatoes is now believed to help prevent prostate cancer, the second most prevalent cancer in men.

• Lack of exercise and its cardiovascular consequences are further consequences of horticultural ignorance. Backyard gardeners have an outdoor gym just seconds away that offers quality exercise for mind and heart. If a garden is available, few urban exercise alternatives are as easy, as cheap, or as likely to be sustainable into old age.

• In land–rich cities such as Houston, we have very large numbers of vacant lots that will not sell at any price. Their maintenance is a financial burden on their owners. At the same time, there are under–employed and unemployed people who might be employed in market gardening. Such urban farming might be attractive to the semi-retired, people with few educational skills, non-English speakers, some people with disabilities, school and college students, parolees, homemakers, and so forth. We have evidence that at least some can make good money this way.

• Too many urbanites today have only the vaguest notion of insect or disease ecologies, distinctions between pests and beneficials, or appropriate and safe control strategies. They rely too heavily on pesticides, buy pesticides indiscriminately, apply them without training or even reading the label, and usually get a poor result. Affluent neighborhoods particularly (and those down stream and down wind from them) suffer from pesticide abuse.

• Water–soluble fertilizers are polluting ground water.

• Rainfall is not retained where it falls and is often encouraged to run off with the topsoil and pollutants into water courses. This encorages subsidence and coastal salt infiltration of our soils.

You are here.

Step into a tropical world filled with living color. Where thousands of live butterflies flutter overhead, dancing on air, surrounding you in a mosaic of shimmering light. And high above, a majestic waterfall cascades past lush jungle foliage. It's the Cockrell Butterfly Center. An amazing tropical paradise where imagination takes flight.

• Irrigation is frequently wasteful; rather than apply it subsurface, it is usually allowed to evaporate before reaching the roots.

• Too much of urban land is in lawn, too much garden labor is in lawn-mowing, and mowers and blowers create too much noise and air pollution. Yard wastes are often sent to landfills rather than composted or mulched.

• Urban habitat for birds, butterflies and other creatures declines when people don't know how to promote their survival. Because too few schools have outdoor wildscapes, urban children learn about nature only secondhand and from an occasional field trip, so the next generation will grow up as ignorant as the present one.

These conditions have prompted a recent surge in community gardens, with a variety of goals:

Combat hunger and malnutrition: Various authorities estimate our own metropolitan area's hungry in the 200,000 to 400,000 range. If they were all lined up into one food line, it would be 60 to 100 miles long! Many of these hungry are unlikely to become gardeners no matter what we do. Yet if most urban people knew how to grow food, food would be abundant and low–income relatives of the hungry could help them more than they do.

Improve the immediate environment: Pesticide contamination of the land, air, water, buildings, and food can have serious health effects, both known and unknown including a litany of cancers, and disorders connected with the reproductive, immune, and neurological systems. Least-toxic approaches, or ideally, organic ecological approaches, could reduce these hazards greatly.

Use land more efficiently: There are many secondary effects that a reintroduction of food-growing skills would have in cities once they created significant income. Land in low–income neighborhoods would increase in value both because of its economic value and because the neighborhood would increase in beauty; income earned would no doubt produce more education, more stable families, less crime, better health care. Most importantly, money that now leaves the urban area with every food dollar, would recycle back into local businesses.

Eat what we grow: There are 14,000 or more varieties of vegetables that gardeners can grow and thousands of fruits. Many of these make wonderful food.

What does one need to improve urbanscaping? Obviously, we need adequate funding, and some common vision. And we need practical, efficient, effective neighborhood-based means for teaching and inspiring wise land use. Excellent demonstrations should be developed and outreach learning created through festivals, open houses and workshops. This positive contagion would reintroduce local land-use knowledge back into the landscape, and America might once again be a place where horticulture, and its many benefits to the city, thrives at everyone's home, business, or institution.

Editor's note: For information on community-garden organizations near you, see "Where To Find It" at the end of the regional section for your area. (See page 7 for page numbers for each region of Texas.)

VEGETABLE IMPROVEMENT CENTER

By Cynthia Thomas

The man standing in the carrot patch isn't wearing a pocket protector, but he could use one for the cluster of pens sprouting out of his shirt pocket. A plant breeder and director of Texas A&M's Vegetable Improvement Center, Dr. Leonard Pike doesn't look like the kind of guy who would pop up in a fashion magazine. But a full-page picture of the Aggie professor — standing in the dirt — appeared in last month's *Self* magazine, along with stories on fabulous abs, lipstick lessons and casual-dress tips.

* * * * *

Thirteen years after the Texas 1015 sweet onion made its debut — driving food writers wild — its creator is still making headlines. His current sensation also grows below ground, a maroon carrot named 'Beta Sweet.' Months before 'Beta Sweet' would appear on a grocery shelf, it had aroused so much interest that Pike appeared in magazines from *Progressive Farmer* to *Bon Appetit*. Countless TV troops have marched through his Weslaco carrot patch, including crews from CNN, MacNeil-Lehrer and local stations from Dallas to Portland, Ore. How many other plant breeders remove their caps when a photographer starts to take a picture, knowing it casts shadows across the face?

The 56-year-old scientist is more soft-spoken than your typical publicity hound. He sounds like the Texas-transplanted Arkansas country boy that he is. His eyes don't twinkle, and his conversation isn't seeded with sound bites. But Pike is not just some academic egghead measuring chemical levels in carrots, either. His re-search is practical, not theoretical. He envisions his new creation as a uniquely packaged — and highly marketable — ready-to-eat product.

The color draws the curious, but the most newsworthy element is the composition of 'Beta Sweet.' The maroon carrot is one of a new breed of veggies that scientists are producing to have boosted levels of nutrients that may help fight such killers as cancer and heart disease.

On a cloudy February day, seed company scouts and representatives from Gerber, Campbells and Pillsbury are perusing Pike's carrots as workers pull them from the ground. These are not the sexy maroons, just the familiar orange vegetables that fuel the food industry. The center continues to breed crops in pursuit of the perfect carrot, which would have a smooth shape, plentiful nutrients and a built-in ability to fight pests and disease.

The seed people examine the rows of "fresh-market" carrots, sleek and slim and destined for supermarkets. The shorter, squatter carrots are ogled by scouts from the corporations that will chop them up for soups or strain them for baby food. The misshapen, the knobby, the hairy and the grotesque — carrots that look like pairs of Barbie-doll legs (without the high-heeled feet) — are left in the field.

As Pike evaluates the uprooted orange carrots and answers the questions of industry reps, the buried maroon carrots, which aren't scheduled to be harvested yet, beckon. "I'm half-tempted to go lift them right now," he says. He orders a tractor to churn up a row and starts yanking maroon carrots out of the ground. Emerging from the earth, they look like a cross between a radish and a salami.

VEGETABLE IMPROVEMENT CENTER

Pike pulls out a penknife, scrapes off the dirt and slices a carrot open to reveal a crayon-yellow center surrounded by a ring of deep orange and enclosed by an outer circle that bleeds the vibrant magenta of a beet. With the colors of a New Mexico sunset, it looks like a Georgia O'Keeffe painting or an edible poker chip.

He doles out slices of the psychedelic vegetable.

It tastes, as one of the gathered industry reps says, "like a carrot."

But it has a lighter, crisper, less woody texture.

"It just shatters in your mouth," says its creator.

These carrots are the parents of the first maroon carrots that will reach the consumer next winter. After Pike selects the best and the brightest, they will be shipped to Oregon, where they will be planted to produce seeds. Those seeds will get planted in Texas to grow the first commercial crop of maroon carrots.

Until the maroon carrot makes its debut in the marketplace, Pike has to guard his trade secrets. Handing over a maroon carrot to be shot in a Houston photo studio, he says, "Make sure you eat it when you're done." The maroon carrot could yield substantial royalties someday. Several years ago the rules were changed regarding plant engineers and their creations. Now they can profit from their designs just as other engineers can. Pike has received $23,000 in royalties from the 1015, which he turned back in to the vegetable center.

Pike founded A&M's Vegetable Improvement Center four years ago to channel agricultural research in a new direction. While continuing to look for ways to increase yields and produce more uniform-looking plants, the center's goal is to create vegetables that taste better and are packed with extra nutrients.

"We're actually breeding for higher levels of known phytochemicals," says A&M researcher Luke Howard, referring to chemicals found in plants. "The antioxidant research is real exciting. It's something everybody can relate to."

Other researchers are exploring this territory, too. Having conquered the challenge of producing enough food to feed the nation, U.S. researchers are starting to look at ways to create foods that can combat the effects of being overfed.

In "super foods," "designer foods" or "nutraceuticals," foods are manipulated to produce extra nutrients or chemicals that may neutralize dangerous "free radicals," molecules that roam through the body and are suspected of causing diseases like cancer. The vitamins and chemicals that fight the dangerous molecules are antioxidants.

A&M's Institute of Biosciences and Technology is investigating how different foods impact prostate cancer. The University of Wisconsin created an orange cucumber that buoys the nutritionally weak vegetable with beta carotene, but since plant breeding is a slow process, the cuke is several years away from commercial production. Scientists at Cornell University are boosting vitamin and mineral levels in grains to combat deficiencies in populations that get enough calories but not enough nutrients. Food companies are conducting their own research into designer foods, as is the National Cancer Institute.

But Pike's program is the only one that

VEGETABLE IMPROVEMENT CENTER

shepherds the veggies from concept to consumer. That means plant breeders and pathologists, geneticists, biotechnologists, medical doctors, little seed companies, big growers, giant food corporations, supermarkets and restaurant chains are all in the same room. Members of the center, who pay for most of the research, get first dibs on the patented vegetables the center creates.

"I like it because of the team approach," says Jim Breinling from Gerber, which funds agricultural projects at 13 universities. The baby-food company is always looking for a sweeter carrot and one that is more resistant to disease and needs fewer pesticides.

When Pike's latest creation finally hits the stores, it won't be the first time advance publicity has caused a product to be rushed to market. But it will be the first time the product is a carrot. And it won't really be finished. Think of it as the vegetable equivalent of a newly designed car that isn't fully equipped yet, lacking air bag and stereo. The carrot will be maroon, but the super-high levels of beta carotene and extra sweetness will get put in later.

"We have to be cautious in how fast we introduce new things. Because once you introduce them, if they're good, they last

for many years," Pike says. "The 1015 was released in 1983. Here it is 1996, and people are still writing stories about them." But if he waits too long, he fears people may lose interest in the maroon carrot. So he wants to get it out soon and then perfect it later.

"We have carrots that are equally as good or better than the maroon carrot right now," he says. "An orange carrot is an orange carrot to people. But if we go one step further and change the color so that when we promote it, when you walk in that store and you see it, you'll say, 'Oh, that's the one right there.' "

Pike sees the carrot as an eye-catching ready-to-eat product. The new carrots won't be sold whole but will be cut into slices, which will expose their exotic-colored innards, and packed in clear plastic bags. Like the ready-to-eat "baby carrots," which were introduced in California several years ago and made it easier for people to eat carrots, the maroon carrots will require no washing or chopping.

"There's something about having something totally new that adds to the marketability of it. It's like the new Taurus. It gives Ford Motor Co., the ability to promote that car a little more. So I think our new designer foods are going to have to

> ❝ SPORTING THE COLORS OF A NEW MEXICO SUNSET, THE 'BETA SWEET' CARROT LOOKS LIKE A GEORGIA O'KEEFE PAINTING OR AN EDIBLE POKER CHIP.❞

be different enough, in addition to having improved quality, that they can be identified easily and promoted."

He hopes to get the beta carotene count up to 200-plus parts per million (vs. about 150 parts per million in a typical orange carrot) in several years. "Then it's going to be something you can really hang your hat on."

The maroon carrot started as a fluke. Noticing the maroon shoulders of some carrots from Brazil, Pike decided to breed some to create a carrot in the colors of the university. Then he figured he could make the carrot something more than a novelty product by boosting the nutrients. (Ironically, in old botany books, carrots were maroon, but they evolved into the modern orange variety.)

Pike also figures that if he creates a vegetable that people will eat more of, then they will ingest more nutrients anyway, from sheer volume. Take the 1015 onion, which is actually lower in some sulpher compounds believed to be beneficial. The sulphurous stuff that stinks up the onion and sticks to the tongue is actually good for you.

"This was one of my first discussions with Dr. (Michael) Wargovich at the M.D. Anderson Cancer Center. He was saying, 'Leonard, you need to develop onions with a lot of these compounds, because they're good for you.' And I said, 'Dr. Wargovich, people don't eat a lot of these strong onions. If we make it less pungent but still have the good compounds in there, then people eat more of them. They'll actually get more intake than if they had a lot in there.' And he said, 'Well, I hadn't really thought of it that way.' "

Wargovich has spent time in the spotlight as one of the first medical doctors to investigate the cancer-fighting power of foods. His research has focused on compounds in garlic and onions. "I think the evidence is becoming very, very conclusive that there is an interaction between fruits and vegetables that provides a lot of benefit," he says.

"So with that kind of knowledge, we can work with people like Leonard Pike to say, 'OK, we've done an analysis of let's say the garlic and onion group of vegetables, and there are a long list of agents that do prevent cancer. Is there a possibility of working with the plant breeders to see if we can re-engineer or rebreed for produce that might be enriched in these chemicals?' "

While the relationship between Pike and Wargovich is mostly informal at this point, they do have a grant proposal outstanding, asking for $5 million to study the effects of some of the chemicals found in vegetables, including anthacyanin, which is found in maroon but not orange carrots.

Onions are loaded with chemicals that scientists are just discovering are probably good for you. Quercetin, like vitamin C and beta carotene, is believed to be an antioxidant.

Five years ago Pike had never heard of quercetin. Now he's trying to make onions with higher levels of it. With quercetin and other newfound ingredients proving healthful, products such as picante sauce are emerging as powerful health foods. Containing tomatoes, onions and jalapenos (some of which have more vitamin C than an orange and are bursting with other beneficial chemicals), it's a micronutrient cocktail.

VEGETABLE IMPROVEMENT CENTER

Ben Villalon, the A&M professor who revolutionized the picante sauce industry by creating a mild jalapeno that was easier to handle, has created a super-jalapeno that has two times the vitamin C and quercetin of a normal jalapeno. But so far, Villalon's yellow jalapeno hasn't attracted the interest that Pike's carrot has, even though it's a nutritional gangbuster.

Today, wholesale sales of the 1015 are around $30 million annually, according to the Texas Department of Agriculture, which measures its total economic impact on South Texas at about $100 million annually. The novelty carrot could mean big bucks, too.

"He's about to make a tremendous impact on the carrot industry," says W.M. "Mike" Gower, vice president of McAllen-based Griffin & Brand, who credits Pike with reinvigorating Texas' onion industry with the introduction of the 1015.

"He gave us an almost completely new item to sell," Gower says. "It's almost like having a new sports car on the floor."

Othal Brand, mayor of McAllen and founder of Griffin & Brand, a large vegetable grower and shipper, started funding Pike's research in 1970. Brand got growers to donate a part of their sales on each 50-pound bag of onions to research. Over the years they've given more than $2 million to fund Pike's onion research at A&M.

Now Gower is excited about Pike's 'Texas Early White,' which came out two years ago. The size of a softball, the Early White is enticing to restaurant chains that cut the top off so it blossoms like a flower, then fry or bake it and serve it whole.

Pike keeps working on his previous inventions and less exciting new ones. One experimental carrot is a floppy two feet long and earned the name the "buggy whip." It could be the perfect carrot from which to make baby carrots, because a grower could get twice as many baby carrots from the same amount of space.

He continues to work on the 1015 but wants to find a way to make it exciting again.

"I'm improving the 1015 every year, but it's still just the 1015 to everybody. But if I come out with a new 1015 pink, people are going to say, `Oh, we've heard about that,' and they're going to go for it."

> " **PIKE'S 'EARLY TEXAS WHITE' IS NOW A POPULAR RESTAURANT APPETIZER: THE "BLOOMING ONION." THE CHEF CUTS THE TOP OFF SO THE ONION OPENS UP LIKE A FLOWER.**

This article originally appeared in the Sunday Houston Chronicle's Texas Magazine. © Copyright 1996 Houston Chronicle

This region includes the following cities:

Beaumont/Port Arthur
Corpus Christi
Galveston
Houston
Victoria

Beneath Our Feet

Physical regions of this part of Texas include coastal plains, piney woods and post oak "savannah." Pine and hardwood forests give way to oaks as one travels from east to west. Soils vary widely: "clay gumbo" is uttered frequently by Houston-area gardeners after a string of unprintable adjectives. Soils with high amounts of sand or loam pocket the metropolitan area, and sandy, acidic soils are common in the piney woods area north of Beaumont.

Low flatlands, dense soils, flood-prone areas and high humidity all combine to make raised beds very desirable in many areas. Awareness of landscape drainage is critical, and plants should be selected and situated based on their relative enthusiasm for wet feet.

Agriculture/Forestry

Cotton, rice, grain sorghum and soybeans are important coastal crops. In the piney woods, three native pines — longleaf, shortleaf and loblolly — are staples of the timber industry. So is the introduced slash pine, although this tree has been criticized for changing the overall ecoystem of the area. Hardwoods include elm, hickory, magnolia, sweet and black gum, tupelo and, of course, oaks. A little inland, the post oak savannah region is drier and features higher elevations: blackjack oaks compete with post oaks and elms on a near-even footing. Pecans and walnuts thrive in riverbeds and watershed areas.

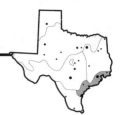

Local Climate Data

	Corpus Christi	Galveston	Houston	Beaumont/ Port Arthur
Mean Max. July	93°	87°	92°	92°
Mean Min. January	45°	47°	43°	42°
Record High	104°	101°	107°	107°
Record Low	13°	8°	7°	12°
Avg. Last Freeze, Spring	Feb. 9	Jan. 24	Feb. 14	Mar. 11
Avg. First Freeze, Fall	Dec. 15	Dec. 25	Dec. 11	Nov. 16
Normal Growing Season	309 days	335 days	300 days	250 days
Normal Precipitation, January	1.7	3.3	3.3	2.8
Normal Precipitation, February	2.0	2.3	3.0	3.4
Normal Precipitation, March	.9	2.2	2.9	3.2
Normal Precipitation, April	1.7	2.4	3.2	3.5
Normal Precipitation, May	3.3	3.6	5.2	5.7
Normal Precipitation, June	3.4	.4	5.0	5.6
Normal Precipitation, July	2.4	4.0	3.6	5.4
Normal Precipitation, August	3.3	4.5	3.5	5.3
Normal Precipitation, September	5.5	5.9	4.9	6.3
Normal Precipitation, October	3.0	2.8	4.3	4.3
Normal Precipitation, November	1.6	3.4	3.8	4.9
Normal Precipitation, December	1.3	3.5	3.5	4.8
Normal Precipitation, ANNUAL	30.1	42.3	46.1	57.2

Temperature Records

	Record High	Month & Year	Record Low	Month & Year	No. Days Max 90° & Above	No. Days Min. 32° & Below
Corpus Christi	104°	7/39	13°	12/89	101.9	6.6
Galveston	101°	7/32	8°	2/99	12.2	3.6
Houston	107°	8/80	7°	12/89	94.2	21.2
Beaumont/Port Arthur	107°	8/62	12°	12/89	81.2	16.3

Chill Hours

According to USDA statistics, the Upper Texas Gulf Coast typically experiences 400-500 chill hours (temperatures between 32° and 45°) from fall to early spring. North Houston frequently gets more than 500 chill hours; Corpus Christi will sometimes record less than 400.

9E GULF COAST

Annual Rainfall

Normal
East Texas .... 45.67"
Upper Coast .... 47.63"

One-Year Sample (1994)

	J	F	M	A	M	J	J	A	S	O	N	D
East Texas	3.31	4.89	3.44	2.60	6.56	2.91	4.22	4.05	2.18	11.14	3.36	7.43
Upper Coast	3.03	1.64	2.69	2.74	6.19	5.50	1.47	5.59	3.15	13.28	1.08	6.06

NOTE: "Normal" rainfalls are based on figures from a 30-year period; currently 1961-1990, while "average" rainfalls are calculated from the entire historical record. While "normals" generally are considered more reliable than averages, they may be no more or less useful than last year's numbers alone. In the sample year 1994, the total annual rainfall was substantially higher than the "normal," and substantial different than the previous years' precipitation. East Texas, for instance, got almost 4 inches less rain in July '93 than in July '94, and the '93 total rainfall was only 29.0 inches.

Recommended Vegetable Varieties*

Asparagus
Jersey Giant
UC 157

Beans (Snap Bush)
Blue Lake 274
Top Crop
Tendercrop
Contender
Tendergreen
Derby

Beans (Pinto)
Improved Pinto

Beans (Lima Bush)
Henderson Baby Bush
Jackson Wonder

Beans (Lima Pole)
Florida Speckled
King of the Garden

Cucumbers (Slicer)
Fanfare (compact plants, fine for pot culture)
Soo Yoh Long (big and weird, but very good)
Sweet Slice (burpless, very prolific)
Sweet Success

Cucumbers (Pickling)
Fancipak Hybrid
Pickalot Hybrid (early)
Pickle-Dilly Hybrid (trellis)
Pioneer (gynoecious)
Saladin (All-America)

Note: Readers in the Corpus Christi area should also consider varieties recommended for Region 9W - South Texas (see page 193).

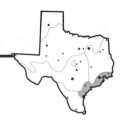

Recommended Vegetable Varieties (cont'd)

Eggplants
Classic (big black)
Ichiban (long, thin)
Listada de Gandia
Thai Long Green
Louisiana Long Green

Leeks
American Flag
Electra
Titan

Lettuce (Leaf)
Salad Bowl
Simpson Elite
Red Sails
Paris Island
Red Fire
Green Ice

Lettuce (Butterhead)
*(among the most
heat-resistant lettuces,
butterhead types can
be planted in January or
even later and success-
fully harvested.)*
Bibb
Buttercrunch
White Boston
Mantilla

Lettuce (Cos/Romaine)
Romaine

Lettuce (Head)
Great Lakes 659-MT
Ithaca
Mission
Summertime (resists bolting)

Melons (Cantaloupe)
French Charantais

Melons (Crenshaw)
Early Hybrid Crenshaw

Melons (Israeli)
Israeli

Melons (Muskmelons)
Ambrosia
(local favorite)
Magnum 45 Hybrid
Saticoy Hybrid
Super Star (8-9 lb. melons)

Melons (Watermelons)
Moon & Stars
Tri-X Seedless
Black Diamond
Jubilee
Queen of Hearts (seedless,
yellow)

Okra
Burgundy
Cowhorn
Clemson Spineless
Flower Bed
Zee Best
Emerald
Lee

Onions (Bulbing)
White Granex
Yellow Granex
Granex 33
TAMU Supersweet
(1015Y)
Burgundy
Red Grano

Peas (English)
Daybreak
Green Arrow
Maestro
Spring

Peas (Edible Pod)
Early Snap
Oregon Sugar Pod 2 (trellis)
Sugar Bon
Sugar Pop
Sugar Snap (old favorite,
still hard to beat)
Super SugarMel

9E GULF COAST

Recommended Vegetable Varieties (cont'd)

Peas (Southern)
Purple Hull Pinkeye
Dixie Lee
California #5
Champion Cream
Cream 40
Crowder
Mississippi Silver (note:
the newer black-eye
varieties have better
disease resistance)

Peppers (Bell/Sweet)
Laparie
Spanish Spice
Jingle Bells
Rio Grande
Puerto Rico
Super Red (pimiento,
roasts beautifully)
Gator Bell
Big Bertha
Orobelle

Peppers (Hot)
Jalapeno
TAMU Jalapeno
Habanero
Hidalgo
Long Red Cayenne
Serrano
many others (there are no
hot peppers that would
rather be grown in New
Jersey than in Texas)

Pumpkins
Spookie Hybrid
Big Max
Jackpot
Small Sugar

Radishes
Champion
Red Prince
Summer Cross
White Icicle

Squash (Summer, Green)
Seneca
Cocozelle
Gold Rush (yellow
zucchini)
Traboncino

Squash (Summer, Yellow)
Butterstick
Multipik
Dixie

Squash (Summer, White)
Patty Pan
St. Pat Scallop

Squash (Winter)
Tahitian
Blue Hubbard
Buttercup
Vegetable Spaghetti

Sweet Corn
Florida Staysweet
Funk's Sweet G-90
Silver Queen

Sweet Potatoes
Centennial
TAMU Cordner
Jewel
Topaz

Tomatoes (Cherry)
Baxter's Early Bush (not
sugar-sweet)
Chello Yello
Red Cherry
Sweet Chelsea
Sweet 100
Toy Boy
Yellow Pear
Yello Currant (itty-bitty but
yummy; also red and pink
varieties)

Tomatoes (Canning/Paste)
Bellestar
Enchantment
Chico III
Napoli
Roma
Viva Italia

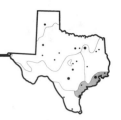

Recommended Vegetable Varieties (cont'd)

Tomatoes (Large Fruit)

Better Boy
Better Bush Improved
Big Beef Hybrid
Bigset
Bingo
Black Krim
Carmello
Carnival
Celebrity (local favorite for consistency and quality)

Champion
Crimson Fancy
Dona
Fantastic
Green Zebra
Heat Wave
Merced
Miracle Sweet
Persimmon
President

Spring Giant
Summer Flavor 5000
Valencia
Whirlaway

9E GULF COAST

Vegetable Harvest

	J	F	M	A	M	J	J	A	S	O	N	D
Artichokes				•								
Beans (Bush & Pole)					•	•	•			•		
Beans (Long)								•	•	•		
Beets					•							
Bok Choy			•									
Broccoli	•	•	•	•								•
Brussels Sprouts		•										
Cabbage	•	•	•									•
Carrots						•	•					
Cauliflower												•
Chard	•	•										
Collards	•	•										
Corn						•	•				•	
Cucumbers						•	•	•	•	•		
Eggplant								•	•			
Garlic					•							
Kale	•	•										
Lettuce (Other Greens)	•	•	•							•	•	
Malabar Spinach								•	•	•		
Melons						•						
Mustard	•	•	•								•	
Okra								•	•	•	•	
Onions (Green)	•	•										
Onions					•							
Pak Choy												•
Parsley	•	•										
Peppers							•	•	•	•		
Potatoes (Irish)					•							
Potatoes (Sweet)								•	•	•	•	•
Squash						•	•			•		
Southern Peas								•	•	•		
Sugar Snap Peas				•								
Tomatoes					•	•				•	•	
Turnips	•	•	•									•

9E GULF COAST

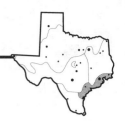

NOTE: This Vegetable Harvest chart is deliberately conservative, designed to illustrate what most home gardeners can expect to harvest when planting is done at the proper times (see page 98 for spring planting schedules, and page 138 for fall planting schedules). Aggressive gardeners willing to gamble may harvest tomatoes as early as April and as late as December: good on ya! Many cabbage and greens growers stretch harvests longer than shown here; these are folks who understand that "the best fertilizer is the gardener's shadow." If you do not tend the vegetable garden daily (at least with an inspection), do not expect a longer than normal season, either early or late.

Recommended Fruit & Nut Varieties

Apples**
Anna
Chandler
Dorsett Golden
Rev. Morgan

Apricots*
Goldkist
Harriet

Bananas
(needs 15 months above 28° to bear fruit)
Gran Nain
Orinoco Victoria

Blackberries
Apache (thornless erect)
Black Satin (semi-erect)
Brazos
Hull (semi-erect)
Navaho (thornless, erect)
Shawnee
Rosborough

Blueberries (Rabbiteye)**
Delite
Tiflue
Climax
Brightwell

Citrus
(some need protection below 26°; most need trifoliate orange rootstock to ensure hardiness)
Armstrong Early Satsuma
Atlas Honey Mandarin
Calamondin
Meiwa Kumquat
Meyer Lemon (on own roots)
Nagami Kumquat
Pummelo Grapefruit
Rio Farms Flame Grapefruit
Rio Red Grapefruit
Tangelo
Tangor Temple Orange
Thomasville Citrangequat

Figs
BA-1
Black Mission
Celeste
Kadota
LSU Purple
Royal Vineyard
San Piero
Texas Everbearing (Brown Turkey)

Grapes (Bunch)
BN5-101
BN12-101
Orlando Seedless
Champarnel
Black Spanish

9E GULF COAST

Recommended Fruit & Nut Varieties (cont'd)

Grapes (Muscadine)***
Darlene
Fry
Cowart (pollinator)
Granny Vail
Ison
Jumbo
Scuppernong
Sugargate (pollinator)
Southland (pollinator)
Triumph

Jujubes
Li
Lang

Mayhaws
Big Red (rust resistant)
Rosy Apple
Super Spur
Warren Superberry

> * If soil is deep sand,
> variety should be
> grafted onto
> Nemaguard or
> Nemared rootstock.
> ** Need more than one
> variety for pollination
> *** Certain muscadines
> can be self-fertile or
> female only; plant
> one self-fertile variety
> for every six female
> varieties.

Nectarines*
(minimum chill hours
needed to set fruit in
parenthesis)
Mayglo (500-600)
Nectar Babe (500-600)
Sungold (200-300)
Sunred (150-200)
Sungem (150-200)

Pawpaws
Common pawpaw
Small-flower pawpaw
Dr. Potter (hybrid)
Earlygold (hybrid)
Overleese
Rebecca's Gold
Sunflower

Peaches*
(minimum chill hours
needed to set fruit in
parenthesis)
Babcock (300-500)
Earligrande (200-300)
Floridacrest (400-500)
LaPercher (400-500)
Mid-Pride (200-300)
Red Baron (500-600)
Texroyal (600)
Tropic Snow (150-200)
Tropic Sweet (150-200)

Pears**
Atlas Comice Royal
Ayers
Cascade
Honey Dew
Honey Sweet
Kieffer
LeConte
Moonglow
Orient
Savannah
South African Bartlett
Tennessee 37-20
Tyson
Warren

Pears (Asian)**
Ho Sui
Monica Harris
Niji Seiki (20th Century)
Shinko
Shin Li
Shin Seiki (New Century)
Ya Li

Pecans
Caddo
Cape Fear
Cheyenne
Choctaw
Desirable
Elliott (home orchard only)
Jubilee
Moreland
Pawnee
Shawnee

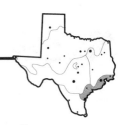

Recommended Fruit & Nut Varieties (cont'd)

Persimmons
(A = astringent)
Brad Sample
Chocolate
Eureka (best commercial)
Giombo
Hachiya (A, may be seedless)
Honan Red
Saijo
Suruga
Tane-nashi (A)
Yokono
Yotsumizo

Plums*
Allred
A.U. Amber (home use)
Methley
Ozark Premier
Santa Rosa

Pomegranates
Flavorful
Wonderful

Raspberries
Dormanred

Strawberries
Chandler (commercial)
Cardinal (home)
Pajaro (commercial)
Tioga (home)
Sequoia (home)

9E GULF COAST

WHERE !
TO FIND IT •

ARBORETA & BOTANIC GARDENS
Corpus Christi Botanical Gardens
8510 Staples St.
Corpus Christi, TX 78413
(512) 852-2100
Mercer Arboretum & Botanic Gardens
22306 Aldine-Westfield Rd.
Humble, TX 77338
(713) 443-8731
Moody Gardens
One Hope Boulevard
Galveston, TX 77554
(800) 582-4673
Houston Arboretum & Nature Center
4501 Woodway
Houston, TX 77024
(713) 681-8433

COMMUNITY GARDEN ORGANIZATIONS
Beaumont Community Garden
Roberts Ave United Methodist Church
Beaumont, TX 77701
(409) 833-1831
Contact: Rev. Bruce Felker
Galveston/Hitchcock Community Gardens
Audrey Chadwick
4006-1/2 Highway 6
Hitchcock, TX 77563
(409) 744-1745 x 273

Interfaith Ministries For Greater Houston
3217 Montrose Blvd.
Houston, TX 77006
(713) 522-3955
Target Hunger
(713) 226-4953
Urban Harvest
1900 Kane
P.O. Box 980460
Houston, TX 77098-0460
(713) 880-5540

LOCAL PUBLICATIONS
Gardening the Upper Texas Gulf Coast
By Harris County Master Gardeners; in
Q&A format organized by month.
Approx. $12
Growing Tomatoes in Houston
Booklet published by Urban Harvest
(713) 880-5540
Harris County Tree Registry
Published by The Park People, Inc.
(713) 528-7725
Texas Gulf Coast Gardening
P.O. Box 131
Missouri City, TX 77459
(713) 261-6077
FAX: (713) 261-5999
Water Wise Plants for Houston
P.O. Box 1562,
Houston, TX 77251
(713) 880-2444

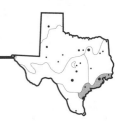

WHERE ! TO FIND IT •

NATURE CENTERS

Armand Bayou Nature Center
8600 Bay Area Blvd.
Houston, TX 77058
(713) 474-3074
Jesse Jones Park & Nature Center
20634 Kenswick Dr.
Humble, TX 77338
(713) 446-8588

PUBLIC GARDENS

Bayou Bend Gardens
1 Westcott St.
Houston, TX 77024
(713) 639-7750; 529-8773
Cockrell Butterfly Center
Museum of Natural Science in Houston
1 Hermann Circle
(713) 639-4600
Houston Garden Center
1500 Hermann Dr.
Houston, TX
(713) 529-5371
Japanese Garden
In Hermann Park
(713) 520-3283
Victoria Rose Gardens
Riverside Park
Victoria, TX 77902-1758

TEXAS AG. EXTENSION SERVICE / MASTER GARDENER PROGRAMS

Brazoria Co. Extension Horticulture
Waverly Jefferson, county agent
1800 County Rd. 171
Angleton, TX 77515
(409) 849-5711, ext. 1558
Ft. Bend Co. Extension Horticulture
Bouche Mickey, county agent
1436 Band Rd.
Rosenberg, TX 77471
(713) 342-3034
Galveston Co. Extension Horticulture
William Johnson, county agent
5115 Highway 3
Dickinson, TX 77539
(713) 534-3413; (409) 762-8621, ext. 196
Harris Co. Extension Horticulture
Williams D. Adams, county agent
Tom LeRoy, county agent
#2 Abercrombie Dr.
Houston, TX 77084
(713) 855-5600
Jefferson Co. Extension Horticulture
Vincent Mannino, county agent
1295 Pearl St.
Beaumont, TX 77701
(409) 835-8461
Nueces Co. Extension Horticulture
Darlene Locke, county agent
710 E. Main St. #1
Robstown, TX 78380
(512) 767-5223

9E GULF COAST

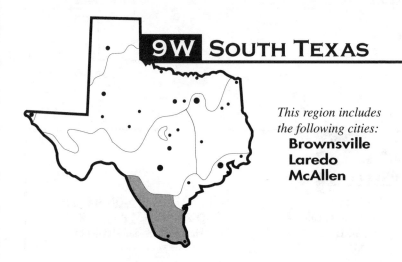

9W SOUTH TEXAS

*This region includes
the following cities:*
**Brownsville
Laredo
McAllen**

Beneath Our Feet

This part of Texas is dominated by the Rio Grande Plain, mostly prairie with grazelands largely replanted in buffalo grass. Other native vegetation includes prickly pear and other cacti, mesquite, huisache and cenizo. The northern region (roughly from Uvalde to Beeville) features red-brown to dark gray clayey soils and some loam, especially in the Winter Garden area. To the west, the alleuvial soils of the river basin support vegetable and sorgum growing, while upland soils largely support grazing beef cattle.

Agriculture/Forestry

The Winter Garden area, north of Laredo and centered in Dimmit and Zavala counties, produces commercial vegetables in late winter and early spring thanks to aggressive irrigation, including corn, cotton, grain sorghum, spinach, carrots and cabbage. To the east, corn, cotton, flax and small grains are also grown. Texas A&M operates a large research station at Weslaco, which has produced a steady stream of onion and pepper cultivars that are commercially grown here and in other parts of Texas. Citrus production has exploded here in recent years.

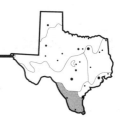

Local Climate Data

	Brownsville	Laredo	McAllen	Uvalde
Mean Max. July	93°	99°	96°	96°
Mean Min. January	50°	43°	49°	36°
Record High	106°	110°	106°	111°
Record Low	16°	13°	17°	6°
Avg. Last Freeze, Spring	Feb. 4	Feb. 7	Feb. 7	Mar. 10
Avg. First Freeze, Fall	Dec. 12	Dec. 26	Dec. 8	Nov. 21
Normal Growing Season	341 days	322 days	327 days	255 days
Normal Precipitation, January	1.6	0.8	1.4	1.1
Normal Precipitation, February	1.1	1.0	1.3	1.4
Normal Precipitation, March	0.5	0.5	0.6	1.1
Normal Precipitation, April	1.6	1.6	1.3	2.3
Normal Precipitation, May	2.9	2.7	2.8	3.3
Normal Precipitation, June	2.7	3.1	2.7	2.8
Normal Precipitation, July	1.9	1.4	1.7	1.9
Normal Precipitation, August	2.8	2.6	2.4	2.7
Normal Precipitation, September	6.0	3.3	4.4	2.8
Normal Precipitation, October	2.8	2.5	2.6	3.0
Normal Precipitation, November	1.5	1.1	1.0	1.3
Normal Precipitation, December	1.3	0.9	1.1	1.1
Normal Precipitation, ANNUAL	26.6	21.4	23.4	24.8

Temperature Records

	Record High	Month & Year	Record Low	Month & Year	No. Days Max 90° & Above	No. Days Min. 32° & Below
Brownsville	106°	3/84	16°	12/89	117.3	2.2
Laredo	110°	7/60, 6/80	16°	12/73	167.0	8.0
McAllen	106°	5/74, 7/79	17°	1/62	157.0	4.0
Uvalde	110°	8/62	6°	1/51	132.0	30.0

Chill Hours

According to USDA statistics, South Texas typically experiences 400 chill hours or less.

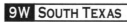

9W SOUTH TEXAS

Annual Rainfall

Normal
Southern Texas .... 23.70"
Lower Rio Grande Valley .... 25.31"

One-Year Sample (1994)

	J	F	M	A	M	J	J	A	S	O	N	D
Southern Texas	1.54	0.74	3.15	1.90	2.64	3.66	0.92	1.07	2.60	4.17	0.27	1.96
Lower Rio Grande Valley	1.86	0.40	1.75	0.82	2.58	3.36	0.26	2.36	3.88	2.98	0.50	2.32

NOTE: "Normal" rainfalls are based on figures from a 30-year period; currently 1961-1990, while "average" rainfalls are calculated from the entire historical record. While "normals" generally are considered more reliable than averages, they may be no more or less useful than last year's numbers alone. In the sample year 1994, the total annual rainfall was substantially higher than the "normal," and substantial different than the previous years' precipitation. East Texas, for instance, got 4 inches less rain in October '91 than in October '94.

Recommended Vegetable Varieties

Asparagus
Jersey Giant
UC 157
UC 72

Beans (Pinto)
Dwarf Horticultural
Improved Pinto
Idaho 114

Beans (Lima Pole)
Florida Speckled
King of the Garden
Sieva Carolina

Beans (Bush)
Contender
Greencrop
Roman
Blue Lake 274
Top Crop
Tendercrop

Beans (Lima Bush)
Dixie Speckled
Dixie White
Henderson Baby Bush
Jackson Wonder

Cabbage
Rio Verde
Ruby Ball
Sanibel
Savoy King
Stonehead

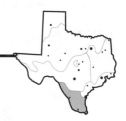

Recommended Vegetable Varieties (cont'd)

Cabbage (Chinese)
Jade Pagoda
Michili

Carrots (Fresh)
Imperator 58
Nantes
Orlando Gold
Short 'n Sweet (baby)
TAM Gold Spike
Trophy

Carrots (Processing)
Danvers 126
Gold King
Spartan Bonus

Cauliflower
Snow King
Snow Crown

Cucumbers (Slicer)
Sweet Slice (burpless, very
   prolific)
Sweet Success
Burpless
Dasher II

Cucumbers (Pickling)
Crispy
Carolina
Liberty

Eggplants
Black Magic
Classic (big, black)
Dusky
Florida Hibush
Florida Market
Ichiban (Asian)
Long Tom (Asian)
Tycoon (Asian)
Listada de Gandia

Leeks
American Flag
Broad
Electra
London
Titan

Lettuce (Leaf)
Buttercrunch
Green Ice
Paris Island
Prizehead
Salad Bowl
Red Fire

Lettuce (Head)
Great Lakes 659 MT
Mission
Red Salad Bowl

Melons (Muskmelons)
Ambrosia
Laguna
Magnum 45
Mission
Perlita
TAM Dew
TAM
Uvalde

Melons (Watermelons)
Allsweet
Black Diamond
Calhoun Gray
Crimson Sweet
Dixielee
Royal Jubilee
Royal Sweet
Yellow Tendersweet

Okra
Clemson Spineless
Emerald
Lee

Onions
White and Yellow Granex
Granex 33
TAMU Supersweet
   (1015Y)
Texas Early Grano 502
Red Burgundy
Red Grano

9W SOUTH TEXAS

Vegetable Harvest

	J	F	M	A	M	J	J	A	S	O	N	D
Aspargus	•	•	•	•	•						•	•
Beans (Green)					•	•	•			•		
Beans (Long)								•	•	•		
Beets					•							
Bok Choy			•									
Broccoli	•	•	•	•								•
Brussels Sprouts		•										
Cabbage	•	•	•	•								•
Carrots						•	•					
Cauliflower												•
Chard	•	•										
Collards	•	•										
Corn						•	•				•	
Cucumbers						•	•	•	•	•		
Eggplant								•	•	•		
Garlic						•						
Kale	•	•										
Lettuce (Other Greens)	•	•	•								•	•
Spinach	•	•	•							•	•	•
Melons							•					
Mustard	•	•	•								•	
Okra								•	•			
Onions (Green)	•	•										
Onions					•							
Pak Choy											•	•
Parsley	•	•										
Peppers							•	•	•	•		
Potatoes (Irish)					•							
Squash						•	•			•		
Southern Peas								•	•			
Sugar Snap Peas				•								
Tomatoes				•	•					•	•	
Turnips	•	•	•									•

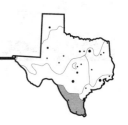

NOTE: This chart is deliberately conservative, designed to illustrate what most home gardeners can expect to harvest when planting is done at the proper times (see page 98 for spring planting schedules, and page 138 for fall schedules). Aggressive gardeners willing to gamble may harvest tomatoes as early as March and as late as Christmas: good on ya!

Many cabbage and greens growers stretch harvests longer than shown here; these are folks who understand that "the best fertilizer is the gardener's shadow." If you do not tend the vegetable garden daily (at least with an inspection), do not expect a longer than normal season, either early or late.

Recommended Vegetable Varieties (cont'd)

Peas (English)
Green Arrow
Little Marvel
Wando

Peas (Edible Pod)
Dwarf Gray Sugar
Sugar Bon
Sugar Pop (bush)
Sugar Rae
Sugar Snap (vine, spring
    only)

Peas (Southern)
California #5
Champion Cream
Cream 40
Purple Hull Pinkeye
Zipper Cream Crowder
Mississippi Silver

Peppers (Bell/Sweet)
Bell Tower
Big Bertha
Emerald Giant
Jupiter Shamrock
Sweet Banana
TAM Bell II

Peppers (Hot)
TAMU Mild Jalapeno
Hidalgo
Hungarian Yellow Wax
Long Red Cayenne
Serrano
many others (there are no
    hot peppers that would
    rather be grown in New
    Jersey than in Texas)

Pumpkins
Connecticut Field
Funnyface
Max
Small Sugar
Spirit

Radishes
Champion
Red Prince
Summer Cross
White Icicle

Squash (Summer)
Dixie
Elite
Multipik
Senator
Traboncino
Zucco

Recommended Vegetable Varieties (cont'd)

Squash (Summer Pan)
Sunburst (yellow)
Patty Pan (white)
Peter Pan (green)

Squash (Winter)
Blue Hubbard
Butternut
Sweet Mama
Table Ace
Table King
Tahitian
Vegetable Spaghetti
Waltham

Sweet Corn
Calumet
Capitan
Honeycomb
Merit
Kandy Korn
Summer Sweet 7800
Sweet G-90 (bi-color)

Tomatoes (Cherry)
Cherry Supreme
Porter Improved
Porter's Pride
Red Cherry
Small Fry
Texas Wild

Tomatoes (Canning/Paste)
Napoli
Roma

Tomatoes (Large Fruit)
Bigset
Bingo
Carnival
Celebrity
Crimson Fancy
Jackpot
Merced
Spring Giant

Turnips (Spring/Fall)
Tokyo Cross
Royal Globe II
White Globe
Just Right

Recommended Fruit & Nut Varieties

Apples**
Anna
Ein Sheimer
Golden Dorsett

Apricots*
Blendheim
Royal

Avocados
Lula
Mexican strain seedlings
   (ornamental)

Blackberries
Brazos
Brison
Rosborough

Citrus (Cold Hardy)
Calamondin
Changsha Tangerine
Eustis Limequat
Kumquat (Nagami, Meiwa,
   Hongkong)
Satsuma
Meyer Lemon
Tangelo
Tangor Temple Orange

Figs
Alma
Celeste
Texas Everbearing

Grapefruit
Ruby Red
Henderson
Ray Ruby
Star Ruby

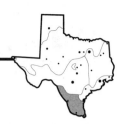

Recommended Fruit & Nut Varieties (cont'd)

Grapes (Bunch)
Black Spanish
Blanc du Bois
Carman
Champanel
Favorite
Herbemont
Orlando Seedless

Grapes (Muscadine)***
Carlos
Cowart
Fry
Higgens
Jumbo
Magnolia
Regale
Scuppernong
Summit

* If soil is deep sand, variety should be grafted onto Nemaguard or Nemared rootstock.
** Need more than one variety for pollination
*** Certain muscadines can be self-fertile or female only; plant one self-fertile variety for every six female varieties.

Jujubes
Li
Lang

Oranges
Marrs (navel)
Hamlin
Navel
Valencia

Peaches*
(chill hours needed in parenthesis)
Earligrand (200)
Rio Grande (450)
Florida Grande (100)
Floridaking (450)
Tropic Beauty (150)
Tropic Sweet (175)
Tropic Snow (200)
Vallegrand (200)

Pears**
Fan Still
Garber (Oriental hybrid)
Kieffer
LeConte
Monterrey
Orient (Oriental hybrid)
Pineapple (Oriental hybrid)
Savannah
Warren

Persimmons
(A= astringent)
Eureka (best commercial variety)
Fuyu Fugaki
Hachiya (A, can produce seedless fruit)
Tamopan (A)
Tane-nashi (A)

Plums*
Bruce
Gulfruby
Gulfgold
Methley
Santa Rosa

Pecans
Caddo
Cape Fear
Cheyenne
Choctaw
Desirable
Kiowa
Pawnee
Shawnee

Strawberries
Chandler (commercial)
Douglas
Pajaro (commercial)
Tioga (home)
Sequoia (home)

9W SOUTH TEXAS

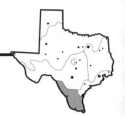

WHERE ! TO FIND IT

<u>TEXAS AG. EXTENSION SERVICE /
MASTER GARDENER PROGRAMS</u>

Cameron Co. Extension Horticulture
Terry Lockamy, agriculture agent
650 E. Highway 77
San Benito, TX 78586-3869
(210) 399-7757

Hidalgo Co. Extension Horticulture
Brad Cowan, county agent
Box 600
Edinburg, TX 78540
(210) 383-1026

TAES Horticulture
Dr. Julian Sauls
Fruit & Pecan Specialist
2401 E. Highway 83
Weslaco, TX 78596
(210) 968-5581
(210) 969-2115

TAES Horticulture
Dr. Larry Stein
Fruit & Pecan Specialist
P.O. Box 1849
Uvalde, TX 78802
(210) 278-9151
(210) 278-1570

Uvalde Co. Extension Horticulture
Kenneth G. White, county agent
Drawer 1708
Uvalde, TX 78802-1708
(210) 278-6661

Webb Co. Extension Horticulture
George Gonzales, county agent
7209 E. Saunders, # 5
Laredo, TX 78040
(210) 721-2626

OTHER
Emergency Pollution Reports
24 hours
(800) 832-8224

**Texas National Resource Conservation
Commission**
Harlingen: Tony Franco
(210) 968-3165

The Perfect Gift

For... **A Gardening Friend**

It Keeps Giving All Year Long!

This *1997 Texas Garden Alamanac* is the perfect
Texas gift for anyone who loves the joys of gardening.
Get your shopping done early. *Order direct by calling . . .*

(713) 261-6077

— or —

(800) 310-7047

*Or tear out the
postage-paid card in
this almanac
and mail it
TODAY!*

1997
TEXAS
GARDEN ALMANAC

From the publishers of *Texas Gulf Coast Gardening*

*Great
Value!*
$10.95
*Plus $3.00 Shipping
& Handling*

*Additional
copies also available
at your local bookstore.*

8E EAST TEXAS

This region includes the following cities:
Bryan/College Station
Dallas
Longview
Texarkana
Tyler

Beneath Our Feet

Physical regions of this part of Texas include the bulk of our piney woods, some post oak "savannah" and the biggest and richest part of the blackland belt. Sandy, acid soils nurture pine and hardwood forests in the east, while the post oak belt features sandy loams in the uplands (often thin over clay subsoils) and alluvial loam and clay soil series in the bottomlands. In the blacklands to the west, very friable soils of the rolling plains mark was once the heart of Texas' cotton country. (Since the 1930s, however, mechanization and irrigation have pushed other parts of Texas to the forefront in farm output. Bottomland soils in the blackland belt tend to clay; elm, hackberry and pecan trees populate stream bottoms.

Agriculture/Forestry

A wide range of grasslands, featuring both native and cultivated species, offer grazing lands for cattle in the piney woods area. Three native pines — longleaf, shortleaf and loblolly — are staples of the timber industry. So is the introduced slash pine, although this tree has been criticized for changing the overall ecosystem of the area. Hardwoods include elm, hickory, magnolia, sweet and black gum, tupelo and, of course, oaks. A little inland, the post oak savannah region is drier and features higher elevations: blackjack oaks compete with post oaks and elms on a near-even footing. Pecans and walnuts thrive in riverbeds and watershed areas in both the post oak and blackland regions; in the latter, horseapple and mesquite also are numerous.

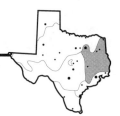

Local Climate Data

	Bryan/ College Station	Dallas	Texarkana	Tyler
Mean Max. July	94°	96°	93°	94°
Mean Min. January	39°	35°	35°	33°
Record High	110°	113°	101°	108°
Record Low	-3°	1°	-6°	0°
Avg. Last Freeze, Spring	Mar. 1	Mar. 23	Mar. 21	Mar. 7
Avg. First Freeze, Fall	Nov. 30	Nov. 13	Nov. 11	Nov. 21
Normal Growing Season	274 days	235 days	235 days	259 days
Normal Precipitation, January	2.7	1.8	3.6	3.0
Normal Precipitation, February	2.6	2.3	3.3	3.3
Normal Precipitation, March	2.6	3.2	4.2	3.5
Normal Precipitation, April	3.4	3.9	5.1	4.9
Normal Precipitation, May	4.8	5.0	4.4	4.9
Normal Precipitation, June	3.7	3.5	3.9	3.3
Normal Precipitation, July	2.3	2.4	3.5	2.8
Normal Precipitation, August	2.4	2.3	3.2	2.5
Normal Precipitation, September	4.9	3.6	3.6	4.1
Normal Precipitation, October	3.8	3.9	2.8	3.3
Normal Precipitation, November	3.2	2.4	3.9	3.8
Normal Precipitation, December	2.8	1.9	3.9	3.7
Normal Precipitation, ANNUAL	39.1	36.1	45.3	43.1

Temperature Records

	Record High	Month & Year	Record Low	Month & Year	No. Days Max 90° & Above	No. Days Min. 32° & Below
Bryan/College Station	110°	7/17	-3°	1/49	103.0	29.7
Dallas	113°	6/80	-1°	12/89	96.2	40.9
Shreveport, LA*	107°	8/62	3°	1/62	90.1	36.2

* Texas State Climatologist uses this station's data to approximate East Texas.

Chill Hours

According to USDA statistics, the East Texas area typically experiences 600-1,000 chill hours (temperatures between 32° and 45°) from fall to early spring. Dallas frequently gets more than 900 chill hours; Conroe, at the southern extreme of this region, is more likely to get 500.

8E EAST TEXAS

Annual Rainfall

Normal

East Texas .... 45.67"
North Central .... 33.99"

One-Year Sample (1994)

	J	F	M	A	M	J	J	A	S	O	N	D
East Texas	3.31	4.89	3.44	2.60	6.56	2.91	4.22	4.05	2.18	11.14	3.36	7.43
North Central	1.27	2.40	1.78	2.79	7.01	1.68	3.69	1.88	3.14	6.53	4.88	3.37

NOTE: "Normal" rainfalls are based on figures from a 30-year period; currently 1961-1990, while "average" rainfalls are calculated from the entire historical record. While "normals" generally are considered more reliable than averages, they may be no more or less useful than last year's numbers alone. In the sample year 1994, the total annual rainfall was substantially higher than the "normal," and substantial different than the previous years' precipitation. East Texas, for instance, got almost 4 inches less rain in July '93 than in July '94, and the '93 total rainfall was 29.0 inches.

Recommended Vegetable Varieties

Asparagus
Jersey Giant
UC 157

Beans (Snap Bush)
Blue Lake 274
Top Crop
Tendercrop
Contender
Tendergreen
Derby

Beans (Pinto)
Improved Pinto

Beans (Lima Bush)
Henderson Baby Bush
Jackson Wonder

Beans (Lima Pole)
Florida Speckled
King of the Garden

Cucumbers (Slicer)
Sweet Slice (burpless, very
    prolific)
Sweet Success
County Fair 87
Burpless
Dasher II
Slicemaster

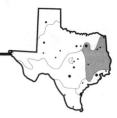

Recommended Vegetable Varieties (cont'd)

Eggplants
Classic (big, black)
Florida Market
Tycoon (Asian)
Listada de Gandia
Thai Long Green
Louisiana Long Green

Leeks
American Flag

Lettuce (Leaf)
Black-Seeded Simpson
Buttercrunch
Salad Bowl
Red Sails
Paris Island
Red Fire
Green Ice

Lettuce (Head)
Classic
Park's Mission

Lettuce (Cos/Romaine)
Romaine

8E EAST TEXAS

Recommended Vegetable Varieties (cont'd)

Melons (Muskmelons)
Ambrosia
Caravelle
Minnesota Midget (bush)
Explorer

Melons (Watermelons)
Crimson Sweet
Jack of Hearts (triploid)
Royal Jubilee

Okra
Blondie
Clemson Spineless
Emerald
Lee

Onions
(short-day varieties best)
Burgundy
Crystal Wax
Red Granex
TAMU Supersweet (1015Y)
Red Grano

Peas (English)
Little Marvel
Wando
Dwarf Gray Sugar

Peas (Edible Pod)
Sugar Ann (bush)
Sugar Pop (bush)
Super SugarMel (vine)
Sugar Snap (vine, spring
only)

Peas (Southern)
Blackeye #5
Purple Hull Pinkeye
Zipper Cream Crowder
Mississippi Silver

Peppers (Bell/Sweet)
Big Bertha
Cubanelle
Golden Summer (yellow)
Jupiter
Purple Belle (purple)
Super Red (pimiento, roasts
beautifully)

Peppers (Hot)
Jalapeno
TAMU Jalapeno
Hidalgo
Hungarian Yellow Wax
Long Red Cayenne
Serrano
many others (all hot peppers
would rather be grown in
Texas than in New Jersey)

Pumpkins
Autumn Gold
Connecticut Field
Jack Be Little (ornamental)
Small Sugar
Spirit

Radishes
Champion
Cherry Belle
Inca
Snow Belle
White Icicle

Squash (Summer)
Burpee's Butterstick
Dixie
Multipik
Seneca
Sun Drops
Gold Rush
Traboncino

Squash (Summer Pan)
Sunburst (yellow)
Patty Pan (white)
Peter Pan (green)

Squash (Winter)
Acorn
Early Butternut
Cream of the Crop
Sweet Mama
Tahitian

Sweet Corn
Florida Staysweet (yellow)
Golden Queen (yellow)
Guadalupe Gold (yellow)
Sweet G-90 (bi-color)
Honey & Pearls (bi-color)
How Sweet It Is (white)
Silver Queen (white)

8E EAST TEXAS

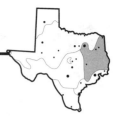

Recommended Vegetable Varieties (cont'd)

Tomatoes (Cherry)
Cherry Grande
Small Fry
Sweet 100
Yello Currant (itty-bitty but
  yummy)
Texas Wild

Tomatoes (Canning/Paste)
Roma
San Marzano

Tomatoes (Large Fruit)
Carnival
Celebrity
Champion
Crimson Fancy
First Lady
President
Quick Pick
Simba
Superfantastic

Turnips
Tokyo Cross
Royal Globe II
White Lady
Just Right (Fall only)

8E EAST TEXAS

Mark Your Calendar!

May 17, 1997

for the

GARDEN GALA

at the

Stephen F. Austin State University Arboretum
Nacogdoches, Texas

• • • *More than 20 display gardens* • • •

9 a.m. 'til dusk

Plant sale all day (first come, first served), booths,
student-led guided tours, refreshments and a good time for all!
For more information: (409) 468-3705

Vegetable Harvest

	J	F	M	A	M	J	J	A	S	O	N	D
Asparagus	•	•	•								•	•
Beans (Green)					•	•	•			•		
Beans (Long)							•	•		•		
Beets					•							
Bok Choy			•									
Broccoli	•	•	•	•								•
Brussels Sprouts		•										
Cabbage	•	•	•									•
Carrots						•	•					
Cauliflower												•
Chard	•	•										
Collards	•	•										
Corn						•	•				•	
Cucumbers						•	•	•	•	•		
Eggplant								•	•	•		
Garlic					•							
Kale	•	•										
Lettuce (Other Greens)	•	•	•								•	•
Spinach	•	•	•							•	•	•
Melons							•					
Mustard	•	•	•								•	
Okra							•	•	•	•		
Onions (Green)	•	•										
Onions				•								
Pak Choy											•	•
Parsley	•	•										
Peppers							•	•	•	•		
Potatoes (Irish)					•							
Squash						•	•			•		
Southern Peas								•	•	•		
Sugar Snap Peas				•								
Tomatoes					•	•				•	•	
Turnips	•	•	•									•

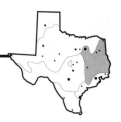

NOTE: This Vegetable Harvest chart is deliberately conservative, designed to illustrate what most home gardeners can expect to harvest when planting is done at the proper times (see page 98 for spring planting schedules, and page 138 for fall planting schedules). Aggressive gardeners willing to gamble may harvest tomatoes as early as April and as late as December, depending on when the first frost hits. Good on ya! Many cabbage and greens growers stretch harvests longer than shown here; these are folks who understand that "the best fertilizer is the gardener's shadow." If you do not tend the vegetable garden daily (at least with an inspection), do not expect a longer than normal season, either early or late.

Recommended Fruit & Nut Varieties

Apples**
Gala
Granny Smith
Holland
Jerseymac
Mollie's Delicious

Apricots*
Bryan
Hungarian
Moorpark
Peggy
Wilson

Blackberries
Apache (new in '92, thornless erect)
Black Satin (semi-erect)
Brazos
Hull (semi-erect)
Navaho (thornless, erect)
Shawnee
Rosborough

Black Walnuts
Ogden
Ohio
Myers (thinnest shell)

Blueberries (Rabbiteye)**
Delite
Tiflue
Climax
Brightwell

Chestnuts (Chinese Hybrid)
American x Chinese
Dustan hybrids

Citrus
(containers only, protect in winter)
Calamondin
Kumquat
Mandarins (Satsuma, Owari)
Meyer Lemon
Tangelo
Tangor Temple Orange

Figs
Texas Everbearing (Brown Turkey)
Celeste

Grapes (Bunch)
Orlando Seedless
Champarnel
Black Spanish

8E EAST TEXAS

Recommended Fruit & Nut Varieties (cont'd)

Grapes (Muscadine)***
Granny Vail
Jumbo
Scuppernong
Sugargate
Triumph

Jujubes
Li
Lang

Mayhaws
Big Red (rust resistant)
Super Spur

Nectarines*
(chill hours needed
to set fruit in parenthesis)
Armking (400-500)
Crimson Gold (600-700)
Redgold (850)

* If soil is deep sand, variety should be grafted onto Nemaguard or Nemared rootstock.
** Need more than one variety for pollination
*** Certain muscadines can be self-fertile or female only; plant one self-fertile variety for every six female varieties.

Pawpaws
Common pawpaw
Small-flower pawpaw
Dr. Potter (hybrid)
Earlygold (hybrid)

Peaches*
(chill hours needed
to set fruit in parenthesis)
Belle of Georgia (850, white flesh)
Derby (750)
Loring (650-750)
Oachita Gold (850)
Redskin (750)
Ruston Red (800)
Texroyal (600)
Springold (750)
Summergold (750)

Pears**
Ayers
Kieffer
LeConte
Moonglow
Orient
Savannah
Warren

Pears (Asian)**
Shinko
Tsu Li
Ya Li

Persimmons
(A = astringent)
Eureka (best commercial)
Hachiya (A, may be seedless)
Tane-nashi (A)
Chocolate

Plums*
Allred
A.U. Amber (home use)
Methley
Ozark Premier
Santa Rosa

Pecans
Caddo
Cape Fear
Cheyenne
Choctaw
Desirable
Elliott (home orchard only)
Pawnee

Pomegranates
Flavorful
Wonderful

Raspberries
Dormanred

Strawberries
Chandler (commercial)
Cardinal (home)
Pajaro (commercial)
Tioga (home)
Sequoia (home)

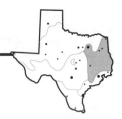

WHERE TO FIND IT !

ARBORETA & BOTANIC GARDENS
Dallas Horticulture Center
P.O. Box 152537
Dallas, TX 75315
Contact: Michael Cheever
(214) 428-7476
Dallas Arboretum & Botanic Garden
8617 Garland Rd.
Dallas, TX 75218
Contact: L. Landon Scarlett
(214) 327-8263
Stephen F. Austin Arboretum
Stephen F. Austin State University
P.O. Box 13000
Dept. of Agriculture & Horticulture
Nacogdoches, TX 75962-3000
(409) 468-3705

COMMUNITY GARDEN ORGANIZATIONS
Gardeners in Community Development
Dr. Don Lambert
901 Greenbriar Ln
Dallas, TX 75080
(214) 231-3565

EDUCATION
Stephen F. Austin State University
Dept. of Agriculture & Horticulture
P.O. Box 13000
Nacogdoches, TX 75962-3000
Contact: David Creech
(409) 468-3705

Texas A&M University Horticulture Dept.
Dr. Sam Cotner, chairman
225 Hort/Forestry Bldg.
College Station, TX 77843-2134
(409) 845-7341
FAX: (409) 845-8906
Trinity Valley Community College
Department of Horticulture
500 S. Prairieville
Athens, TX 75751
Contact: Sam Hurley
(903) 675-6258

MASTER COMPOSTER PROGRAMS
East Texas Council of Governments, Kilgore
Kevin Glanton
(903) 984-8641
Montgomery Co. Extension Horticulture
Karen Overgaard
(409) 539-7824

INTERNET
Howard Garrett
www.wbap.com
Local Extension Service
Aggie-horticulture.tamu.edu/cohort/
hansen.html
Local Extension Service
Aggie-horticulture.tamu.edu/imagemap/
taexmap/smith/smith.html

8E EAST TEXAS

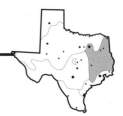

WHERE TO FIND IT !

TEXAS AG. EXTENSION SERVICE / MASTER GARDENER PROGRAMS

Brazos Co. Extension Horticulture
Katie Beth Harris, county agent
2619 Hwy 21 West
Bryan, TX 77803
(409) 823-0129

Collin Co. Extension Horticulture
Lynn Rawe, county agent
210 S. McDonald, Ste 6 22
McKinney, TX 75069
(214) 548-4232

Dallas Co. Extension Horticulture
Stacey Reese, county agent
10056 Marsh Lane, Suite B-101
Dallas, TX 75229
(214) 904-3053

Denton Co. Extension Horticulture
Nancy Brown, county agent
306 N. Loop 288 #222
Denton, TX 76201
(817) 565-5537

Montgomery Co. Extension Horticulture
Robert "Skip" Richter, county agent
9020 FM 1484
Conroe, TX 77303
(409) 539-7823; (713) 353-9791

Smith Co. Extension Horticulture
Keith Hansen, county agent
1517 W. Front St., 116 Cotton Belt Bldg.
Tyler, TX 75702-7897
(903) 535-0885

Texas A&M Extension Horticulture
Marvin L. Baker
Drawer 38
Overton, TX 75684
(903) 834-6191

Texas A&M Extension Horticulture
CEMAP program
Steve George
17360 Coit Rd.
Dallas, TX 75252-6599
(214) 904-3050

PUBLIC GARDENS

Tyler Municipal Rose Gardens
420 Rose Park Dr.
Tyler, TX 75702
(903) 531-1212

OTHER

Dogwood Festival (April)
Tyler County Chamber of Commerce
201 N. Magnolia
Woodville, TX 75979
(409) 283-2632

Texas Natural Resource Conservation Commission
Tyler: Leroy Biggers
(903) 595-5466

Tyler Rose Festival (October)
Tyler Chamber of Commerce
(903) 592-1661

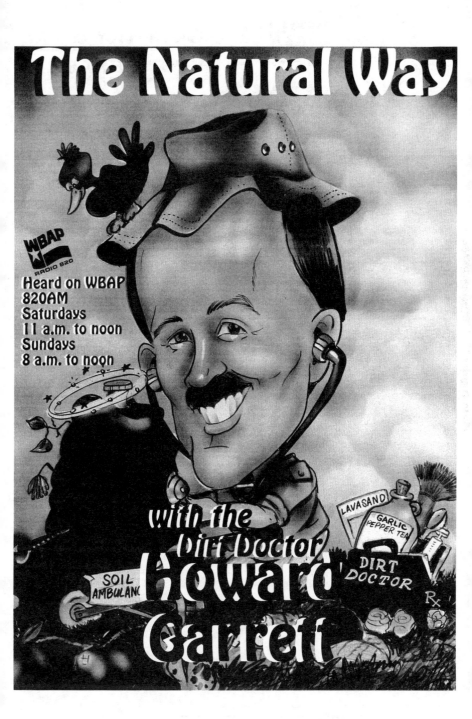

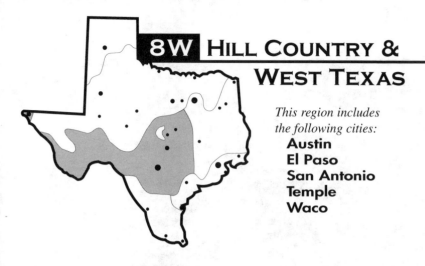

8W HILL COUNTRY & WEST TEXAS

*This region includes
the following cities:*
**Austin
El Paso
San Antonio
Temple
Waco**

Beneath Our Feet

The Llano Basin, the Edwards and Stockton plateaus and the Trans-Pecos are the key geographies of this region. Much of the Edwards Plateau is crusted with a soil layer dominated by limestone but also including dark clays and some loams, the latter more present and useful in lowland areas. Trans-Pecos uplands feature soils of reddish to brown clay loams and some sand, usually very alkaline, while lowlands are darker, alluvial soil types including silt loams with some salt content. Thanks to the vagaries of climate and geology that make it hard to generalize about Texas, this USDA region does not include the westernmost extention of West Texas (Zone 7) except for El Paso.

Agriculture/Forestry

Some crops compete with grazing land in the Edwards Plateau area. Live oak, mesquite, cedar and (in alleuvial areas) cypress dominate the vegetation. Sheep, goats and cattle represent the bulk of agriculture production.

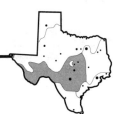

Local Climate Data

	Austin	El Paso	San Antonio	Waco
Mean Max. July	95°	96°	95°	97°
Mean Min. January	39°	29°	38°	34°
Record High	109°	114°	108°	112°
Record Low	-2°	-8°	0°	-5°
Avg. Last Freeze, Spring	Mar. 3	Mar. 9	Mar. 6	Mar. 16
Avg. First Freeze, Fall	Nov. 28	Nov. 12	Nov. 26	Nov. 24
Normal Growing Season	270 days	248 days	265 days	253 days
Normal Precipitation, January	1.7	0.4	1.7	1.7
Normal Precipitation, February	2.2	0.4	1.8	2.1
Normal Precipitation, March	1.9	0.3	1.5	2.3
Normal Precipitation, April	2.6	0.2	2.5	3.2
Normal Precipitation, May	4.8	0.3	4.2	4.6
Normal Precipitation, June	3.7	0.7	3.8	3.3
Normal Precipitation, July	2.0	1.5	2.2	2.0
Normal Precipitation, August	2.1	1.6	2.5	1.7
Normal Precipitation, September	3.3	1.7	3.4	3.5
Normal Precipitation, October	3.4	0.8	3.2	3.4
Normal Precipitation, November	2.4	0.4	1.5	2.4
Normal Precipitation, December	1.9	0.6	1.4	1.9
Normal Precipitation, ANNUAL	31.9	8.8	31.0	32.0

Temperature Records

	Record High	Month & Year	Record Low	Month & Year	No. Days Max 90° & Above	No. Days Min. 32° & Below
Austin	109°	7/54	-2°	1/49	105.0	21.1
El Paso	114°	7/94	-8°	1/62	104.0	65.0
San Antonio	108°	8/86	0°	1/49	110.8	22.7
Waco	112°	8/69	-5°	1/49	108.5	35.2

Chill Hours

According to USDA statistics, the Hill Country area typically experiences 500-800 chill hours (temperatures between 32° and 45°) from fall to early spring. Parts of West Texas may get 1,000.

8W HILL COUNTRY & WEST TEXAS

Annual Rainfall

Normal
South Central .... 34.49"
Edwards Plateau .... 24.00"
Trans Pecos .... 13.01"

One-Year Sample (1994)

	J	F	M	A	M	J	J	A	S	O	N	D
South Central	1.26	1.54	2.94	2.87	5.61	2.75	0.31	3.68	3.71	9.78	0.88	4.88
Edwards Plateau	1.95	1.18	1.69	1.47	3.96	1.30	1.68	0.99	2.77	3.22	2.03	2.46
Trans Pecos	0.62	0.28	0.52	0.30	1.67	0.70	1.12	0.69	1.18	0.80	0.39	0.56

NOTE: "Normal" rainfalls are based on figures from a 30-year period; currently 1961-1990, while "average" rainfalls are calculated from the entire historical record. While "normals" generally are considered more reliable than averages, they may be no more or less useful than last year's numbers alone. In the sample year 1994, the total annual rainfall was substantially higher than the "normal" in South Central Texas, but much lower in the Trans Pecos.

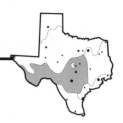

Recommended Vegetable Varieties

Asparagus
Jersey Giant
UC 72
UC 157

Beans (Snap Bush)
Blue Lake 274
Contender
Derby
Goldcrop
Greencrop
Improved Golden Wax
Top Crop
Tendercrop
Tendergreen

Beans (Pinto)
Dwarf Horticultural
Idaho 114
Improved Pinto

Beans (Lima Bush)
Dixie Speckled
Dixie White
Henderson Baby Bush
Jackson Wonder
Thorogreen

Beans (Lima Pole)
Florida Speckled
King of the Garden
Sieva Carolina

Beets
Pacemaker II
Ruby Queen

Broccoli
Galaxy
Green Comet
Explorer
Premium
Southern Comet

Brussels Sprouts
Prince Marvel

Cabbage
Rio Verde
Ruby Ball
Sanibel
Savoy King
Stonehead

Cabbage (Chinese)
Jade Pagoda
Michili

Carrots
Imperator 58
Nantes
TAM Gold Spike

Cucumbers (Slicer)
Sweet Slice (burpless, very
    prolific)
Sweet Success
County Fair 87
Burpless
Dasher II
Slicemaster

Eggplants
Black Magic
Classic (big, black)
Dusky
Florida Market
Ichiban (Asian)
Listada de Gandia
Long Tom (Asian)
Louisiana Long Green
Thai Long Green
Tycoon (Asian)

Kohlrabi
Early White Vienna
Grand Duke Hybrid

Leeks
American Flag
Electra
Titan

Lettuce (Leaf)
Black-Seeded Simpson
Buttercrunch
Green Ice
Paris Island
Prizehead
Red Sails
Red Fire
Salad Bowl

Lettuce (Head)
Classic
Great Lakes 659 MT
Park's Mission
Ruby

Recommended Vegetable Varieties (cont'd)

Lettuce (Cos/Romaine)
Romaine

Melons (Muskmelons)
Ambrosia
Caravelle
Explorer
Minnesota Midget (bush)
Uvalde

Melons (Watermelons)
Crimson Sweet
Jack of Hearts (triploid)
Royal Jubilee

Okra
Blondie
Clemson Spineless
Emerald
Lee

Onions
   (*short-day varieties best*)
Burgundy
Crystal Wax
Granex 33
Red Granex
Red Grano
TAMU Supersweet (1015Y)
White Granex
Yellow Granex

Peas (English)
Green Arrow
Little Marvel
Wando

Peas (Edible Pod)
Dwarf Gray Sugar
Sugar Ann (bush)
Sugar Pop (bush)
Super SugarMel (vine)
Sugar Snap (vine, spring
   only)

Peas (Southern)
Blackeye #5
Champion Cream
Cream 40
Crowder
Mississippi Silver
Purple Hull Pinkeye
Zipper Cream Crowder

Peppers (Bell/Sweet)
Bell Tower
Big Bertha
Cubanelle
Emerald Giant
Golden Summer (yellow)
Grand Rio 66
Jupiter
Pip
Purple Belle (purple)
Shamrock
Super Red (pimiento, roasts
   beautifully)
Sweet Banana

Peppers (Hot)
Jalapeno
TAMU Jalapeno
Hidalgo
Hungarian Yellow Wax
Long Red Cayenne
Serrano
many others (all hot peppers
   would rather be grown in
   Texas than in New Jersey)

Pumpkins
Autumn Gold
Big Max
Connecticut Field
Funny Face
Jack Be Little (ornamental)
Jack O'Lantern
Small Sugar
Spirit

Radishes
Champion
Cherry Belle
Inca
Red Prince
Snow Belle
Summer Cross
White Icicle

Spinach
Coho
Green Valley II

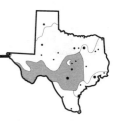

Recommended Vegetable Varieties (cont'd)

Squash (Summer)
Burpee's Butterstick
Dixie
Multipik
Seneca
Sun Drops
Gold Rush
Traboncino

Squash (Summer Pan)
Sunburst (yellow)
Patty Pan (white)
Peter Pan (green)

Squash (Winter)
Acorn
Early Butternut
Cream of the Crop
Sweet Mama
Tahitian

Sweet Corn
Calumet (yellow)
Capitan (yellow)
Golden Queen (yellow)
Guadelupe Gold (yellow)
Honey & Pearls (bi-color)
Honeycomb (yellow)
How Sweet It Is (white)
Silver Queen (white)
Summer Sweet 7800 (yellow)
Sweet G-90 (bi-color)

8W HILL COUNTRY & WEST TEXAS

Vegetable Harvest

	J	F	M	A	M	J	J	A	S	O	N	D
Aspargus	•	•	•	•							•	•
Beans (Green)					•	•	•			•		
Beans (Long)								•	•	•		
Beets					•							
Bok Choy			•									
Broccoli	•	•	•	•								•
Brussels Sprouts		•										
Cabbage	•	•	•									•
Carrots						•	•					
Cauliflower												•
Chard	•	•										
Collards	•	•										
Corn						•	•				•	
Cucumbers						•	•	•	•	•		
Eggplant								•	•	•		
Garlic						•						
Kale	•	•										
Lettuce (Other Greens)	•	•	•								•	•
Spinach	•	•	•							•	•	•
Melons							•					
Mustard	•	•	•								•	
Okra							•	•	•	•		
Onions (Green)	•	•										
Onions					•							
Pak Choy											•	•
Parsley	•	•										
Peppers							•	•	•	•		
Potatoes (Irish)					•							
Squash						•	•				•	
Southern Peas								•	•	•		
Sugar Snap Peas				•								
Tomatoes					•	•				•	•	
Turnips	•	•	•									•

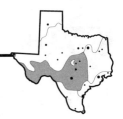

NOTE: This Vegetable Harvest chart is deliberately conservative, designed to illustrate what most home gardeners can expect to harvest when planting is done at the proper times (see page 98 for spring planting schedules, and page 138 for fall planting schedules). Aggressive gardeners willing to gamble may harvest tomatoes as early as April and as late as November: good on ya! Many cabbage and greens growers stretch harvests longer than shown here; these are folks who understand that "the best fertilizer is the gardener's shadow." If you do not tend the vegetable garden daily (at least with an inspection), do not expect a longer than normal season, either early or late.

Recommended Vegetable Varieties (cont'd)

<u>Sweet Potatoes</u>
Centennial
Cordner
Jewel

<u>Tomatoes (Cherry)</u>
Cherry Grande
Small Fry
Sweet 100
Yello Currant (itty-bitty but yummy)
Texas Wild

<u>Tomatoes (Canning/Paste)</u>
Roma
San Marzano

<u>Tomatoes (Large Fruit)</u>
Carnival
Celebrity
Champion
Crimson Fancy
First Lady
President
Quick Pick
Simba
Superfantastic

<u>Turnips</u>
All Top (greens)
Just Right (Fall only)
Purple Top
Royal Globe II
Tokyo Cross
White Globe
White Lady

Recommended Fruit & Nut Varieties

Apples**
Red Delicious
Golden Delicious
Fuji
Gala
Granny Smith
Holland
Jerseymac
Mollie's Delicious

Apricots*
Bryan
Hungarian
Moorpark

Blackberries
Arapaho (thornless, erect)
Arkansas
Brazos
Comanche
Humble
Navaho (thornless, erect)
Shawnee
Rosborough

Cherries (Sour)
Montmorency

Citrus
*(containers only, protect
in winter; plants may be
moved outside into full
sun when temperatures
exceed 26°)*
Satsuma

Figs
Alma
Brown Turkey
Celeste
Green Ischia
Kadota
Mission
Negrone
San Piero

Grapes (Bunch)
Barbera
Beacon
Black Spanish (Lenoir)
Blanc du Bois
Champanel
Ellen Scott
Favorite
Fredonia
French Colombard
Golden Muscat
Golden Seedless
Herbemont
Petite Sirah

**Grapes (French-
American Hybrids)**
Aurelia
Seibel 9110
Seyve-Villard 12-375

Jujubes
Li
Lang

* If soil is deep sand,
variety should be
grafted onto
Nemaguard or
Nemared rootstock.
** Need more than one
variety for pollination
*** Certain muscadines
can be self-fertile or
female only; plant
one self-fertile variety
for every six female
varieties.

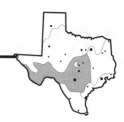

Recommended Fruit & Nut Varieties (cont'd)

Peaches*
*(chill hours needed in
parenthesis)*
Bicentennial
Derby (750)
Redskin (750)
Springold (750)
Summergold (750)
Belle of Georgia (850,
    white flesh)
Oachita Gold (850)
Ruston Red (800)

Peaches (Dwarf)
*(full-sized fruit on dwarf
plants)*
Bonanza II
Early Golden Glory

Pears*
Ayers
Garber
Kieffer
LeConte
Maxine
Moonglow
Orient
Savannah
Warren

Pears (Asian)**
*(rootstocks to request:
Calleryana, Old Home)*
Hosui
Shinko
20th Century
Tsu Li
Ya Li

Pecans
Caddo
Cape Fear
Choctaw
Desirable
Kiowa
Pawnee

Persimmons
(A= astringent)
Eureka (A, best
    commercial variety)
Hachiya (A, can produce
    seedless fruit)
Tamopan (A)
Tane-nashi (A)
Chocolate
Fuyu (more susceptible to
    cold)

Plums*
*(rootstock to request:
Lovell for alkaline soils,
Nemaguard for acid,
sandy soils)*
Bruce (requires cross-
    pollinator)
Morris
Methley
Ozark Permier

Quinces
all varieties

Raspberries
Dorman Red

**Strawberries
    (Everbearing)**
Allstar
Cardinal (home variety)
Gem
Ozark Beauty
Ogallala
Sunrise

WHERE ! TO FIND IT

ARBORETA & BOTANIC GARDENS
Chihuahuan Desert Research Institute
P.O. Box 1334
Alpine, TX 79831
Contact: Dennie Miller
National Wildflower Research Center
4801 La Crosse Ave.
Austin, TX 78739
(512) 292-4200
Texas Botanical Garden Society
P.O. Box 5642
Austin, TX 78763
Contact: Sol Steinberg
(512) 478-0010
San Antonio Botanical Garden
555 Funston Place
San Antonio, TX 78209
(210) 829-5360
Zilker Botanical Gardens
2220 Barton Springs Rd.
Austin, TX 78746
(512) 477-8672

COMMUNITY GARDEN ORGANIZATIONS
Austin Community Gardens
4814 Sunshine Dr.
Austin, TX 78756
(512) 458-2009
Sustainable Food Center
434 Bastrop Hwy
Austin, TX 78741
(512) 385-0080
Contact: Kay Fitzgerald
Bexar Co. Extension Service
Calvin Finch, county agent
3427 NE Pkwy
San Antonio, TX78218
(210) 930-3086
By far the largest school gardening program in the state.
Dr. Joseph Novak
Texas A&M University
Department of Horticulture
College Station, TX 77843-2133
(409) 845-3915

EDUCATION
Southwest Texas State University
Department of Biology
San Marcus, TX 78666
(512) 245-2178

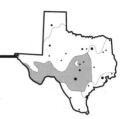

WHERE ! TO FIND IT ●

TEXAS AG. EXTENSION SERVICE / MASTER GARDENER PROGRAMS

Bexar Co. Extension Horticulture
Calvin Finch, county agent
Jerry Parsons, horticulture specialist
3247 Northeast Pkwy
San Antonio, TX 78218
(210) 930-3086

El Paso Co. Extension Horticulture
John White, county agent
1030 N. Zaragosa, Suite A
El Paso, TX 79907
(915) 859-7725

McLennan Co. Extension Horticulture
Charlotte A. Talley
420 N. 6th St.
Waco, TX 76701
(817) 757-5180

Travis Co. Extension Horticulture
Ted Fisher, county agent
1600-B Smith Rd.
Austin, TX 78721
(512) 473-9600
(512) 473-9226

Waller Co. Extension Horticulture
David E. McGregor, county agent
846 6th St.
Hempstead, TX 77445
(409) 826-3357

Washington Co. Extension Horticulture
Spencer D. Tanksley, county agent
100 E. Main St., #7
Brenham, TX 77833-3798
(409) 277-6200

OTHER

Bluebonnet Festival
Washington County Chamber of
Commerce
314 S. Austin
Brenham, TX 77833
(409) 836-3695
April in Chappell Hill

Emergency Pollution Reports
24 hours
(800) 832-8224

Texas Natural Resource Conservation Commission
Austin: Larry Smith
(512) 339-2929
El Paso: Frank Espino
(915) 778-9634
San Antonio: Richard Garcia
(210) 490-3096
Waco: Gene Fulton
(817) 751-0335

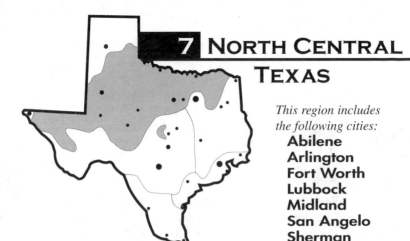

7 NORTH CENTRAL TEXAS

*This region includes
the following cities:*
**Abilene
Arlington
Fort Worth
Lubbock
Midland
San Angelo
Sherman
Wichita Falls**

Beneath Our Feet

In the eastern part of this region is the "grand prairie" of the Dallas/Ft. Worth metroplex. (By the USDA map, Ft. Worth is in Zone 7 and Dallas is in Zone 8, another case of nature having the impertinence to ignore the lines we humans have drawn.) The east and west "cross timbers" areas flank the grand prairie; moving west, the topography evolves into the central plains of North Texas, an extenion of lowlands that stretch from Texas to Canada. In the Lone Star State, this topography ranges from the Red River to the Colorado River. Farther west are rolling prairies (with red to grayish brown sandy loams and clays), the "great plains," the Pecos Valley, and the rangelands of West Texas up to but not including El Paso, which belongs to Zone 8.

Agriculture/Forestry

This region includes neither Texarkana nor El Paso, but it does include almost everything in between. Cattle feed and small grains dominate the agriculture of the north central prairies. To the east, commercial production is more diverse: crops of the cross timbers regions include grain sorghums, small grains, peaches, peanuts, pecans and vegetables, while the grand prairie communities also produce corn.

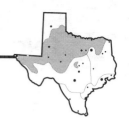

Local Climate Data

	Abilene	Fort Worth	Lubbock	Wichita Falls
Mean Max. July	95°	96°	92°	97°
Mean Min. January	31°	35°	25°	28°
Record High	110°	108°	114°	117°
Record Low	-9°	4°	-16°	-8°
Avg. Last Freeze, Spring	Mar. 31	Mar. 26	Apr. 9	Mar. 27
Avg. First Freeze, Fall	Nov. 11	Nov. 11	Nov. 3	Nov. 11
Normal Growing Season	225 days	230 days	208 days	229 days
Normal Precipitation, January	1.0	2.0	0.4	1.0
Normal Precipitation, February	1.2	2.2	0.7	1.5
Normal Precipitation, March	1.4	2.5	0.9	2.2
Normal Precipitation, April	1.9	3.6	1.0	3.0
Normal Precipitation, May	3.0	4.6	2.4	4.1
Normal Precipitation, June	2.9	3.0	2.8	3.5
Normal Precipitation, July	2.1	1.8	2.4	1.7
Normal Precipitation, August	2.8	1.7	2.5	2.5
Normal Precipitation, September	3.2	2.5	2.6	3.8
Normal Precipitation, October	2.5	2.6	1.9	2.7
Normal Precipitation, November	1.5	2.5	0.8	1.5
Normal Precipitation, December	1.0	2.4	0.5	1.3
Normal Precipitation, ANNUAL	24.4	31.3	18.7	28.9

Temperature Records

	Record High	Month & Year	Record Low	Month & Year	No. Days Max 90° & Above	No. Days Min. 32° & Below
Abilene	110°	7/78	-9°	1/47	96.6	53.6
Fort Worth	113°	6/80	-1°	12/89	96.2	40.9
Lubbock	114°	6/94	-16°	1/63	78.6	94.6
Wichita Falls	117°	6/80	-8°	2/85	105.9	68.1

Chill Hours

According to USDA statistics, North Texas typically experiences 1,000-1,200 chill hours (temperatures between 32° and 45°) from fall to early spring.

7 NORTH CENTRAL TEXAS

Annual Rainfall

Normal

High Plains .... 18.88"
Low Rolling Plains .... 23.77"
North Central .... 33.99"
Edwards Plateau .... 24.00"
Trans Pecos .... 13.01"

One-Year Sample (1994)

	J	F	M	A	M	J	J	A	S	O	N	D
High Plains	0.54	0.13	0.91	1.68	3.35	1.17	2.86	1.80	1.49	1.10	0.88	0.44
Low Rolling Plains	0.85	1.03	0.95	2.01	4.86	0.60	1.58	0.70	2.58	2.49	2.05	0.85
North Central	1.27	2.40	1.78	2.79	7.01	1.68	3.69	1.88	3.14	6.53	4.88	3.37
Edwards Plateau	1.95	1.18	1.69	1.47	3.96	1.30	1.68	0.99	2.77	3.22	2.03	2.46
Trans Pecos	0.62	0.28	0.52	0.30	1.67	0.70	1.12	0.69	1.18	0.80	0.39	0.56

NOTE: "Normal" rainfalls are based on figures from a 30-year period; currently 1961-1990, while "average" rainfalls are calculated from the entire historical record. While "normals" generally are considered more reliable than averages, they may be no more or less useful than last year's numbers alone. In the sample year 1994, the total annual rainfall was substantially higher than the "normal," and substantial different than the previous years' precipitation. East Texas, for instance, got almost 4 inches less rain in July '93 than in July '94, and the '93 total rainfall was 29.0 inches.

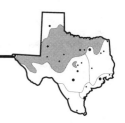

Recommended Vegetable Varieties

Asparagus
Jersey Giant
UC 157

Beans (Snap Bush)
Blue Lake 274
Top Crop
Tendercrop
Contender
Tendergreen
Derby

Beans (Yellow Bush)
Goldcrop
Improved Golden Wax

Beans (Pinto)
Improved Pinto

Beans (Snap Pole)
Blue Lake
Kentucky Wonder

Beans (Lima Bush)
Henderson Baby Bush
Jackson Wonder

Beans (Lima Pole)
Florida Speckled
King of the Garden

Beets
Pacemaker III

Broccoli
Premium Crop (spring only)
Emperor (spring only)
Green Comet
Galaxy
Packman
Baccus
Early Dawn

Brussels Sprouts
Prince Marvel
Royal Marvel

Cabbage
Early Jersey Wakefield
    (spring only)
Sanibel
Rapid Ball
Savoy Ace (wrinkled leaves)
Ruby Ball (red)

Cabbage (Chinese)
Jade Pagoda
Michihili
China Flash
China Pride

Carrots
Royal Chantenay
Burpee's Toudo
Park's Nandor
Danvers 126

Cauliflower
Snow Down

Swiss Chard
Rhubarb (red color)
Lucullus
Fordhook

Collards
Blue Max
Georgia

Cucumbers (Slicer)
Sweet Slice (burpless, very
    prolific)
Sweet Success
Burpless
County Fair 87
Dasher II
Slicemaster

Cucumbers (Pickling)
County Fair 87
Liberty
Saladin

Eggplants
Florida Market
Tycoon (Asian)
Listada de Gandia

Garlic
Texas White

Kale
Dwarf Blue Curled
Blue Knight

7 NORTH CENTRAL TEXAS

Recommended Vegetable Varieties (cont'd)

Kohlrabi
Grand Duke

Leeks
American Flag

Lettuce (Butterhead)
Buttercrunch
Tom Thumb (fall only)

Lettuce (Leaf)
Black-Seeded Simpson
Salad Bowl
Red Sails
Paris Island
Red Fire
Green Ice

Lettuce (Head)
Classic
Park's Mission

Lettuce (Cos/Romaine)
Romaine

Melons (Muskmelons)
Ambrosia
Caravelle
Explorer
Magnum 45
Minnesota Midget (bush
    type, good in containers)
Mission
Perlita (non-hybrid)
Uvalde (non-hybrid)

Melons (Watermelons)
Crimson Sweet
Jack of Hearts (triploid)
Orange Golden
Royal Jubilee
Royal Sweet
Star Brite
Sugarbaby
Supersweet 5032 (triploid)
Tiffany (triploid)

Okra
Blondy
Clemson Spineless
Emerald
Lee

Onions
    (short-day varieties best)
Burgundy
Crystal Wax
Red Granex
TAMU Supersweet (1015Y)
Red Grano
White Granex
Yellow Granex

Onions (Bunching)
Beltsville Bunching

Peas (English)
Little Marvel
Wando
Dwarf Gray Sugar

Peas (Edible Pod)
Sugar Ann (bush)
Sugar Pop (bush)
Super SugarMel (vine)
Sugar Snap (spring only)

Peas (Southern)
Blackeye #5
Purple Hull Pinkeye
Zipper Cream Crowder
Mississippi Silver

Peppers (Bell/Sweet)
Big Bertha (red bell)
Cubanelle
Golden Summer (yellow
    bell)
Gypsy
Jupiter (red bell)
Purple Belle (purple bell)
Summer Sweet 860 (yellow
    bell)
Sweet Pickle
Super Red (pimiento, roasts
    beautifully)
Top Banana

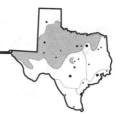

Recommended Vegetable Varieties (cont'd)

Peppers (Hot)
Jalapeno
TAMU Jalapeno
Hidalgo Serrano
Hungarian Yellow Wax
Long Red Cayenne
Super Chili
many others (there are no
  hot peppers that would
  rather be grown in New
  Jersey than in Texas)

Potatoes (Irish)
Norland (red, early)
Red LaSoda (red,
  midseason)
Kennebec (white, late)

Potatoes (Sweet)
Centennial
Jewell
Vardaman

Pumpkins
Autumn Gold
Connecticut Field
Jack Be Little (ornamental)
Small Sugar
Spirit

7 NORTH CENTRAL TEXAS

Vegetable Harvest

	J	F	M	A	M	J	J	A	S	O	N	D
Asparagus	•	•	•	•							•	•
Beans (Green)					•	•	•					
Beans (Long)								•	•	•		
Beets					•							
Bok Choy			•									
Broccoli	•	•	•	•								•
Brussels Sprouts		•										
Cabbage	•	•	•									•
Carrots						•	•					
Cauliflower												•
Chard	•	•										
Collards	•	•										
Corn						•	•				•	
Cucumbers						•	•	•	•	•		
Eggplant								•	•			
Garlic						•						
Kale	•	•										
Lettuce (Other Greens)	•	•	•								•	•
Spinach	•	•	•								•	•
Melons						•						
Mustard	•	•	•								•	
Okra							•	•	•	•		
Onions (Green)	•	•										
Onions					•							
Pak Choy											•	•
Parsley	•	•										
Peppers							•	•	•	•		
Potatoes (Irish)					•							
Squash						•	•			•		
Southern Peas								•	•			
Sugar Snap Peas				•								
Tomatoes					•	•					•	•
Turnips	•	•	•									•

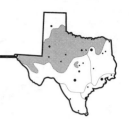

NOTE: This Vegetable Harvest chart is deliberately conservative, designed to illustrate what most home gardeners can expect to harvest when planting is done at the proper times (see page 98 for spring planting schedules, and page 138 for fall planting schedules). Aggressive gardeners willing to gamble may harvest tomatoes as early as April and as late as December: good on ya! Many cabbage and greens growers stretch harvests longer than shown here; these are folks who understand that "the best fertilizer is the gardener's shadow." If you do not tend the vegetable garden daily (at least with an inspection), do not expect a longer than normal season, either early or late.

Recommended Vegetable Varieties (cont'd)

Radishes
Champion
Cherry Belle
Inca
Snow Belle
White Icicle

Squash (Summer)
Burpee's Butterstick
Dixie
Multipik
Sun Drops
Traboncino

Squash (Summer Pan)
Sunburst (yellow)
Patty Pan (white)
Peter Pan (green)

Squash (Winter)
Acorn
Early Butternut
Cream of the Crop
Sweet Mama
Table Ace
Tahitian

Sweet Corn
Florida Staysweet (yellow)
Frontier (white)
Golden Queen (yellow)
Guadelupe Gold (yellow)
Sweet G-90 (bi-color)
Honey & Pears (bi-color)
How Sweet It Is (white)
Silver Queen (white)

Tomatoes (Cherry)
Cherry Grande
Small Fry
Sweet 100
Yello Currant (itty-bitty but yummy)
Texas Wild (also tiny, plant as decoy crop for birds)

Tomatoes (Canning/Paste)
Roma
San Marzano

Tomatoes (Large Fruit)
Carnival
Celebrity
Champion
Crimson Fancy
First Lady
Heatwave
President
Quick Pick
Simba
Superfantastic
Surefire

Turnips
Just Right (fall only)
Tokyo Cross
Royal Globe II
White Lady

7 NORTH CENTRAL TEXAS

NORTH CENTRAL TEXAS

Recommended Fruit & Nut Varieties

Apples**
Red Delicious
Golden Delicious
Fuji
Gala
Granny Smith
Holland
Jerseymac
Mollie's Delicious

Apricots*
Bryan
Hungarian
Moorpark

Blackberries
Arapaho (thornless, erect)
Brazos
Navaho (thornless, erect)
Shawnee
Rosborough

---

* If soil is deep sand,
variety should be
grafted onto
Nemaguard or
Nemared rootstock.
** Need more than one
variety for pollination
*** Certain muscadines
can be self-fertile or
female only; plant
one self-fertile variety
for every six female
varieties.

Cherries (Sour)
Montmorency

Citrus
*(containers only, protect
in winter; move plants
outside into full sun when
temperatures exceed 26°)*
Satsuma

Figs
Texas Everbearing (Brown
Turkey)
Celeste

Grapes (Bunch)
*(these are resistant to
Pierce's disease)*
Black Spanish
Blanc du Bois
Champarnel
Golden Seedless

Jujubes
Li
Lang

Nectarines*
*(chill hours needed
to set fruit in parenthesis)*
Double Delight (700-800)
Durbin (850)

Peaches*
*(chill hours needed
to set fruit in parenthesis)*
Bicentennial (800-900)
Derby (750)
Dixieland (700-800)
Frank
Fayette
Majestic (800)
Milam
Ranger
Redskin (750)
Sentinel (650-750)
Springold (750)
Summergold (750)
Belle of Georgia (850, white
flesh)
Oachita Gold (850)
Ruston Red (800)

Peaches (Dwarf)
*(full-sized fruit on dwarf
plants)*
Bonanza II
Early Golden Glory

Pears**
Ayers
Garber
Kieffer
LeConte
Maxine
Moonglow
Orient
Savannah
Warren

NORTH CENTRAL TEXAS

232   *1997 Texas Garden Almanac*

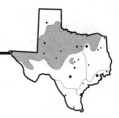

Recommended Fruit & Nut Varieties (cont'd)

Pears (Asian)**
(rootstocks to request:
Calleryana, Old Home)
Hosui
Shinko
20th Century
Tsu Li
Ya Li

Pecans
Caddo
Cape Fear
Choctaw
Desirable
Kiowa
Pawnee

Persimmons
(A= astringent)
Eureka (A, best commercial
   variety)
Hachiya (A, can produce
   seedless fruit)
Tamopan (A)
Tane-nashi (A)
Chocolate
Fuyu (more susceptible to
   cold)

Plums*
(rootstock to request:
Lovell for alkaline soils,
Nemaguard for acid,
sandy soils)
Bruce (requires cross-
   pollinator)
Morris
Methley
Ozark Permier

Raspberries
Dorman Red

Strawberries
Allstar (everbearing)
Chandler (annual,
   commercial)
Cardinal (everbearing,
   home)
Douglas (annual)
Sequoia (annual, home)
Sunrise (everbearing)

7 NORTH CENTRAL TEXAS

WHERE ! TO FIND IT •

ARBORETA & BOTANIC GARDENS
Ft. Stockton Desert Gardens
  P.O. Drawer 430
  Ft. Stockton, TX 79735
Living Desert Botanic Gardens
  P.O. Box 64
  Ft. Stockton, TX 79735
Fort Worth Botanic Garden
  3220 Botanic Garden Blvd.
  Fort Worth, TX 76107-3496
  (817) 871-7686

COMMUNITY GARDEN ORGANIZATIONS
Gardens Minifarms Network
  P.O. Box 1901
  Lubbock, TX 79408-1901
  (806) 744-8517
  Contact: Ken Hargesheimer

EDUCATION
Texas Tech University
  Plant & Soil Science Dept.
  P.O. Box 42122
  Lubbock, TX 79409-2122
  (806) 742-2837

TEXAS AG. EXTENSION SERVICE / MASTER GARDENER PROGRAMS
Ector/Midland Co.
Extension Horticulture
  Deborah Benge, county agent
  1010 E. 8th St.
  Odessa, TX 79761
  (915) 335-3071
Grayson Co. Extension Horticulture
  W. Mark Arnold, county agent
  Courthouse
  100 W. Houston St.
  Sherman, TX 75090
  (903) 813-4206
Hale Co. Extension Horticulture
  Robert C. Benson, county agent
  Box 680
  Plainview, TX 79073-0680
  (806) 291-5267
Lubbock Co. Extension Horticulture
  Stanley Young, county agent
  1418 Avenue G
  Lubbock, TX 79401
  (806) 767-1190

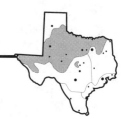

WHERE !
TO FIND IT :

Tarrant Co. Extension Horticulture
Dottie Woodson, county agent
103 Commerce St.
Ft. Worth, TX 76102-7205
(817) 884-1944

Taylor Co. Extension Horticulture
Gary Bomar
Old County Courthouse
Abilene, TX 79602
(915) 674-1321

Tom Green Co. Extension Horticulture
John Begnaud, county agent
113 W. Beauregard
San Angelo, TX 76903
(915) 659-6522

Wichita Co. Extension Horticulture
Mark Terning, county agent
1002 5th St.
Wichita Falls, TX 76301
(817) 716-5580

OTHER
Botanical Research Institute of Texas
509 Pecan St.
Fort Worth, TX 76102-4060
(817) 332-4441
FAX: (817) 332-4112

Emergency Pollution Reports
24 hours
(800) 832-8224

Texas National Resource Conservation Commission
Abilene: Winona Henry
(915) 698-9674
Arlington: Melvin Lewis
817) 732-5531
Lubbock: Jim Estes
(806) 796-7092
Odessa: Jed Barker
(915) 362-6997
San Angelo: John Haagensen
(915) 655-9479

7 NORTH CENTRAL TEXAS

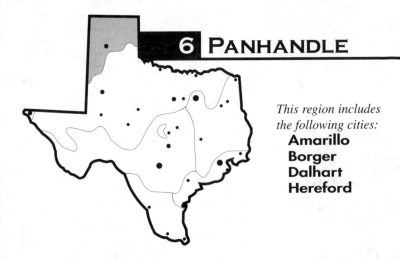

6 PANHANDLE

*This region includes
the following cities:*
**Amarillo
Borger
Dalhart
Hereford**

Beneath Our Feet

From the eastern edge of the Panhandle there is a gradual descent from high to low plains. Canyons and other unfriendly topography make the north end of the Panhandle less hospitable for farming than the south.Most soils are deep clay loams, with some sandy loams and sand. Subsoils may include lime deposits at varying depths. Short grasses, well suited to the fine-textured soils and essential to prevent wind erosion, cover much of the region.

Agriculture/Forestry

Hale County is one of the most productive counties in the state: cotton is the major crop, followed by wheat, sorghum and corn. North of Hale County, the land is less hospitable for cotton and wheat and sorghum are the principal commodities.

Local Climate Data

	Amarillo	Borger	Dalhart	Hereford
Mean Max. July	92°	93°	92°	90°
Mean Min. January	21°	23°	19°	20°
Record High	108°	107°	107°	108°
Record Low	-14°	-12°	-21°	-17°
Avg. Last Freeze, Spring	Apr. 17	Apr. 20	Apr. 23	Apr. 16
Avg. First Freeze, Fall	Oct. 24	Oct. 24	Oct. 18	Oct. 28
Normal Growing Season	190 days	187 days	178 days	195 days
Normal Precipitation, January	0.5	0.5	0.4	0.4
Normal Precipitation, February	0.6	0.9	0.5	0.6
Normal Precipitation, March	1.0	1.3	0.8	0.8
Normal Precipitation, April	1.0	1.3	1.1	0.8
Normal Precipitation, May	2.5	2.8	2.6	1.9
Normal Precipitation, June	3.7	3.4	2.4	3.0
Normal Precipitation, July	2.6	2.7	3.1	1.9
Normal Precipitation, August	3.2	2.9	3.1	3.1
Normal Precipitation, September	2.0	2.0	1.9	2.1
Normal Precipitation, October	1.4	1.3	1.0	1.4
Normal Precipitation, November	0.7	0.8	0.7	0.8
Normal Precipitation, December	0.4	0.5	0.4	0.4
Normal Precipitation, ANNUAL	19.6	20.3	17.9	17.2

Temperature Records

	Record High	Month & Year	Record Low	Month & Year	No. Days Max 90° & Above	No. Days Min. 32° & Below
Amarillo	108°	6/90	-14°	2/51	63.8	110.7

Chill Hours

According to USDA statistics, the Panhandle typically experiences 1,200 or more chill hours (temperatures between 32° and 45°) from fall to early spring.

Annual Rainfall

Normal
High Plains .... 18.88"

One-Year Sample (1994)

	J	F	M	A	M	J	J	A	S	O	N	D
High Plains	0.54	0.13	0.91	1.68	3.35	1.17	2.86	1.80	1.49	1.10	0.88	0.44

NOTE: "Normal" rainfalls are based on figures from a 30-year period; currently 1961-1990, while "average" rainfalls are calculated from the entire historical record. While "normals" generally are considered more reliable than averages, they may be no more or less useful than last year's numbers alone. In the sample year 1994, the total annual rainfall was substantially higher than the "normal," and substantial different than the previous years' precipitation. East Texas, for instance, got almost 4 inches less rain in July '93 than in July '94, and the '93 total rainfall was 29.0 inches.

Recommended Vegetable Varieties

Asparagus
Jersey Giant
UC 157

Beans (Snap Bush)
Blue Lake 274
Top Crop
Tendercrop
Contender
Tendergreen
Derby

Beans (Yellow Bush)
Goldcrop
Improved Golden Wax

Beans (Pinto)
Improved Pinto

Beans (Snap Pole)
Blue Lake
Kentucky Wonder

Beans (Lima Bush)
Henderson Baby Bush
Jackson Wonder

Beans (Lima Pole)
Florida Speckled
King of the Garden

Beets
Pacemaker III

Broccoli
Premium Crop (spring only)
Emperor (spring only)
Green Comet
Galaxy
Packman
Baccus
Early Dawn

Brussels Sprouts
Prince Marvel
Royal Marvel

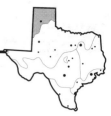

Recommended Vegetable Varieties (cont'd)

Cabbage
Early Jersey Wakefield
  (spring only)
Sanibel
Rapid Ball
Savoy Ace (wrinkled leaves)
Ruby Ball (red)

Cabbage (Chinese)
Jade Pagoda
Michihili
China Flash
China Pride

Carrots
Royal Chantenay
Burpee's Toudo
Park's Nandor
Danvers 126

Cauliflower
Snow Down

Swiss Chard
Rhubarb (red color)
Lucullus
Fordhook

Collards
Blue Max
Georgia

Cucumbers (Slicer)
Sweet Slice (burpless, very
  prolific)
Sweet Success
Burpless
County Fair 87
Dasher II
Slicemaster

Cucumbers (Pickling)
County Fair 87
Liberty
Saladin

Eggplants
Florida Market
Tycoon (Asian)
Listada de Gandia

Garlic
Texas White

Kale
Dwarf Blue Curled
Blue Knight

Kohlrabi
Grand Duke

Leeks
American Flag

Lettuce (Butterhead)
Buttercrunch
Tom Thumb (fall only)

Lettuce (Leaf)
Black-Seeded Simpson
Salad Bowl
Red Sails
Paris Island
Red Fire
Green Ice

Lettuce (Head)
Classic
Park's Mission

Lettuce (Cos/Romaine)
Romaine

Melons (Muskmelons)
Ambrosia
Caravelle
Explorer
Magnum 45
Minnesota Midget (bush
  type, good in containers)
Mission
Perlita (non-hybrid)
Uvalde (non-hybrid)

Melons (Watermelons)
Crimson Sweet
Jack of Hearts (triploid)
Orange Golden
Royal Jubilee
Royal Sweet
Star Brite
Tiffany (triploid)

6 PANHANDLE

Recommended Vegetable Varieties (cont'd)

Okra
Blondy
Clemson Spineless
Emerald
Lee

Onions
(short-day varieties best)
Burgundy
Crystal Wax
Red Granex
TAMU Supersweet (1015Y)
Red Grano
White Granex
Yellow Granex

Onions (Bunching)
Beltsville Bunching

Peas (English)
Little Marvel
Wando
Dwarf Gray Sugar

Peas (Edible Pod)
Sugar Ann (bush)
Sugar Pop (bush)
Super SugarMel (vine)
Sugar Snap (spring only)

Peas (Southern)
Blackeye #5
Purple Hull Pinkeye
Zipper Cream Crowder
Mississippi Silver

Peppers (Bell/Sweet)
Big Bertha (red bell)
Cubanelle
Gypsy
Jupiter (red bell)
Purple Belle (purple bell)
Summer Sweet 860 (yellow bell)
Sweet Pickle
Super Red (pimiento, roasts beautifully)
Top Banana

Peppers (Hot)
Jalapeno
TAMU Jalapeno
Hidalgo Serrano
Hungarian Yellow Wax
Long Red Cayenne
Super Chili
many others (there are no hot peppers that would rather be grown in New Jersey than in Texas)

Potatoes (Irish)
Norland (red, early)
Red LaSoda (red, midseason)
Kennebec (white, late)

Potatoes (Sweet)
Centennial
Jewell
Vardaman

Pumpkins
Autumn Gold
Connecticut Field
Jack Be Little (ornamental)
Small Sugar
Spirit

Radishes
Champion
Cherry Belle
Inca
Snow Belle
White Icicle

Squash (Summer)
Burpee's Butterstick
Dixie
Multipik
Sun Drops
Traboncino

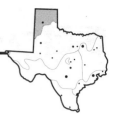

Recommended Vegetable Varieties (cont'd)

Squash (Summer Pan)
Sunburst (yellow)
Patty Pan (white)
Peter Pan (green)

Squash (Winter)
Acorn
Early Butternut
Cream of the Crop
Sweet Mama
Table Ace
Tahitian

Sweet Corn
Florida Staysweet (yellow)
Frontier (white)
Golden Queen (yellow)
Guadelupe Gold (yellow)
Sweet G-90 (bi-color)
Honey & Pears (bi-color)
How Sweet It Is (white)
Silver Queen (white)

Tomatoes (Canning/Paste)
Roma
San Marzano

Tomatoes (Cherry)
Cherry Grande
Small Fry
Sweet 100
Yello Currant (itty-bitty but yummy)
Texas Wild (also tiny, plant as decoy crop for birds)

Tomatoes (Large Fruit)
Carnival
Celebrity
Champion
Crimson Fancy
First Lady
Heatwave
President
Quick Pick

Turnips
Just Right (fall only)
Tokyo Cross
Royal Globe II
White Lady

6 PANHANDLE

Recommended Fruit & Nut Varieties

Apples**
Red Delicious
Golden Delicious
Fuji
Gala
Granny Smith
Holland
Jerseymac
Mollie's Delicious

Apricots*
Bryan
Hungarian
Moorpark

Blackberries
Arapaho (thornless, erect)
Brazos
Navaho (thornless, erect)
Shawnee
Rosborough

---

* If soil is deep sand, variety should be grafted onto Nemaguard or Nemared rootstock.
** Need more than one variety for pollination
*** Certain muscadines can be self-fertile or female only; plant one self-fertile variety for every six female varieties.

Cherries (Sour)
Montmorency

Figs
Brown Turkey
Celeste

Grapes (Bunch)
(these are resistant to Pierce's disease)
Black Spanish
Blanc du Bois
Champarnel
Golden Seedless

Jujubes
Li
Lang

Nectarines*
(chill hours needed to set fruit in parenthesis)
Double Delight (700-800)
Durbin (850)

Peaches*
(chill hours needed to set fruit in parenthesis)
Bicentennial (800-900)
Derby (750)
Dixieland (700-800)
Majestic (800)
Belle of Georgia (850, white flesh)
Oachita Gold (850)
Ruston Red (800)

Peaches (Dwarf)
(full-sized fruit on dwarf plants)
Bonanza II
Early Golden Glory

Pears**
Ayers
Garber
Kieffer
LeConte
Maxine
Moonglow
Orient
Savannah
Warren

Pears (Asian)**
(rootstocks to request: Calleryana, Old Home)
Hosui
Shinko
20th Century
Tsu Li
Ya Li

Pecans
Caddo
Cape Fear
Choctaw
Desirable
Kiowa
Pawnee

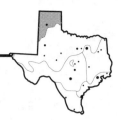

Recommended Fruit & Nut Varieties (cont'd)

Persimmons
(A= astringent)
Eureka (A, best commercial
  variety)
Hachiya (A, can produce
  seedless fruit)
Tamopan (A)
Tane-nashi (A)
Chocolate

Plums*
*(Lovell rootstock for alkaline
  soils, Nemaguard for
  acid, sandy soils)*
Bruce (requires cross-
  pollinator)
Morris
Methley

Raspberries
Dorman Red

Strawberries
Allstar (everbearing)
Chandler (annual,
  commercial)
Cardinal (everbearing,
  home)
Douglas (annual)
Sequoia (annual, home)
Sunrise (everbearing)

WHERE !
TO FIND IT :

**TEXAS AG. EXTENSION SERVICE /
MASTER GARDENER PROGRAMS**
Brewster Co. Extension Horticulture
  Rebel Royall
  Briscoe County
  Box 730
  Silverton, TX 79257
  (806) 823-2131
Dallam Co. Extension Horticulture
  Michael Bragg
  Dallam County Courthouse, Box 9377
  Dalhart, TX 79022-2798
  (806) 249-4434

Deaf Smith Co. Extension Horticulture
  Dennis W. Newton
  Deat Smith County
  Box 953
  Hereford, TX 79045
  (806) 364-3573
Potter Co. Extension Horticulture
  James I. Allison
  Charles Walton
  3301 E. 10th
  Amarillo, TX 79104
  (806) 372-3829

6 PANHANDLE

Cont'd from page 256 —

ample, of feeding chickens with regular tiny doses of nux vomica (*Strychnos nux-vomica*, or strychnine, used in 19th-century medicine as a central nervous system tonic), thus rendering them systemically toxic to hawks without — he said — seriously harming the barnyard fowl. What this might have actually done to the chickens is not nearly as unnerving as the possible effects on humans eating those chickens and their eggs.

Affleck was obliged to admit complete bafflement now and then; he once wrote to the editorial column of a newspaper for advice on how to treat cat fits. He "cannot like," he wrote, "the local custom of cutting off the tail to bleed the cat to health, though a tailless cat is certainly better than no cat at all." While waiting to hear from more knowledgeable correspondents, he announced that he would be taking partial clipping measures, "economizing the tail" as much as possible!

In spite of these very occasional lapses, his writings alone qualify Thomas Affleck for a permanent niche in the horticulturists' hall of fame. They display him to advantage as a well-informed, thoughtful man — with, perhaps, a little urgency to

be paid for his services, but also a great deal of heart with which to serve.

Affleck was born in an agricultural valley in Southern Scotland on July 13, 1812. His father was a shipping merchant, apparently very well to do, for his dock yards opening onto Solway Firth were large enough that he was able to give young Thomas a corner for himself in which to garden. An anonymous eulogy, written for the *Houston Telegraph* about a year after Affleck's death in 1868, gives intriguing details of his early years. The eulogizer claims to have known Affleck well, and tells that "as soon as he could handle a hoe and rake...it was his boyish pride to place on his mother's table the earliest vegetables, the finest and first fruits —

> " **AFFLECK HAD STARTED HIS OWN AGRICULTURAL ALMANAC BY 1845 AND MADE SURE TO INCLUDE LISTINGS FROM HIS NURSERY CATALOG WITHIN IT.** "

his flowers, his strawberries, and all the other productions of his little garden."

The youngster seems to have been loosely educated at home, perhaps by a tutor, for the eulogizer adds that "horticultural books, articles in encyclopedias, many not generally found in private libraries, attracted his youthful mind, and his manuscript copies of many of them, made when from eight to fourteen years of age, are still in the possession of his family." Thus Thomas' early schooling was centered on actual gardening, reading about horticulture and copying out the works by hand.

From age 15 through 20, Affleck worked as an accountant in the National Bank of Scotland under his maternal uncle, the bank's president — good background for the *Plantation Account Books* he would later produce. He studied briefly in Edinburgh during that period — his father wished him to become a surgeon, but this seems to have been the only career Affleck ever tackled that he actively disliked. His father allowed him to return to banking, and Affleck filled his off hours with studies more to his taste, primarily botany and ornithology. He even became a taxidermist of note. This early skill with the knife must have come in useful when Affleck, as a nurseryman, became a talented grafter of fruit trees.

In 1832, at age 20, Affleck sailed for New York. There were family businesses there, but Affleck was most excited by the prospect of American bird study. The journey appears to have been sort of a coming-of-age tour; he immediately headed for Pennsylvania and wandered about the state for quite a while on foot with only his gun and knapsack. When ready at last to settle down, he took a commercial job in Pittsburgh and married Margaret Bruce, the daughter of university president Dr. Robert Bruce.

He soon moved his family to Indiana. Engaged in commercial business once again, he was joined by his father's family while becoming a father in his own right. Then disaster struck: within three years "he lost his wife, child, mother and two brothers, and his own health to such a degree that he was forced to leave."

This complete obliteration of his family sent Affleck back East, perhaps with the intention of making his way home to Scotland. Never naturally despondent, however, he got as far as Cincinnati, then seems to have decided to comfort himself with a return to the interests of his youth. Purchasing land just on the Kentucky side of the Ohio River, Affleck went to work and soon built both a cottage and a reputation in agriculture and horticulture. He accepted an editorial position at the *Western Farmer and Gardener* in 1840, and was soon able to purchase the magazine and edit it completely. In a classic summing up of the man's talents, Affleck's eulogizer wrote that "his accurate knowledge, fluent style, and above all his untiring energy soon gave it a wide circulation."

In 1841 Affleck was invited by the organizing committee to attend the Agricultural Fair at Washington, Mississippi. He went down with some blood livestock, found the local Natchez society conge

nial, and decided to resettle. This plan may have been aided by the presence of the widow Anna (Dunbar) Smith, who became his second wife in April of 1842. Anna, daughter of Issac Dunbar and Elizabeth Wilkinson Dunbar, was also a niece of Jane Long, known as the "Mother of Texas."

With the marriage, Affleck acquired plantations and debt in equal degree, and was closely pressed to make ends meet financially. This led him to become involved in a number of speculative agricultural schemes, including the craze for mulberry trees for silk production, which seem generally to have fallen through with a crash. Perhaps if Affleck had been able to finance the projects himself he would have been more successful; instead, he frequently had to regroup when his partners pulled out or went bankrupt.

Cut back to a 40-acre homestead and deploring the habit of Northern nurseries to send their second-rate goods to the South — poorly packed and incorrectly labeled, according to Affleck — he now undertook to support his new family by opening his Southern Nurseries. While establishing the business and developing stock he continued to write on his favorite topics, with regular paid columns in both the *New Orleans Commercial Times* and the *New Orleans Picayune* as well as the *Natchez Times* and a number of other papers. The *Southern Rural Register* not only printed Affleck's work but largely advertised his nursery.

Never content with the efforts of others, Affleck started his own innovative agricultural almanac by 1845 and made sure to include listings from his nursery catalog within it.

For the next nine years Affleck appears to have been content to concentrate on building up Southern Nurseries, soon famous for offering warm-climate adapted plants that were backed by his name. He admits in the preface to his catalog that his prices were higher than in the North, but he has no trouble with the justification: "The advantages are so many, of being able to purchase good, thrifty trees and plants, of Southern growth, thoroughly suited to the climate, and from a responsible party, near enough at hand to correct any errors that might occur, and whose manifest interest it is to grow and sell stock which will do credit to his establishment; together with the still greater advantages of avoiding the expense and loss arising from distant and tedious transportation, and from insufficient and injudicious packing, that the greater first cost is but a secondary matter."

His hand-labeled packages were often to be seen on the New Orleans and Galveston steamers, heading out to a customer base that reached from Maryland to Texas. He did a great deal of experimentation, especially with fruit trees and roses, and reported regularly on the performance results while adding to his list of good varieties for the South. His 1851-52 catalog, for example, contains listings for 166 described and approved varieties of pears, with 63 new and untested types also available. Affleck developed an excellent reputation for skill in grafting, and taught this vital art to as many as his writings could reach. His eulogist tantalizingly shares the information that he had "a rose bush with fifty varieties budded upon it, blooming at once, many of them the finest tea roses."

In 1855, following a trip out to Texas, Affleck and his family decided to move to a homestead they selected in the valley of New Year's Creek, near Brenham, a place they christened "Glenblythe." One of his biographers reports that debt connected to his wife's plantations (and his own failed ventures) was the primary impetus, though the connection to Jane Long may have been a minor factor. Affleck's friend and eulogist states that the reason for discontent in Mississippi was unsatisfactory soil, "loose and friable, melting like sugar in every rain, and requiring incessant labor to preserve it." The new property, purchased dear at $3 per acre, was built up by Affleck into a substantial settlement. Not only the main house but all of the outbuildings — including hospital and church — necessary to a large plantation and all of the businesses such as saw mill, smithy, cotton gin and winery to make it completely productive and self sufficient were included. Livestock was numerous and farm machinery, including several of the most recent advances in plows and other equipment, was extensive.

It took time to develop all this, plus his new nursery, and to dismantle and pack the Mississippi site. During the first period of transition a severe drought in Texas destroyed thousands of his stock trees.

Then his stepson died and left Affleck with the draining chore of dissolving his estate and transporting the extra slaves to Texas.

Worst of all was the disaster that came at the end of five years of trying to get resettled. The final and largest shipment of his rare and valuable plants, "to lift and pack which had taken himself and two gardeners, with a number of hands, several weeks," was loaded onto the steamboat 'Charmer,' in the spring of 1860. She was burned the night after leaving Natchez — his loss was total and uninsured.

This event, as any plantsperson would agree, was nearly on a par with losing so many of his family members back in Indiana. Even his eulogizer admits that "he came home disheartened."

The almost immediate start, in 1861, of the Civil War hampered Affleck greatly in overcoming his losses, and he was in fairly low financial straits by the end of the war. He wasn't ever completely without resource — he supplied General Waul's Legion with everything from "beeves" to a hospital (to be returned to him in good condition when the conflict ended) while the Confederate troops were headquartered at New Year's Creek. His record books for the period also show continuing small sales of fruit trees and ornamen

98   SOUTHERN RURAL ALMANAC.—AUGUST.

THE GREAT
AMERICAN BRICK MACHINE!

It saves over 50 per cent. in labor; makes the finest of Brick; cannot get out of order; and is so simple that a child of ten years can work it.

It tempers the mortar, and moulds the Brick with great rapidity; and is pronounced by those who have them in use the best Brick Machine in the world.

No better evidence of their merit could be wanted than the fact that since the first machine was sold, the orders have come in faster than they could be built.

☞ Send for Descriptive Circular.

Price $250. in New Orleans. Terms, *Net Cash,* or approved paper bearing interest. Address all orders to

S. A. Hubbs,
Sole Manufacturer under the Patent, 97 COMMON STREET, NEW ORLEANS.

PATENTED September 21st, 1858, by Dr. JOHN BOOTH.

This Machine has peculiar claims upon the people of the South, being the invention of a Southern gentleman who has spent years of time in perfecting it; it is also manufactured in the South.

tal plants, especially to customers in Houston, which must have been somewhat helpful. But an advertisement in the *New York Herald* from 1865 describes Glenblythe in detail and offers the plantation for lease. Even so, in the midst of the general devastation of Southern plantation lifestyle that followed the Civil War, Affleck himself remained positive and energetic and was one of the first to take the oath of amnesty and get on with new projects for recovery. It was at this point that the replacement labor scheme made him a target of vituperation from some critics.

Travelling back and forth to England in fruitless pursuit of capital to transport the Scottish cottars, Affleck encountered a newly patented kind of carbolic sheep dip which he felt to be of great potential value. He found, on returning to the States, that this cysrelic compound had been discovered and patented simultaneously in this country, so he had to drop his scheme to personally control its American introduction.

He remained involved in the business, however, and spent several weeks in Galveston at the end of 1868 discussing manufacturing and marketing plans. There, his eulogizer states, "from lack of accustomed home comforts" he caught cold. By December 30th, at only 56 years of age, he was dead.

Affleck's writings continued to be circulated and even published for some time (an article he did on pasture grasses is included in the *U.S. Senate Executive Documents* from 1879). But his enormous effort to educate his readers, even if it meant doing all their thinking for them, has gradually faded from sight. Because he so wisely chose to promote varieties that were acclimated to the warm climate, at least some plants from his nursery are part of the surviving landscape in both Natchez and Brenham, and there are probably many more scattered across the Southern landscape.

> " **BECAUSE HE SO WISELY CHOSE TO PROMOTE VARIETIES THAT WERE ACCLIMATED TO THE WARM CLIMATE, SOME PLANTS FROM HIS NURSERY ARE PART OF THE SURVIVING LANDSCAPE IN BOTH NATCHEZ AND BRENHAM.**"

Editor's note: The 1860 edition of Affleck's almanac was reprinted in a limited edition in 1986 by the New Year's Creek Settlers Association, Rt. 4, Box 437, Brenham, TX 77833

Bed & Breakfasts Of Texas

AUSTIN
AUSTIN'S WILDFLOWER INN
512/477-9639; FAX 512/474-4188
1200 West 22 1/2 St, Austin, TX 78705
4 units. Rates from $50-75. CC: AE, MC, Visa. Host on property. Four rooms with two shared baths and two private baths. Rates include hearty full breakfast. New England decor, beautiful grounds and gardens, antique furnishings, and beautiful oak hardwood floors. No pets allowed, no children, no smoking.

BRENHAM
NUECES CANYON INN
409/289-5600; FAX 409/289-2411
9501 US 290 West, Brenham, TX 77833
Rates $75 and up. CC: AE, MC, Visa. Host on property. Sleeps 50 in 15 rooms with 1 shared bath and 13 private baths. Continental breakfast. 135 acres of wooded & rolling hiking trails, hayrides, campfires with BBQ facilities, pond fishing, catering services for all occasions, meeting room, fax, and copier service available. Full R.V. accomodations available. No pets. Children welcome. Smoking and non-smoking rooms available.

GLEN ROSE
YE OLE MAPLE INN B&B
817/897-3456
1509 Van Zandt, PO Box 1141,
Glen Rose, TX 76043.
2 Units. Rates from $65-$80. CC: AE, MC, Visa. A quiet getaway in the country. Enjoy a large yard with pecan trees dating from 300 to 500 years old. Enjoy porch with swing and rockers overlooking Paluxy River. Full breakfast is served. Evening desserts. Ice tea and soft drinks always available. Sleeps 4 peole in 2 rooms with private bath. Host on property. No pets, no children, no smoking.

HAMILTON
HAMILTON GUEST HOTEL
109 N. Rice
Hamilton, TX 76531
CALL 800-876-2502

Hamilton Guest Hotel
Inn on the Square

• TEA GARDEN
• BED & BREAKFAST
• Relax and enjoy a sophisticated luncheon
• Browse through our lobby shops
• Plan your reception, tea party, wedding, shower or family reunion
• Stay overnight in our historic bed & breakfast

LEDBETTER
LEDBETTER BED & BREAKFAST
800/240-3066; 409/249-3066;
Fax 409/249-3330
PO Box 212, Ledbetter, TX 78946
22 Units. Rates from $55-$166. CC: AE, MC, Visa. Hosts on property. Sleeps 80+ in 22 rooms, with 6 shared baths and 19 private baths. Choice of full or continental breakfast, indoor-heated pool, volleyball, horseshoes, washer pitching, barnyard animals, walking and nature paths, and juke box. Reunion accomodations available. Children allowed. No pets. No smoking. Minimum of 3 nights required on some weekends. Some restrictions may apply.

MINEOLA
NOBLE MANOR BED AND BREAKFAST
903/569-5720; Fax 903/569-0472
411 East Kilpatrick, Mineola, TX 75773
Rates from $80 to $125. CC: AE, MC, Visa. Host on property. Sleeps 22 people in 9 rooms each with a private bath. Full breakfast. 90 miles east of Dallas or West of Shreveport. 8 antique furnished rooms and a private cottage with garden hot tub. Library, king and queen beds, whirlpool baths, and porches. No pets. Children 10 and older welcome. Smoking outside.

SAN ANTONIO
SAN ANTONIO - RIVERWALK
• Elegant, quiet 1857 Antebellum mansion
• On 1-1/2 acres in the King William Historic District
• 10 King or Queen bedrooms with European antiques
• All rooms with TV's, telephones, A/C, refrigerator
• Fireplaces, porches and luxury amenities
Featured in: Texas Monthly, Texas Highways, N.Y. Times, Victoria, Glamour, Southern Living
Mobil 3-Star   IIA Rated
Oge´ House on the Riverwalk
800/242-2770

ROYAL SWAN GUEST HOUSE
800/368-3073; 210/223-3776
236 Madison, San Antonio, TX 78204
5 units. Rates from $75 -$135. CC: AE, MC, Visa, Discover. Host on property. Sleeps 12 in 5 rooms, each with private bath. Full breakfast. Victorian elegance, antique furnishings, some with verandas. Located in historic district. 2 blocks to Riverwalk and trolleys. No pets. Children over 12 welcome. No smoking. 2 night minimum over Saturday.

INDEX

Abilene
  best veg./fruit/nut varieties 227
  growing conditions 224
  Texas Ag. Ext. Service 234
  weather records 225
Affleck, Thomas 256
All America Selections 76
Allison, Christine 17
Almanac eras 11
Amarillo
  best veg./fruit/nut varieties 238
  freeze dates 98, 138
  growing conditions 236
  Texas Ag. Ext. Service 243
  weather records 237
Ambrosia, South Texas 50
Anaerobic 94
Anise hyssop 43
Aphelion 97
Aphids
  on fruit trees 32
  organic control 68
April
  astronomy in 117
  Daylight Savings Time 10
  events in, 116
  journal 119
  in verse 111
  moon phases 116, 118
  moon rise, set times 117
  mow dates 118
  plant/fertilize dates 118
Apogee 97
Arbor Day 12
Armand Bayou Nature Center 189
Arugula 43
Arlington
  best vegetable varieties 227
  best fruit/nut varieties 232
  growing conditions 224
  Texas Ag. Ext. Service 234
  weather records 225
Ash Wednesday 111
Atwood, Margaret 122
August
  astronomy in 135
  events in, 134
  fertilizing dates 136
  journal 137
  moon phases 134, 136
  moon rise, set times 135
  mowing dates 136
  planting dates 136
Austin
  best veg./fruit/nut varieties 215
  Community Gardens 222

freeze dates 98, 138
growing conditions 212
Sustainable Ag. Center 222
Texas Ag. Ext. Service 223
weather records 213
Zilker Botanical Garden 222
Ayenia, Texas 50
Aztec calendar 11, 14

Bachelor's button 43
Bagworms
  organic control 68
Basil
  planting 22
  'Siam Queen' 78
Bat Conservation International 80
Bayou Bend Gardens 189
Beans, bush
  days to maturity 98, 138
  fall planting 138
  planting depth 98, 138
  spacing 98, 138
  spring planting 98
  thinning 98, 138
Beans, lima
  days to maturity 98, 138
  fall planting 138
  planting depth 98, 138
  spacing 98, 138
  spring planting 98
  thinning 98, 138
Beans, pole
  days to maturity 98, 138
  fall planting 138
  planting depth 98, 138
  spacing 98, 138
  spring planting 98
  thinning 98, 138
Beaumont
  best vegetable varieties 180
  best fruit/nut varieties 185
  Community Garden 188
  growing conditions 178-180
  Texas Ag. Ext. Service 189
  weather records 179
Beck, Malcolm 93
Beets
  days to maturity 98, 138
  fall planting 138
  planting depth 98, 138
  spacing 98, 138
  spring planting 98
  and temperature 28
Beneficial insects 70
Biennials 28
Blackberries 143

Bladderpod, white 50
Bloodmeal 93
Bluebonnet
  festival 223
  legends 49
  planting 49
  scarifying 49
  state flower 48, 112
Bonemeal 93
Borage 43
Borger 236
Botanical Research Institute of
  Texas 80, 84, 235
Brand, Othal 177
Breinling, Jim 175
Brazos River flood, 126
Broccoli
  days to maturity 98, 138
  fall planting 138
  planting depth 98, 138
  spacing 98, 138
  spring planting 98
  and temperature 28
  thinning 98, 138
Brown rot 34, 36, 36
Browing, Robert 146
Brownsville
  best veg./fruit/nut varieties 196
  growing conditions 190
  Texas Ag. Ext. Service 198
  weather records 191
Bryan/College Station
  best vegetable varieties 202
  best fruit/nut varieties 207
  growing conditions 201
  Texas Ag. Ext. Service 209
  weather records 201
Brussels sprouts
  days to maturity 98, 138
  fall planting 138
  planting depth 98, 138
  spacing 98, 138
  spring planting 98
  thinning 98, 138
Budbreak 31
Byzantine 11

Cabbage
  days to maturity 98, 138
  Dynamo 77
  fall planting 138
  planting depth 98, 138
  spacing 98, 138
  spring planting 98
  and temperature 28
  thinning 98, 138

INDEX

INDEX

INDEX

INDEX

INDEX

Spider mites
  organic control 68
Spinach
  days to maturity 100, 140
  fall planting 140
  planting depth 100, 140
  spacing 100, 140
  spring planting 100
  and temperature 28
  thinning 100, 140
Spring Equinox 110
Squash (summer/winter)
  days to maturity 100, 140
  edible flowers 44
  fall planting 140
  planting depth 100, 140
  spacing 100, 140
  spring planting 100
  thinning 100, 140
Standard Time Zones 152
Stephen F. Austin State Univ. 209
  Arboretum 209
Stewart, George 1
Summer
  solstice 124
Sun 97
Sunshine by city 30
Sustainable Agriculture Center 222
Sweet potatoes
  (see Potatoes, sweet)
Swiss chard (see Chard, Swiss)

Tea, herb 169
Teeth and the moon 21
Texarkana
  best veg./fruit/nut varieties 207
  freeze dates 98, 138
  growing conditions 201-2
Texas A&M University 80
Texas Ag. Ext. Service 85
  Gulf Coast 189
  East Texas 209
  Hill Country 223
  North Central Texas 234
  Panhandle 243
  South Texas 198
  West Texas 223
Texas Assn. of Landscape
  Contractors 80
Texas Assn. of Nurserymen 80
Texas Botanical Garden Society 80, 222
Texas Dept. of Agriculture
  Organic Cert. Program 81
Texas Forest Service 81
Texas Natural Resource

Conservation Commission 81
Texas Organic Growers Assn., 81
Thyme
  cooking with 163-4, 166
  culture 163
  edible flowers 44
  English 163, 167
  French 163, 167
  lemon 164
  planting, 22
  T. vulgaris 162, 167
  tea 169
  varieties 167-8
Time
  Daylight Savings 113
  Standard 113
Tomatoes
  days to maturity 100, 140
  fall planting 140
  planting depth 100, 140
  pollination 87
  spacing 100, 140
  spring planting 100
  and temperature 28
  thinning 100, 140
Tomatillos, planting 22
Tonalpohualli, 14
Tornadoes 120
Townsend, Charles 14
Trichogramma wasps 68
Trinity Valley Comm. College 209
Transplants, hardening off 46
Tulbaghia 44
Turmeric root, planting 22
Turnips and temperature 28
Tyler
  best veg./fruit/nut varieties 207
  growing conditions 201-2
  Municipal Rose Garden 210
  Rose Festival 210
Turnips
  days to maturity 100, 140
  fall planting 140
  planting depth 100, 140
  spacing 100, 140
  spring planting 100
  thinning 100, 140

Urban Harvest 188
USDA 24
U.S. Naval Observatory 97
Uranus 97
Uvalde
  best veg./fruit/nut varieties 193
  established, 130
  growing conditions 190-2

weather records 191

Vegetable Improvement Ctr., 173
Venus 97
  visibility of 10
Verbena, Large-fruited sand 51, 53
Victoria
  best veg./fruit/nut varieties 180
  growing conditions 178-180
  Rose Gardens 189
Villalon, Ben 177
Violet flowers 44

Watering 6, 88-89
Watermelons
  days to maturity 100, 140
  fall planting 140
  planting depth 100, 140
  spacing 100, 140
  spring planting 100
  and temperature 28
  thinning 100, 140
Weather Bureau 106
Weather records 25
Weaning and the moon 21
Weather
  Record cold 106
  Record snowfall in Houston, Orange 106
Weeding 68
Weight control by the moon, 21
Whiteflies
  organic control 68
Wichita Falls
  best veg./fruit/nut varieties 227
  freeze dates 98, 138
  growing conditions 224
  Texas Ag. Ext. Service 234
  weather records 225
Wildflowers 47
Wild rice, Texas 51

Xiuhpohualli, 14

Yucca 44

Zilker Botanical Garden 222
Zinnia angustifolia
  'Crystal White' 76
Zodiac 19
  for planting by moon 18
  relating to human body 19
  and remedies 20

FIRST TEXAS GARDEN ALMANAC

By Liz Druitt

*"...we think [Thomas Affleck] can
so serve the public good more by
increasing his supply of plum, cherry,
apple and peach trees, as we are fond
of fruit, than in demanding of his
'beloved State' a mission for which
he is certainly unqualified."*
*— anonymous letter writer to the
Houston Telegraph, May 26,1866*

As a respected nurseryman and publisher of *The Southern Rural Almanac and Plantation and Garden Center*, Thomas Affleck was a man who found it easy to guide the daily business of planters, gardeners and all proponents of agriculture and horticulture. His almanacs, his record books and his articles were much sought-after as sources of growing information.

As a social pioneer, however, Affleck found his energy and his ideas to be downright unappreciated. The immigrant Scotsman had moved his nursery from Mississippi to Texas just before the outbreak of the Civil War. When it was over, he had a grand scheme: Texas could replace its lost work force of slaves with Scottish cotters — impoverished, displaced and known for their hard work and thrift. An ideal source of cheap labor? It was not to be.

But as a grower of local and locally acclimated plants, Affleck's myriad ideas

AFFLECK'S

SOUTHERN RURAL ALMANAC,

AND

PLANTATION AND GARDEN

CALENDAR,

FOR

1860:

BEING LEAP YEAR;

AND UNTIL THE FOURTH OF JULY, THE EIGHTY-FOURTH YEAR
OF THE INDEPENDENCE OF THE UNITED STATES.

BY THOMAS AFFLECK,

NEAR BRENHAM,

WASHINGTON CO., TEXAS.

PUBLISHED BY

DAVID FELT, NEW YORK, AND H. G. STETSON & CO.,
84 CAMP STREET, NEW ORLEANS.

enjoyed a wide following. His almanac editions ("published, almost continuously, each year since 1845," he wrote in 1860) contained intelligent essays on every aspect of Southern life, including the value of guano, cultivation of the dahlia, rose training, how to protect fields from erosion and proper ways to use compost, green manures and native grasses. He wrote a book on bee-breeding, and his lengthy articles covered topics as varied as livestock breeding, wine grapes and winemaking in Texas, erosion control, and hedging plants to replace (before barbed wire) the scarce resource of wood.

There was no topic too large for Affleck to approach, and no detail too small to consider. As a Southern plantation owner himself, he was able to write clearly and knowledgeably about the positive care and management of Negroes in his *Plantation Record & Account Books*, guiding overseers firmly away from practices that made the condition of slavery viciously and unnecessarily cruel. At the same time, he didn't forget to remind customers that upon receiving a shipment of plants, they should attend to removal of the copper-wired tag before it cut through a growing branch.

It is true that, in writing so much, Affleck occasionally got himself out on a conceptual limb. He had the idea, for ex

— Cont'd on page 244